A COMPANION TO
Beowulf

A COMPANION TO

Beowulf

Ruth Johnston Staver

Greenwood Press
Westport, Connecticut · London

Library of Congress Cataloging-in-Publication Data

Staver, Ruth Johnston.
  A companion to Beowulf / Ruth Johnston Staver.
    p. cm.
  Includes bibliographical references and index.
  ISBN 0–313–33224–X (alk. paper)
  1. Beowulf—Handbooks, manuals, etc. 2. Epic poetry, English (Old)—History and
criticism—Handbooks, manuals, etc. 3. Scandinavia—In literature—Handbooks, manuals,
etc. 4. Monsters in literature—Handbooks, manuals, etc. 5. Dragons in literature—
Handbooks, manuals, etc. 6. Heroes in literature—Handbooks, manuals, etc. I. Title.
  PR1585.S73 2005
  829'.3—dc22   2005006568

British Library Cataloguing in Publication Data is available.

Library of Congress Catalog Card Number: 2005006568
ISBN: 0–313–33224–X

First published in 2005

Greenwood Press, 88 Post Road West, Westport, CT 06881
An imprint of Greenwood Publishing Group, Inc.
www.greenwood.com

Printed in the United States of America

The paper used in this book complies with the
Permanent Paper Standard issued by the National
Information Standards Organization (Z39.48–1984).

10 9 8 7 6 5 4 3 2 1

COPYRIGHT ACKNOWLEDGMENTS

Beowulf manuscript facsimile (folio 129r of Cotton Vitellius A.xv) is reproduced by permis-
sion of The British Library. Images from the graphic novel *The Collected Beowulf* by Gareth
Hinds (Cambridge: The Comic.com, 1999–2000) appear by permission of Gareth Hinds.
Selections from the translation *Beowulf: A New Verse Translation*, R. M. Liuzza (Peterborough,
Ontario: Broadview Press, 2000), are reprinted by permission of Broadview Press.

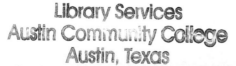

For my sons,

and for all who would be heroes in a difficult world

Contents

Acknowledgments

Special thanks to John Osborne, Steve Pollington, and Peter Fox for their help with detail questions; to Belinda Jenks and her English class at Miami Trace High School in Washington, Ohio, for giving feedback on portions of the manuscript; to the artists, Levi Staver, Ellen McHenry, and Andrew McHenry, who worked with detailed and sometimes mysterious material; and to The English Companions for many comments along the way.

Preface

WHY SHOULD ANYONE READ *Beowulf* more than a thousand years after it was written? Students and scholars have been asking that question since the manuscript came to light around 1800. What is *Beowulf* about, and why is it important?

It is much easier to state why it is not important. These reasons are quickly apparent to any modern student who has to read it for class in a limited amount of time.

1. It has been translated, unlike most works in "English Lit."
2. Its poetic style is difficult, and if the translation imitates the style, the sentences are hard to understand.
3. Its culture is foreign.
4. Its narrative style is hard to follow.
5. Its story is about physical conquest of monsters rather than psychological conquest of inner conflicts.

Scholars lodged other objections to *Beowulf.* J. R. R. Tolkien, writing in 1935, summarized the objections that had been made throughout the nineteenth century:

1. Its plot seems jumbled.
2. Its religion seems confused.
3. Its historical details are sometimes clear, and sometimes fuzzy.
4. It uses legends, mixed with folktales, so that you cannot tell what was "original" story and what may have been added.

With all of these objections lodged against it, why does it continue on English reading lists? Why do some enthusiasts study Old English to be able to read its original text? What makes *Beowulf* important, and why is it important to us?

Beowulf was produced in a time that exhibits many parallels to our own. Its author lived in a great civilization but looked back to a time when, as it seemed, noble fighting men had to administer the justice of the frontier. He knew stories of these heroes, the way stories are still told of early American soldiers like Ethan Allen or pioneers like Davy Crockett. They were men from a different time, a time when the challenges were plainer, choices were simpler, and many things were possible.

The author's time, like ours, was filled with impossible problems, limited choices, and moral dilemmas. Filled with concerns for the future, he looked back to the past. The poem's characters make decisions and hope for the best—but the poem, written with hindsight, knows that heartbreak will come. The characters face ethical crisis and use an old value system for choosing what to do—but is it enough, as times change? The poem presents the difficulty of taking action when you have limited knowledge. Sometimes it works out well, but sometimes it doesn't. *Beowulf* floats in time; ancient to us, it looks backward and forward along linear time and poses questions that we have never quite answered.

Violence is always near at hand. There is accidental death, and how do you place blame for that? When revenge gets out of hand, where should it stop? Each party feels justified; how much blood can be spilled? If a man kills his relatives, by accident or in anger, to what extent is that man a pariah—are we, the innocent, after all, any better? If a proud king becomes corrupt and misuses his power, who can judge him? The ethical judgments of *Beowulf*, like the judgments of our time, are never simple or easy.

One of the great challenges of our time is blending different religious cultures. How can we keep our own convictions while valuing what is strong in others? *Beowulf* faces this challenge, as the narrator is clearly Christian, but his characters are just as clearly pagans. It could have been written as a tract against pagan beliefs, but instead it presents the complex, shifting picture that earlier critics called confusing. Perhaps, in a later time more distant from the certainties of the nineteenth century, we can read with open minds and open arms. Like the *Beowulf* poet, we can find much to admire in those with whom we disagree.

In a time that values the individual, we can understand the *Beowulf* poet's emphasis on the young man who challenges himself to take risks that no one has yet been able to handle. We can understand the value of naming the individual victims of the monster and in showing the old king's grief as he finds the severed head of his best friend. We can understand, too, the changing circumstances for an aging hero who chooses to face a new monster, and probable death, to protect his people. If he protects his people and dies, then they will be without a protector in the future, saved as they are from this one danger. How much is his individual life worth? Is it his to spend, or does it belong to others? To what extent can the community tell him how much risk to take?

Do you face destructive forces in your life? Do you think you can't overcome them? Try. Perhaps you will fail, but people will see and praise the effort, and it will inspire others to try. Perhaps someone will come to your aid, or perhaps you will succeed by the skin of your teeth. The effort, says *Beowulf*, is worth it, not because success is assured, but just because it's worth it. That message, in the end, is why we read *Beowulf*.

How to Use This Book

THIS BOOK is arranged with the convenience of a busy reader in mind. Each chapter is followed by a list of books that are suggested for further study of that topic. There are many books and articles for students to choose from; the lists here can only give some direction.

For the student who only needs a general idea of the context of *Beowulf* and has only a half hour to read in the library, Chapter 1 may be enough information to understand the poem on its own. This introduction covers the time and place in which the poem's action takes place, the time and place of the people who preserved the poem in written form, and the unique discovery and translation of the manuscript. Chapter 2 discusses choices that translators must make, with a brief review of some of the many translations.

For readers who want a more complete discussion of the poem, the main commentary follows in Chapters 3, 4, 5, and 6. Each chapter introduces characters and explains the action as it follows the poem's structure. Students who are reading a shortened form of the poem in a literature textbook may find that some sections do not apply to their version and may use the section headings to guide them in their choice of what to read.

Following the commentary, Chapters 7, 8, and 9 cover the more technical issues of literary techniques (Chapter 7), the controversial issue of when the poem may have been composed (Chapter 8), and the language of the original poem (Chapter 9). Chapter 9 includes discussion of both the poetic meter of the poem and the Old English language in general. While a serious consideration of these technical and linguistic issues is beyond the scope of this work, these chapters introduce topics and explain the context of the questions. The information will be of interest to readers who hope that this work will be an introductory gateway to further study.

Chapters 10 and 11 provide a discussion of Anglo-Saxon culture for readers who desire an understanding of the society in which the poem and its writing took place. Chapter 10 discusses the culture's religion, examining the evidence for religious beliefs and how religious ideas connect in *Beowulf*. Chapter 11 covers daily work, the role of women, and the clothing, food, education, buildings, and weapons of the time.

Chapters 12 and 13 explain modern adaptations and offshoots of *Beowulf*. These modern works include books, graphic art, and film; several images from Gareth Hinds' graphic novel illustrate Chapter 12. Finally, the last chapter examines how the world of J. R. R. Tolkien's *Lord of the Rings* presents a surprising number of ties with Tolkien's scholarly specialty, *Beowulf*.

I

Introduction to the Context of *Beowulf*

"Listen!" The opening lines of *Beowulf* signal that what follows will be a marvelous tale from the past: "We have heard of the glory in bygone days / of the folk-kings of the spear-Danes, / how those noble lords did lofty deeds." As ancient as the poem is to us, to its audience it spoke of something older still, an already half-forgotten tale to be heard and retold. To put *Beowulf* in a setting and come to grips with its meaning, a reader must understand how the poem bridges between three time periods: the ancient North Germanic past, the "contemporary" Anglo-Saxon period, and our time, as we read it in modern English. This chapter covers these times in a general way, showing how *Beowulf* links them together.

THE NORTH GERMANIC TRIBES

The poem's story is set in the past and opens in the land of Denmark. The Danes were one of the many Germanic groups living in the area of Northern Europe, from central Germany to the coasts of Norway, in the years of the late Roman Empire. The Roman historian Tacitus described some of these tribes around AD 70, and as the custom of written histories spread through conversion and education, the Germanic peoples themselves began to keep histories. From these histories, as well as from archeological evidence, we can estimate the location of the major nations and tribes during the seventh century.

The story of Beowulf begins in the land of the Danes, but Beowulf has traveled from the land of the Geats. ("Geat" should be pronounced with the "g" making the sound of a "y," something like "Yay-aht.") You can see Geatland in southern Sweden, although the island to the east of Sweden bears their name, Götland, suggesting that the Geats pulled back to a safer island home. Positioned in southern Sweden, they had the fierce Swedes to their north, as well as other potentially hostile groups to their south. Balancing their relationships with all of these groups was a key concern for leaders of the Geats, and Beowulf's journey to the land of the Danes could be seen as a means to strengthen relations with peaceful allies on whom they could later rely.

Other peoples who appear on the map are named in the poem as either allies or enemies. Hrothgar's daughter will marry the prince of the Heathobards on their southern border, while Hygelac (Beowulf's king) will die during a raid on the Franks at the mouth of the Rhine. The power of Rome had never reached beyond the Franks, so while the Frankish Empire had begun to extend its power into the territory of modern France and Germany (on the coastlands to the north), the rule was still that every tribe must do its best for itself. There was no central authority, only territories and spheres of influence.

Because there are contemporary histories, we can give the story (or some of its characters) an approximate date. Late in the poem, Beowulf tells how his king, Hygelac, died while attacking the land of the Franks. The history of Gregory of Tours mentions that in 521 there was an attack on the Rhine River by a northern leader named Chlochilaichus. This spelling is recognizable as a foreigner's attempt to write down the name of Hygelac, adding, of course, the Latin "-us" at the end. Historians accept that the two are the same person. The character of Beowulf could be fictional, but if he existed, we can set the dates of his life and the poem's action as having occurred approximately between 515 and 570.

The culture of the Germanic peoples was quite different from the Roman culture that first recorded them in history. Tacitus described a people who were tall, most with red hair and blue eyes. They loved war and typically carried weapons, and they spent as little time as possible doing what Tacitus considered real work, such as building or farming. They had very strict morals and a code of loyalty. With democratic traditions, they governed themselves in small groups under local kings who were chosen by their people. To Tacitus, accustomed to dark-haired Italians who were primarily farmers under a large central government, these Germanic traits were astounding. He was probably exaggerating: there must have been some brown-haired Germans, as well as Germans with less

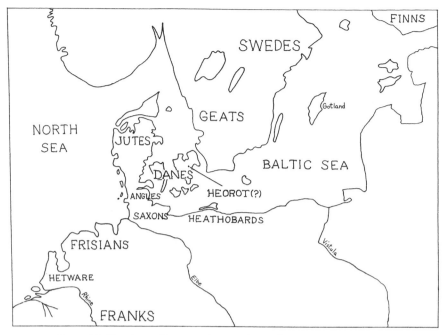

Beowulf's Northern Europe. Approximate location of nations in
Northern Europe around AD 500. Heorot may have been located at Lejre,
on the island of Sjaelland (Zealand).

strict morals or a greater turn for farming. Tacitus was certainly correct
in two points, that the Germanic peoples were almost always armed, and
that they followed a code of loyalty above all.

There were two main loyalty bonds: loyalty within a family, and loyalty to the king or other lord. They held marriage in great honor, marrying only one wife, and expecting a complete sharing of goals and life
between husband and wife. Marriages for their rulers usually crossed
borders, because the marriage bond was considered so strong that it would
bring about peace between formerly warring peoples. Loyalty to the king
was an even higher value for the warriors.

The central image of early Germanic society is that of a war leader
with a band of warriors who are loyal to the death. This loyalty was not
free, for the expected duty of a king was to give gifts. In *Beowulf*, the
throne is the "gift-chair," and it represents the way their social ties worked.
The warriors served their lord and were given lavish gifts as reward. The
higher they rose, the more lavish the gifts were, and the more loyalty
they owed. This relationship was even more intense for those warriors
who were related to the king, because the ties of gratitude and loyalty

were doubled by their ties of kinship. The most shocking acts in the Germanic culture's stories involve betrayals of these ties, and many of the side stories in *Beowulf* reflect this cultural fascination with doing the unthinkable. These reciprocal ties of generosity and loyalty held Germanic society together. (See Chapter 11, "Anglo-Saxon Culture," for more details on Germanic cultural life.)

Tacitus considered the Germanic peoples to be native to the lands where the Romans found them, because, as he asked, who would leave a pleasant land like Asia or Italy for the wild weather and frontier life of Germany? Linguistic evidence, however, tells us that Tacitus was wrong. The Germanic languages are related to a number of other European and Asian languages, and they share some common cultural aspects. Starting from a point of origin near the Black Sea, around 4,000 BC, all of these peoples fanned out. Some went east into Persia and India, while many went west into Greece, Italy, and the rest of Europe. The Germanic peoples arrived after the Celts had already settled parts of modern-day France and Germany. By the time of Tacitus, the Celts still lived in these lands, but some had crossed the English Channel, where they were part of the Roman colony of Britain. Germanic tribes became dominant in Europe.

A survey of Germanic peoples around the year 500 would find the Swedes, Geats, Danes, and Jutes in Scandinavia (modern-day Denmark, Norway, and Sweden). To the south, the Franks were also Germanic, but because the Romans colonized them and imported Latin as their written language, the Frankish Empire developed the offshoot of Latin now known as French ("Frankish"). To the south and east of the territory on Map 1, several groups of Goths had invaded southward to Italy itself and had taken over the Roman Empire. These Goths intermarried and blended into Spain, Italy, and parts of Romania, and their descendants are still living in these places today. The Goths eventually disappeared as an ethnic group and as a nation.

To the west of the territory shown on Map 1, a group of Germanic peoples had migrated to the island of Britain. By 500, they were actively migrating, leaving the marshy coastlands of Denmark and Frisia. (Hygelac may have seen them as he passed by in 521.) Shown on Map 1 are the Jutes, who migrated to the southern coast of Britain (as the county of Kent). The region between the Danes and the Heathobards was called Angeln, and the Angles, as well as the Saxons (inland and to the south), migrated in large numbers to Britain. They are not mentioned in the poem of *Beowulf*, except in one important way: the entire poem is written in their language.

ANGLO-SAXON ENGLAND

Contemporary histories tell us that the Jutes, Angles, and Saxons originally came to Britain at the invitation of the Britons; the Celts who had
moved to Britain partly under pressure from migrating Germanic tribes.
With Roman power fading, the Britons were suffering from raids by
their rival neighbors, the Picts. At the time, it seemed like a good idea
to ask the Germanic coast-dwellers to come for a short time and help
fight the Picts. However, it turned out to be a bad idea: a larger wave
of Germanic immigration followed, and then came a possibly brutal sup-
pression of the British themselves. Many of the British pulled back into
the hills of Wales or crossed into France to establish Brittany. The Jutes,
Angles, and Saxons became the dominant inhabitants of most of the island,
and they eventually spread northward into southern Scotland as well.

The Germanic invader-immigrants to Britain blended their cultures
and languages and became what we call the Anglo-Saxons. They settled
into several kingdoms, partly based on their original ethnic groups and
partly based on local geography and sheer political and military power.
The major kingdoms were Northumbria (north of the Humber River),
Mercia (central and bordering on Wales), Wessex ("West Saxons"), East
Anglia (Angles), and Kent (Jutes).

These kingdoms were at first pagan, worshipping the Earth and honoring Woden, Thor, and the other Germanic gods. Latin-speaking missionaries from Rome began to arrive in 597. Coming first to Kent, they
found that the pagan king had married a Frankish princess who was
already a Christian, with a chapel and a priest. With this friendly base at
Canterbury, they traveled to the other cities and kingdoms. Meanwhile,
missionaries came from Ireland, which had converted to Christianity
through the work of St. Patrick in the 400s. Christianity spread rapidly
and peacefully, although not all kingdoms accepted it at once. Even
kings who chose to remain pagan were tolerant and allowed priests to
travel and build churches. By 700, most pagan practices were a memory.
Instead, stone churches filled the land, and the imagery of saints and the
Bible influenced the culture and literature. (See Chapter 10, "Religion
in *Beowulf*," for more detail.)

With Christian conversion came writing, as the Latin monks used Latin
letters, combined with some of the traditional runic symbols, to capture
the spoken language. In Anglo-Saxon times, words were written precisely the way they were said, and spelling varied. The written language
of Mercia varied from those of Kent and Wessex, and spelling varied
from place to place, person to person, and even moment to moment.

Major Anglo-Saxon kingdoms around AD 800.

Books were hand-inked by monks and concentrated in cathedral towns and monasteries, which in turn reflected some of the regional dialect differences. The prolific historian and writer Venerable Bede lived near York, in Northumbria; he wrote his many histories and essays in Latin around the year 700. King Alfred of Wessex, who reigned from 871 to

899, promoted the use of his native language by having many Latin works translated. Among them, Bede's history was translated into the dialect and spelling of politically dominant Mercia. Perhaps this is a good snapshot of the linguistic reality: the works of Northumbrian-speaking Bede are memorialized in Mercian, written by West Saxons.

Around King Alfred's time, in Wessex, monks began to keep a continuous history of their times, now called the *Anglo-Saxon Chronicle*. This remarkable history summarized the years up to its inception, and was then kept as a running diary until 1154, noting briefly what key events happened each year. We also have many poems and letters from this time, as well as short texts, that discuss medical treatments and charms. There is even a collection of riddles. Around 1000, someone took a Latin text that had been written to teach daily-life Latin to new monks and wrote the Anglo-Saxon words above the Latin words, the way a student might pencil in English above Spanish. From this translation, we have an extensive vocabulary including many kinds of fish, and the tools of daily occupations like shoemaking, baking, and shepherding.

The Anglo-Saxons, in their histories, began to refer to themselves as "English," a form of "Angle-ish." To differentiate their Latin works from their native works (both are considered "Anglo-Saxon"), we call their language from this period Old English. It appears to be a foreign language to any speaker of Modern English, but a closer examination of the vocabulary shows that there are more connections than first appear. For example, some words, such as "winter," "gold," and "hand," have not changed in over a thousand years. Some words are only different in their spelling, not in their pronunciation. If you know that "sc" is the way the sound "sh" was once spelled, words such as "scip" and "fisc" are not mysterious. While many words in Modern English have a different history— coming from French, or from Latin or Greek, or perhaps even borrowed from Indonesian—the core vocabulary (such as "sit," "stand," "is," "with," or "from") is easily recognized in Old English. (See Chapter 9, "Language and Poetry," for more detail.)

The poem of *Beowulf*, like other works in Latin or Old English, must be translated into Modern English for us to read. Some editions of the poem include the original Old English text on a facing page, so that a reader may look for familiar words or use the book for language study. The inverted and complex wording of the poetic style makes it a challenge for translators. Like a poet of Modern English who is hunting for a rhyme, the poet of *Beowulf* often used unusual words or arrangements to preserve the traditional Germanic rhythm and alliteration. Most translators try to imitate this effect in Modern English, while a few have translated the poem into rhyme or ordinary prose. (See Chapter 2, "Choosing a Translation," for more detail.)

The contradiction inherent in *Beowulf* is that although it is composed in Old English, its subject matter deals with Sweden and Denmark. While the Anglo-Saxons were aware of their roots on the continent, they had a complex relationship with the Scandinavians. Because archeologists have uncovered finely made Swedish weapons in England, we know that some of the Anglo-Saxon kingdoms maintained trade with Scandinavia. But beginning in 793, with the burning and sacking of the monastery on Lindisfarne Island, Danish pirates (vikings) began attacking England. What began as seasonal raids turned into permanent wars and the construction of Danish forts. The various kingdoms fought back, sometimes winning and often losing. Wessex had the most military success, due to the resolve of its kings (chiefly King Alfred), and so gradually Wessex became dominant, controlling territory previously ruled by East Anglia or Mercia. In 886, King Alfred seized and burned London, which had been held by the Danes, and dictated a peace treaty. This treaty allowed the Danes to hold and govern much of the territory they had seized, with mutual recognition of borders and a cessation of fighting. They now ruled a large portion of eastern England and had the responsibility of fighting back unruly pirates. We refer to this arrangement, and the territory that they held, as Danelaw.

But this peace did not last forever, and the warring continued into the tenth century. In the last move of the power struggle between the English and the Danes, Canute of Norway conquered a united English kingdom in 1016 and was crowned its king. Canute (also written as "Cnut") and his sons ruled England until 1042. For the first time, the king ruling in London did not speak Old English, but rather, he spoke Old Norse. During the period of Danelaw, and again in Canute's reign, the Old Norse language influenced Old English. Some Old Norse words were adopted into English, such as "window," "take," and "skill." The garment that the English called a "shirt" was called in Danish a "skirt," and both words have remained in our language, developing different meanings. Old Norse words linger in some regional words of England, and in many English place names. For example, "-by" and "-thorpe" at the end of village names are actually Norse words for "farm" and "settlement."

In 1066, England was attacked on two coasts within a week's time. King Edward, an Anglo-Saxon, had died without a son to succeed him, and the council had elected Harold Godwinson to the kingship. The new king faced an immediate challenge. His brother instigated an attack from the King of Norway on the northeastern coast, while William, the Duke of Normandy, prepared to attack on the southern coast. King Harold successfully repelled the Norse attack at the Battle of Stamford Bridge, but his army had no time to recover before a messenger came with news of an attack across the English Channel. Weakened by fatigue, and arriving too late to stop the invaders from building a fort, Harold died in battle and England was conquered by Normandy. The Normans, descendants of Norse pirates who had formed their own "Danelaw" on the coast of France, changed the course of English life much more dramatically than Danish King Canute had.

With French as the language of the court, and Latin the language of the church, Old English existed only a little longer as a written language. In 1154, almost 100 years later, the last entries in Old English were made in the *Anglo-Saxon Chronicle*. There are a few scattered documents written in English after that, but most were in French or Latin. English continued to exist as a spoken language but changed through increased contact with the Normans. With an Old English core, a new French vocabulary, and a simplified grammar, the new language form picked up its written history again in the fourteenth century. Chaucer's *Canterbury Tales* were written in this new hybrid language. Many of the crumbling Anglo-Saxon manuscripts still existed, but they were buried in monastery libraries and were no longer recopied or read.

THE MODERN ERA

Beowulf was almost lost, like many other manuscripts that succumbed to water, fire, mold, and accident. No one knows how many copies originally existed; if it was an old composition, there should have been more. Regardless, only one manuscript survived, but it was forgotten and almost destroyed. Like the other Anglo-Saxon books, it probably sat in a monastic library as the culture shifted to Anglo-Norman. Through the Middle Ages, it was probably wedged between other books on a shelf or at the bottom of a chest. These books were made of vellum, leather carefully prepared as a writing surface. With the ink no longer carefully freshened and copied, the manuscripts grew faded and worn.

During the Reformation (a violent period in English history), monasteries and cloisters were closed, and their lands were seized and given to loyal Protestants. Many libraries burned, while others were passed into the hands of private collectors. Few people at that time gave thought to the precious history embodied in these curious antique manuscripts, but some people did take care to preserve them. At least one collector, Laurence

Nowell, owned a set of vellum manuscripts, and he wrote his name and date, 1563, onto the front page.

Along with other manuscripts, this particular one passed into the hands of Sir Robert Cotton, a great collector of antique books. Sir Robert had a large library, which he kept in bookcases lining the room. Each bookcase had a bust of a Roman emperor on top, and he named each case after an emperor. The Nowell Codex, as we call it today, sat as the fifteenth book on the top shelf of the bookcase named for the Emperor Vitellius. Someone, perhaps Sir Robert, had it bound with manuscripts that appeared to be related: perhaps they were from the same original collection or had been stacked together; certainly they appear to be in the same handwriting, if they were not originally sewn together. It is doubtful that Sir Robert had any idea what his manuscripts were. By this time, most knowledge of Old English was lost, and even the medieval script was hard to read, with its occasional runic form sprinkled in.

In 1700, Sir Robert's grandson decided to give his entire collection to the government, which was interested in forming a museum. Since the Cotton house was falling into disrepair, and the books were no longer dry and protected, the collection had to be moved, but for the next fifty years, there was no actual British Museum to put them in. Humphrey Wanley went through the collection and made a list of its contents. He described one manuscript as an example of Anglo-Saxon poetry: it was the story of the wars of Beowulf, a Danish prince, against the Swedes. This is not an accurate description of the story, but Wanley did well to decode enough of the words to make an educated guess at the contents of the manuscript. Sir Robert Cotton's collection was later moved into a private house for storage, but in 1731, this house caught fire. As the fire raged out of control, men began to push the heavy bookcases out the windows. Some of them had already caught fire, but most of the collection was saved. Many of them were charred along the edges, as the bookcases had caught fire at the back.

In 1786, an Icelander, Grim Johnson Thorkelin, working as the archivist for the Danish court in Copenhagen, read Humphrey Wanley's list. Thorkelin was in London, searching for manuscripts that might pertain to Danish history. Wanley's description of an Anglo-Saxon poem about a Danish prince seemed to be exactly what he was looking for. The manuscript, now named Cotton Vitellius A.XV (Cotton's library, Vitellius bookcase, shelf A, position 15), was still there, but it was damaged. It was dirty, smudged, water-spattered in places, and even burnt to ash on many edges, but it was still readable.

Because the Icelandic language preserved so many of the old word

The first page of the *Beowulf* manuscript, which is faded and crumbling but is in better condition than some other pages. (By permission of the British Library, folio 129, Cotton Vitellius A.XV.)

forms, Thorkelin understood some of what he read, and he quickly hired a scribe to make a copy. Not long after, he made a copy himself; these two copies are now called Thorkelin A and Thorkelin B. Although these copies contain errors, they preserve something precious, because the burnt edges of the original manuscript crumbled away during the next fifty years. As charred as the pages were, Thorkelin and his copyist could make out the words in those margins, and now these words are completely gone. Fire almost claimed the poem one more time, as Thorkelin prepared to print his copy in Copenhagen. In one stage of the Napoleonic Wars, the British Navy bombarded Copenhagen, and Thorkelin's house caught on fire. He managed to save his handwritten copies of the poem but lost the printing efforts. He was forced to begin again. His printed copies were finally published in 1815, and the manuscript now known as *Beowulf* went public.

Beginning in 1805 with Sharon Turner's partial translation, a series of scholars and poets tried to translate *Beowulf* into Modern English. Turner's difficulties with the language are well illustrated by the fact that a page had been misplaced in the manuscript, and Turner did not comprehend what he read well enough to realize this. Some scholars already had enough knowledge of Old English to read the histories and other straightforward prose, but the challenge was to develop a larger vocabulary and wider grasp of the possibilities inherent in poetry. By the middle of the nineteenth century, scholars' understanding of the poem had improved. Their *Beowulf* translations of 1850 are not significantly different than those produced 150 years later, though they do vary in style. The first complete translation was published in 1837, and perhaps as many as 100 translations have been published since that time. The pace of new publications has only increased: between 1960 and 2000, at least forty new translations were published. Scholarly studies of Old English are now extremely detailed, pinning down the history of change of certain words and sounds in selected regions and detailing minute descriptions of poetic style.

In the modern era, the meaning of *Beowulf* has evolved. It was, at first, mostly significant as a historical document. As early as 1820, a Danish pastor, N. F. S. Gruntvig, identified the historical Hygelac in the history of Gregory of Tours. From that point, most scholarship was dedicated to finding the history behind *Beowulf*, or the finer points of the archaic language, or the sources of the Germanic legends, or the ancient culture suggested by the story. To most critics, the fights with monsters were trivial, since the poem also records short accounts of local feuds. Trying to peer through that tiny keyhole into the Dark Ages, they wished that the poet had told them more about Ingeld or Finn, and less about Grendel. For early archeologists, the glimpses of pagan burials or rituals were tantalizing, and they sought to make the most of what they could learn from these passages. While some readers probably enjoyed the poem as a monster story, the scholars and critics pointedly rejected it as such.

In 1936, J. R. R. Tolkien, an Anglo-Saxon specialist at Oxford, delivered the Sir Israel Gollancz Memorial Lecture to the British Academy. At that time, Tolkien was not famous, as he is now; the publication of *The Hobbit* was still a year away. He was well respected as a *Beowulf* scholar, however, and in delivering the Gollancz lecture, he changed the course of all subsequent scholarship. Citing the consensus that the poem was memorable only as a historical document, he defended the poem as a piece of literature. Critics charged that the poem was poorly constructed and dealt with childish topics. Tolkien asserted, in defiance of this critical opinion, that the poem's construction was poorly understood. The structure was not intended to tell a biographical story, but to poise two halves of an adventure in a balance: youth and old age, success and failure, troll and dragon. The topics, he said, were not childish, but rather, the critics had rejected them before examining their literary value. He particularly defended the dragon and argued that it formed a symbol of all the values that the poem spoke against. Germanic kings and chieftains had to be generous to their followers and not arbitrary or cruel to their people. The dragon, on the other hand, hoarded his gold and burned houses and halls without regard for whose they were. What better symbol of all that a virtuous man must overcome? (For more detail on Tolkien's connections to the world of *Beowulf*, see Chapter 13, "The Beowulfian World of J. R. R. Tolkien.")

By defending *Beowulf* as a genuine piece of poetry, Tolkien challenged a new generation of critics to change their methods of scholarship. Archeology continued to uncover new finds that shed light on the material culture of Beowulf's world, but scholarly efforts with the poem turned more to its meaning as literature. How do the characters interact? What is the meaning of a certain incident? How is imagery used? The traditional tools of literary study—theme, character, language, imagery—were turned toward *Beowulf*, with good effect. It is now possible to read many detailed studies of how the poem fits into the tradition of the time, and how its ideas link it to our time. (For a detailed literary analysis, see Chapter 7, "Literary Techniques.")

This revaluation is why *Beowulf* turns up in so many high school and college English courses. While it is so different from modern works, it contains the essential parts of great literature. It is unique in many ways, just as its manuscript is rare and precious. No other work in English can tie together so many time periods, while still using character and theme in recognizably modern ways. No other work in Old English presents so many levels of complexity. While showing us a different culture, it poses contemporary questions, and raises issues of enduring significance.

IN DEPTH: WHY THE DANES?

Why was the story of Beowulf, set in Denmark and Sweden, written in Old English by an Anglo-Saxon? As far as we know, there is no poem or story about Beowulf in Danish or Swedish, but only in Old English. Given the unpopularity of Danish pirates in England, who would take the trouble to preserve a very long poem about them? Who would want to hear it recited or read out loud? There are a few theories, but no one can give a definitive answer to these questions.

One possibility is that the poem of *Beowulf* was retained from the era when Angles, Saxons, and Jutes lived near Denmark and may have shared culture and history. They may have heard of the fabulously strong and brave prince of Geatland and sung his legendary exploits. These recited poems may have been updated through the years, gradually shifted into more "modern" forms of Old English, and finally written down and copied over. Since a historical Beowulf would have lived around the time that the Anglo-Saxons were migrating, the time needed to recall and preserve this memory before the advent of writing would only have been about 150 years, not a long time by folklore standards.

Another possibility is that the stories of Beowulf existed in some legendary form, but not in the verse forms we have. An Anglo-Saxon poet may have given these stories some thought and put together the long, literary composition we have today, fleshing out the shorter legends into a thoughtful, polished piece and being careful to add some Christian morality. He would have completed this task around 750, well before the name "Dane" came to be synonymous with "viking" and "pirate." The manuscript would have been copied after that, so perhaps its value as literature and history was apparent to the monks, so that they preserved its written form after its content ceased to appeal to audiences. This has been the dominant theory about the creation of the poem, and there are many points of evidence to support it.

Finally, the poem could have been entirely composed during the time of King Canute. The stories might not have come with the Anglo-Saxons, but rather with the Danish poets who recited stories out loud. An English poet, carefully arranging the material he had heard, could have wished to please Canute and his court by writing an English poem with a Danish twist. While this theory is new, there is some evidence to support it. (See Chapter 8, "Placing *Beowulf* on a Timeline," for more detail on the evidence for these theories.)

FURTHER SUGGESTED READING

Baker, Peter S. *The Beowulf Reader.* New York: Garland Publishing, Inc., 2000.

Burlin, Robert B. and Edward B. Irving Jr., eds. *Old English Studies in Honour of John C. Pope.* Toronto: University of Toronto Press, 1974.

Chambers, R. W. *Beowulf: An Introduction to the Study of the Poem with a Discussion of the Stories of Offa and Finn.* Cambridge: Cambridge University Press, 1958.

Clark, George. *Beowulf.* Boston: Twayne, 1990.

Creed, Robert P., ed. *Old English Poetry: Fifteen Essays.* Providence, RI: Brown University Press, 1967.

Fry, Donald K., ed. *The Beowulf Poet: A Collection of Critical Essays.* Englewood Cliffs, NJ: Prentice-Hall, Inc., 1968. (Reprints Tolkien's 1936 lecture, "Beowulf: The Monsters and the Critics.")

Fulk, R. D. *Interpretations of Beowulf: A Critical Anthology.* Bloomington: Indiana University Press, 1991. (Reprints Tolkien's 1936 lecture, "Beowulf: The Monsters and the Critics.")

Garmonsway, G. N. and Jacqueline Simpson. *Beowulf and Its Analogues.* New York: Dutton, 1968. (Includes translations of the many Germanic stories that overlap with *Beowulf.*)

Goldsmith, Margaret E. *The Mode and Meaning of "Beowulf."* London: Athlone Press, 1970.

Green, Eugene. *Anglo-Saxon Audiences.* New York: Peter Lang, 2001.

Greenfield, Stanley B. *Hero and Exile: The Art of Old English Poetry.* London: Hambledon Press, 1989.

——, ed. *Studies in Old English Literature in Honor of Arthur G. Brodeur.* New York: Russell and Russell, 1963.

Greenfield, Stanley B. and Daniel G. Calder. *A New Critical History of Old English Literature.* New York: New York University Press, 1986.

Irving, Edward B. Jr. *Introduction to Beowulf.* Englewood Cliffs, NJ: Prentice-Hall, Inc., 1969.

——. *A Reading of Beowulf.* Philadelphia: University of Pennsylvania Press, 1968.

——. *Rereading Beowulf.* Philadelphia: University of Pennsylvania Press, 1989.

Kiernan, Kevin. *Beowulf and the Beowulf Manuscript.* Brunswick, NJ: Rutgers University Press, 1981.

Nicholson, Lewis E. *An Anthology of Beowulf Criticism.* Notre Dame: University of Notre Dame Press, 1963. (Reprints Tolkien's 1936 lecture, "Beowulf: The Monsters and the Critics.")

Ogilvy, J. D. A. and Donald C. Baker. *Reading Beowulf: An Introduction to the Poem, Its Background, and Its Style.* Norman: University of Oklahoma Press, 1983.

Orchard, Andy. *A Critical Companion to Beowulf.* Cambridge: D. S. Brewer, 2003.

Overing, Gillian and Marijane Osborn. *Landscape of Desire: Partial Stories of the Medieval Scandinavian World.* Minneapolis: University of Minnesota Press, 1994. (Includes an article on mapping the places in *Beowulf.*)

Robinson, Fred C. *Beowulf and the Appositive Style.* Knoxville: University of Tennessee Press, 1985.

———. *The Tomb of Beowulf.* Cambridge: Blackwell Publishers, 1993.

Stanley, Eric Gerald. *In the Foreground: Beowulf.* Cambridge: D. S. Brewer, 1994.

Stitt, J. Michael. *Beowulf and the Bear's Son: Epic, Saga and Fairytale in Northern Germanic Tradition.* New York: Garland, 1992.

Tacitus, Cornelius. *Germania.* (Available online, and in many print editions.)

Thompson, Stephen P., ed. *Readings on Beowulf.* San Diego: Greenhaven Press, 1998.

Whitelock, Dorothy. *The Audience of Beowulf.* Oxford: Oxford Unversity Press, 1951.

2

Choosing a Translation

B_{EOWULF} is one of the most translated of ancient texts. There are over 100 translations spread over the last two centuries, and every year some new translation is published. This prolific activity is far beyond that of the Greek classics such as *The Odyssey*, and even beyond that of the *Bible*. What is it that drives scholars and poets to keep trying their hand at *Beowulf*? And how can one choose well among the many translations?

There are three essential decisions that a translator must make, and these decisions account for the differences among the many versions. Because there is no one decision that can be considered the right one, and because there are many sub-choices, each translation (even if it seems complete and perfect) can most likely be improved. This is why so many translators keep trying: they feel that there is always room for one more translation. The three basic decisions for a translator are: Will I write a prose story, or follow the original as poetry? Will I use fancy or plain language? Will I translate as close to word-for-word as possible, or allow for movement of word order within a large phrase?

The major structural question confronting a translator is whether to preserve the poem's poetic form or change it to something more read-able for a modern audience. It is a question of purpose, as prose is gen-erally easier to read. If a poem is translated to prose, however, has it been changed too much? There is no "right" answer, only personal opinion. Most translators have attempted to keep the verse form, with varying degrees of faithfulness. Some, especially in the nineteenth century, tried to update the verse by rhyming the lines. Most of them have tried to imitate the verse form of the original, which used alliteration, not rhyme, as its main sound effect. The original used three alliterated words in every line: two in the first half of the line, and one in the second half. This is difficult to work out in Modern English, and it can sound very artificial if tried. Inevitably, the choice to keep a natural-sounding modern tone means moving away from the strictest re-creation of the poem's sounds. Prose translations, of course, are freer to sound natural and ignore the poetic sounds.

J. R. R. Tolkien felt that the poem was composed as a modern antique, a story that even in its creation was intended to look and sound old. It made use of legends of the past, and it re-created the pagan atmosphere of the past. For that reason, he felt that antique-sounding words and syntax would best convey the tone of the poem. Tolkien never published his prose translation, and other translators have made the same choice. Francis Gummere's 1909 translation, as well as others of the same period, uses the antiquated language familiar to us through children's classics such as *Robin Hood*. Seamus Heaney's 2000 translation also uses "fancy" language, but in a different vein. Heaney sometimes chooses antique or regional words to convey the tone of the text and to explore the possibilities of English in connecting places and times of the past. For example, the Geats' war-gear becomes "war-graith," and the embattled fortress of Heorot is a "bawn" (an old Irish word for "castle"). (Heaney won the 1999 Whitbread Book Award for his original poetic choices.) On the other hand, a translator who chooses plain language tries to use the current coinage of Modern English to create lines that are equivalent to the original, but without unusual diction or phrasing. In the last fifty years, this choice has been more common, and most translators try to choose words that could be used in everyday speech.

Finally, the original text often uses strained, poetic, and unnatural word order, because the Anglo-Saxon poet, too, had to manipulate words to create the alliterative pattern. A translator must decide how closely the word order will follow the original. Will he try to translate each word as it comes, or will he allow himself to rearrange them within the line? What about rearranging the words within two lines, or perhaps within four or five? For example, if there is a normal sentence structure over four lines, and within that sentence the phrases are all mixed up so as to be poetic in Old English, should the translator rearrange the order according to Modern English, perhaps moving a phrase from the first to the third line? Translators always prefer to stick closely to an original, but here they must choose the amount of trade-off they will permit, and how to balance literalness and readability in the word order.

You can see the difference these choices make in the following excerpts: the question that the Danish Coast Guard asks Beowulf, the first reported speech in the poem (237–240), could be rendered in literal (unreadable) form: "What are you [plural] of war-gear-bearers / by chain mail protected, that thus lofty ship [or 'tall keel'] / over water-street to lead [you] come / hither over waves?" In the original, the first phrase alliterates two s's, the second two b's, the third two l's, and the last two h's.

First, here are four prose translations (published more than a hundred years apart) that illustrate the translators' choices. J. M. Kemble's 1835 translation uses a closely literal word order: "What are ye, of armed men, guarded with mailed coats, that thus have come to lead a foaming keel, over the lake paths, hither over the deeps of the sea?" John Earle's 1892 translation asked, "Who are ye arm-bearing men, fenced with mail-coats, who have come thus with proud ship over the watery highway, hither over the billows?" David Wright's 1957 translation asks in very ordinary, idiomatic Modern English, "What sort of people may you be who have come in arms across the ocean in that great ship?" S. A. J. Bradley's 1982 translation seeks a balance between poetic and ordinary diction: "What sort of armour-bearing men are you, protected by corselets, who have come here in this manner, steering your tall ship over the seaways and over the deeps?" Kemble and Earle left the original "hither" (an Old English word) in its place, Bradley moved it to the center as "here," while Wright omitted it. Earle chose to translate "lofty" in the sense of pride, while Bradley chose a literal meaning of having a tall mast. Kemble chose a different phrase, "foaming keel," to suggest the ship, while Wright called it a "great ship."

It is hard to use "fancier" diction than the kind William Morris chose for his 1895 poetic translation: "What men be ye then of them that have war-gear, / With byrnies bewarded, who the keel high upbuilded / Over the Lake-street thus have come leading, / Hither o'er holm-ways hieing in ring-stem?" The antiquated language allowed Morris to choose words that imitate the exact original alliteration in three lines: byrnies, bewarded, builded; Lake, leading; Hither, holm, hieing. Francis Gummere' 1909 translation asks, "Who are ye, then, ye armed men, / mailed folk, that yon mighty vessel / have urged thus over the ocean ways, / here o'er the waters?" Slightly less antiquated than Morris' diction, Gummere's diction allows for some alliteration while using words that are easily understood. Frederick Rebsamen's 1991 translation asks, "Who might you be in your burnished mailcoats / strutting with weapons? Who steered this warboat / deep-running keel across the wave-swells / here against this shore?" Seamus Heaney's 2000 poetic translation asks,

"What kind of men are you who arrive / rigged out for combat in coats of mail, / sailing here over the sea-lanes / in your steep-hulled boat?" By rearranging the words, both Rebsamen and Heaney imitate some alliteration. Rebsamen uses "might, be, burnished, mail" in the first line, followed by "weapons, Who, warboat, wave-swells" crossing over two lines. Heaney's alliteration also crosses line boundaries, and is not restricted to the visual first letter. It begins with the sound, if not the letter, of *r* ("are, arrive, rigged") in the first sequence, followed by "combat, coats; sailing, sea, steep." Both of these modern poetic translations try to use updated poetic language, leaning toward fancy, rather than plain, diction.

Perhaps the most strictly literal translation is Ben Slade's (2002). He follows the exact word order whenever possible: "What are you armor-wearers / bound in byrnies, who thus your tall keel / over the sea-street leading came, / hither over the waters?" Each phrase remains in the position it has in the original text, with alliteration or readability where it is convenient, but no attempt to smooth it into a modern-sounding question. By contrast, Burton Raffel's well-known 1963 poetic translation is freer with the exact word choices and order: "Whose soldiers are you, / You who've been carried in your deep-keeled ship / Across the sea-road to this country of mine?" By changing the content slightly, adding the phrase "this country of mine," and omitting the reiterations of armor and chain mail, Raffel is able to make a shorter, more direct question, but one that does not imitate (in these line) the alliteration or convey the exact wording of the original. Similarly, Michael Alexander's (1973) Coast Guard asks, "Strangers, you have steered this steep craft / through the sea-ways, sought our coast. / I can see you are warriors; you wear that dress now. I must ask who you are." Frederick Rebsamen's 1991 lines try to strike a balance: "Who might you be in your burnished mailcoats / shining with weapons? Who steered this warboat / deep-running keel across the waveswells / here against this shore?" Alan Sullivan and Timothy Murphy (2004) render the question, "What warriors are you, wearers of armor, / bearers of weapons, daring to bring / your lofty longboat over the sea-lane?" It is impossible to cover every recent translation, but most of them try to find a balance between poetic grace and literal precision.

The translation I use for this book, whenever lines of *Beowulf* need to be quoted, is R. M. Liuzza's poem (2000). Liuzza's choices are moderate, combining easy readability with a good level of literal translation. His Danish Coast Guard asks Beowulf, "What are you, warriors in armor, wearing / coats of mail, who have come thus sailing / over the sea-road in a tall ship, / hither over the waves?" His diction is plain, not fancy, but it seeks to alliterate where possible ("warriors, wearing; coats, come; sailing, sea"). I found his division of the poem into "chapters," headed by Roman numerals, easy on the eyes, and he preserves the line numbers needed for study. In addition to the translations that I had at my disposal, Liuzza provided some unusual excerpts (including some of the translations discussed here) in an appendix. His appendices include many of the texts often discussed in conjunction with *Beowulf*, which makes the edition indispensable to the amateur scholar.

FURTHER SUGGESTED READING

Tinker, Chauncey Brewster. *The Translations of Beowulf: A Critical Bibliography*. New York: Gordon Press, 1967.

3

The Hero Comes to Denmark

MAIN CHARACTER INTRODUCTIONS

Hrothgar: King of the Danes, he lives at a hall called Heorot, which is probably located on the island of Sjaelland in modern Denmark. Hrothgar is growing old, with a wife (Wealhtheow) and three teenage children (Freawaru, Hrethric, and Hrothmund). He is past his years of strength, but in his younger days he was a successful war leader and enriched his people. He is above all wise, and he values traditional customs, generosity, and loyalty. He is cautious about accepting the young stranger, Beowulf, but once he confirms Beowulf's good qualities, he welcomes him as a son. Hrothgar loves beautiful things and has decorated his hall with an inlaid wood floor and tapestries woven with gold. He can play the harp and sing.

Wealhtheow: Queen of the Danes, wife to Hrothgar. Wealhtheow means "foreign servant," perhaps showing that she came from a faraway place as part of a peace treaty between two nations. She is probably younger than Hrothgar and knows she will outlive him, and she worries about the future. Her first concern, of course, is that the monster should stop killing off the men of the court before they become completely vulnerable to enemies. She is attentive to court politics and is careful to reward friends richly.

Beowulf: Nephew to King of the Geats (Hygelac). He is probably around twenty years old and eager to use his strength to combat evil and win fame. Although he is very close to his uncle's family, he must venture out and accomplish something on his own before he can inherit an estate. As a young teenager he may have been impulsive in showing off his strength, but now he shows a steady purpose and unwavering courage. He is developing political smarts, and he looks around at the Danish court to understand who is important there and what is likely to be the next turn of their history.

UNFERTH: This Dane is the "thyle" (*thee-lee*), a kind of spokesman in the Danish court. He sees Beowulf as a threat, and as he becomes somewhat drunk, he verbally challenges Beowulf. Everyone listens, and most likely Unferth is only saying what many are thinking. Later, Unferth will try to make friends with Beowulf by lending him a sword.

GRENDEL: A large, man-eating monster who lives in a swampy lake. He may be a kind of troll. He hates human joy and lives only to wage war against the Danes.

MINOR CHARACTERS: Scyld Scefing is the ancestor of Hrothgar, and his family history occupies the opening lines; an unnamed watchman on the coastline is the first to meet Beowulf; Wulfgar is the noble doorkeeper of Heorot, probably a ceremonial post of honor. An unnamed poet sings a long story about Finn, Hildeburh, Hnaef, and Hengest and compares Beowulf to Sigemund the dragon-slayer and Heremod, a legendary Danish king.

OPENING LINES (1–193)

The story of Beowulf begins, not with Beowulf, but with another story. Like many fairy tales, it begins in the dim, ancestral past, with a legend. Traditionally, fairy tales begin by setting the action "long ago" or "once upon a time." A fairy tale that happened last year would lose its enchantment, and a fairy tale that happened in 1873 would invite precise research and contradiction. Like urban legends, tales of the fantastic must happen in a time somewhat remembered but mostly remote. The opening line of this poem includes the expression "in bygone days," or "in days of yore." The action takes place in a past just before living human memory.

To evoke this past, the poet describes the legendary founding of the royal house where the action will take place. Instead of opening the action with the monster's attacks, he goes back several generations and asks us to picture the legendary King Scyld of the Spear-Danes: "That was a good king!"

We can assume that the audience of *Beowulf* was aware of King Scyld in the same way that you are aware of King Solomon, Richard the Lion-Hearted, or even George Washington. A modern reader would not need more than a few details about George Washington to set the scene in early America, and the audience of *Beowulf* required only a few antique details to carry their minds back to the glorious ancestral past. Most of what they knew is lost to us; we have only hints here and there as to what they knew about King Scyld and his family. If modern scholars have one major criticism of the poet of *Beowulf*, it is that he did not give us enough background. We wish that we knew just what to think of the characters and setting, but we can only tie together the most reasonable construction. What else was known about Hrothgar? Why did a stranger from southern Sweden come to help him with his monster difficulties? Who were the other characters in this story, and when they speak or act, what is the significance?

Scyld's Ship Burial

The death and burial of Scyld Sceafing is the first major business of the poem. Scyld is supposed to be the founder of the royal house. Perhaps he is a real person, but most likely his character is legendary. *Beowulf* tells us that he arrived in a boat after being cast away and lost as a small child or infant. The Danes, seeing him as a gift from the Gods, took the child in and raised him to be their king. He was a successful war leader. When he died, he asked for a burial in a ship so that he might return the way he came and be given back to the sea. His boat was loaded with the riches he had helped the people to gain from raids.

No one is sure exactly when *Beowulf* was composed, but most scholars agree that, by its day, ship burials were rare. Perhaps there was a community memory of the lavishness of these old pagan funerals, just as stories may circulate today about the wastefulness of the super rich: Fountains of champagne! Vats of caviar! Ice sculptures! We are amazed at how different these events are from everyday life. It is clear that the audience of *Beowulf* did not think of ship burials as a normal part of life, and there is a strong indication that the burial of Scyld stood out even among ship burials.

Archeologists have discovered ship burials in England and Scandinavia. The most famous one in England is Mound Three at a place called Sutton Hoo in Suffolk, near the eastern seacoast. There are ship burials in Sweden, and a few have even been identified as the burials of characters mentioned in *Beowulf*. We know, then, that kings were often buried this way at the time of the story's action. However, we know that the pagan Germanic tribes also used cremation, as they believed that fire instantly released the soul to heaven (and kept ghosts from coming back). In 921, the Arab Ibn Fadlan wrote an account of a ship burial among a people he called the Rus, who may have been either Slavic or North Germanic. In the burial he witnessed, the dead king was placed on his ship, but the ship was then burned with the corpse. In other burials, the ship was not burned, but the body may have been. In these mound burials, a structure of timbers was raised over the ship, and then dirt was piled up to cover it.

Scyld's burial was different from these historical burials. Because he had come from the sea as an infant, he was given back to the sea at death. The poem describes exotic treasures heaped around his body, which was laid by the mast. The ship was decked with war-gear, including "byrnies" (coats of chain mail), swords, and spears. It was heaped with imported treasures from distant lands, and a gold banner (or crown) was set over his head. The Danish people were showing Scyld their gratitude for his help in gaining these treasures through raiding and peaceful trade. But why did they set him adrift on the sea? This was a very unusual ship burial. The people knew exactly what might happen to this ship. Ideally, it might sink, giving Scyld and his treasures back to the sea. Realistically, it would drift and tip so that the treasures would wash up on another shore and enrich strangers. There is a suggestion of this outcome in the last lines: "Men do not know / (lines 50–52) who received that cargo."

Some scholars have questioned whether Scyld would really have been set adrift in this way. Newton (1993) argues that because the boat might have just drifted back to shore a mile down the coast (in an unromantic ending); therefore it is implausible that the burial could have taken this form. He argues that it was a metaphor for setting Scyld's soul free, that no one could know what spiritual coast he came to. By this reasoning, the ship must have been buried in a mound like any other. Others accept the ship burial as it is told and reason that it might have been a highly unusual ritual performed in special circumstances. Some see in the story a religious myth with nature symbolism.

Scholars questioned just how exotic Scyld's treasures could have been, until the Sutton Hoo mound was excavated in 1939. The treasures included many imported articles, including coins and jewels. Overall, it was more finely made and richer than anyone believed possible, with the remains of an exquisitely decorated helmet and other weapons. Books showing the Sutton Hoo treasure may be as close as we can get to historical illustrations of Scyld' treasure.

ROYAL FAMILY TREES

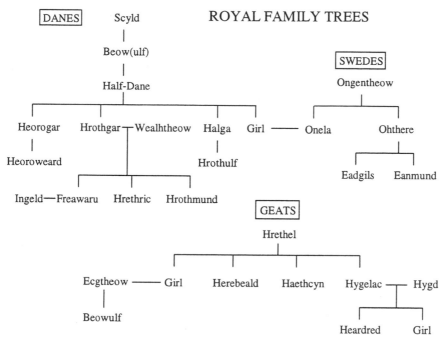

Three royal family trees: Danish, Geatish, and Swedish.

The Scyldings

Using other Germanic sources, scholars have put together a tentative history of the Scyldings. *Beowulf* remains our most detailed source, but some other poems and stories from other times and places can support or modify what we have. If you can understand the history of the Scyldings, then you will find many mysterious lines in the poem easier to interpret.

To indicate a son, Old English added the suffix "-ing." Scyld was the son of Sceaf, and so he is called "Scyld Sceafing" (or "Scefing"). The descendants of Scyld were "Scyldings." The first Scylding is introduced as "Beowulf," although he appears in some other genealogical lists as "Beow." It seems plausible that Beow was originally intended but was mistakenly changed to match the name of the monster-slaying hero. It is confusing to a modern reader, knowing that the story will be about "Beowulf," to find a character with this name so quickly passed over.

Beow's son, Healfdene (or Half-Dane), is the father of four children. We hear little of Healfdene, because the focus is on his children: Heorogar, Hrothgar, Halga, and a girl, said to be married to Onela, the Swedish king. Scandinavian sources describe a certain King Helgi (probably the same person as Halga) as being the most important Scylding king, but in this poem Halga is completely unimportant. "Helgi" is a figure of ambivalent virtue, but this Halga is called "the good"; perhaps to overcome any negative impressions listeners had from other legends. The brothers Heorogar and Halga appear to have died by this time, but Halga's son, Hrothulf, lives at his uncle's court.

The story of the monster-slaying takes place at a time when the succession of the Danish kingdom is in question. We are to understand that Hrothgar is an old man, too old to defend his own hall. Perhaps we are to assume that Hrothgar married late, which would mean he is in his sixties while his children are young and his nephew Hrothulf is possibly twenty-five. Hrothulf is an established warrior, partially raised under his uncle Hrothgar's rule while Hrothgar's own sons are not yet warriors. The daughter, Freawaru, is old enough to marry and has been betrothed to Ingeld, King of the Heathobards. The story takes place while all of these young people are, in retrospect, in the most peaceful time of their lives.

Audiences already knew some of the future story. Choosing this setting was like telling a story of the Hatfields and the McCoys in the time when they were still friends across their boundary river. It was like telling a story of some young men graduating from West Point in 1845, when the North and South had not yet imagined the war that would eventually pit the officers against each other in battle. Every reader of these stories would know what was in store, just by the names and places. The story of the Scyldings was apparently almost as well known, and the narrator could count on his audience to connect the dots.

Two feuds were twined around Hrothgar's young family. The conflict most central to this section of the poem involves the nephew, Hrothulf. Some other sources join *Beowulf* in hinting that Hrothulf became the next king and killed Hrethric, the older boy, after Hrothgar's death. It is possible that Hrothmund escaped from this struggle and chose exile; the name appears in a genealogy list of the Kings of East Anglia. The second feud involved the marriage of Freawaru to Ingeld. Beowulf himself discusses this later (in lines 2020–2069). Beowulf hints that this marriage is intended to settle a feud, but it will not settle it. Eventually, Ingeld's men will take up the feud again, with disastrous results for Freawaru and all.

The question of who will succeed Hrothgar is important in the action of the story. Hrothgar is a good king, but he is old. He does not have any hero on hand with enough strength to stand up to Grendel. His thanes (ranking members of the king's warrior band and men of noble birth) have been killed at a rapid rate, and even in Grendel's last raid he loses one valued counselor. If he dies, he will not leave behind any power structure. His sons are not weak by nature, but they will require loyal followers to support them. Hrothulf is clearly older and stronger than they are. At this time he seems to be loyal to his uncle and bound by gratitude for being raised so well after his father's death; but will he remain loyal?

Hrothgar's Religion

It is worth noting at this point that there is an anomaly in the way Hrothgar is presented in this poem. At times the narrator implies that Hrothgar has knowledge of the God of the Bible, and at other times he implies that Hrothgar worships pagan gods. Lines 90–100 describe how Hrothgar's court poet, or "scop" (*shop*) in Old English, often sings of God's Creation. It is clearly meant to be the creation story of Genesis, not the Norse myth that creation was through a giant and a huge cow. But lines 170–185 describe Hrothgar's despair at Grendel's incessant attacks, and Hrothgar is clearly shown permitting and perhaps joining in pagan worship. The narrator calls the object of this worship "the soul-slayer," meaning the devil. In line 185, he says that they "remembered hell" and did not "know the Maker" and did not even know "how to praise the heavenly Protector."

It is clear, first, that in a factual sense, Hrothgar is a pagan, and that the narrator of *Beowulf* knows this. It is unlikely that Hrothgar's "scop" could have been telling the Genesis story of creation, and the narrator/author of the poem seems sophisticated enough to realize this. Earlier critics considered this dual presentation a mistake; a place where someone had penned in a few lines and neglected to iron out the anomaly. Clearly, critics said, the poem had been pagan and a Christian scribe altered the lines to imply the Genesis account.

However, it is not necessary to suggest altered lines. While the narrator knows that Hrothgar is a pagan, he admires him and wants us to see that there are Christian virtues in him. He is a noble king and a noble pagan. There are poetic versions of Genesis in Old English, and it is likely that these versions were recited in Christian Anglo-Saxon courts, where stories of Woden and Thor were no longer welcome. The narrator of *Beowulf* wishes us to imagine a court where all are noble and all things are done in a civilized, orderly manner. To show the joy and harmony of Heorot when it was first built, the narrator puts into the mouth of Hrothgar's poet the most joyful, harmonious, civilized, orderly song possible: the song of Creation. The narrator expected his audience not to be fooled into believing this was an anachronism. Not a hundred lines later, he expects full agreement with the statement, "they remembered hell in their minds." As noble as they are, Hrothgar and his court are still pagans.

The attitude of the Anglo-Saxons toward the pagans during the eighth, ninth, and tenth centuries was sympathetic. They sent missionaries to the Old Saxons, their distant relatives on the continent. Gradually, through the efforts of devoted missionaries like Boniface and Egbert, the Saxons became Christian. Both groups were aware of their relationship: in 738, Boniface wrote a letter home to the churches in England and said that the Saxons considered them "of one blood and one bone." Sharing many cultural beliefs with the pagan Saxons, the Anglo-Saxons admired them as noble pagans. They earnestly desired their salvation.

Lines 178–188 could express this attitude toward the "noble pagan": the good man who will be hopelessly damned but perhaps would believe in the true God if he could. Is it possible that the author of *Beowulf* was influenced by Boniface's letter and other writings like it? Perhaps he wished that Hrothgar and Beowulf had lived during a time when they might have become Christians, and he felt the goodness of their virtues of loyalty and courage and allowed himself to use more Christian coloring than the facts allowed. (For a more complete discussion, see Chapter 10, "Religion in *Beowulf*.")

Grendel

For eighty-five lines, the poet describes a setting of joy and communal ties, relative peace in a society torn by wars. Then the first note of discord arrives: a "bold demon" waits in the darkness. We are told the demon's name, "Grendel," and little else. Who is Grendel, what does he do, and why?

Grendel's physical appearance is not described, but the reader can conclude that he is both tall and strong. In line 721 he is able to rip open a door that is bound fast with iron. He has no difficulty killing and eating a man. He is able to fit inside the hall with ease, and move about, but the king's hall probably has a high ceiling. Grendel may be twice as big as a normal man, perhaps ten to twelve feet tall. We know that he has claws, as he is able to slit a man open, but these claws could be fingernails that are longer and stronger than usual. We know that much later in the poem, Beowulf is able to carry Grendel's head by the hair, so we can picture hair long enough to serve as a good handle. Apart from these details, we know nothing more about Grendel's appearance. Lines 795–

805 tells us that iron would not work against him. Much later in the poem, Beowulf himself adds that Grendel carried a bag with him that was cleverly made of dragon skins, and that he planned to stuff uneaten victims into this bag and carry them off. Perhaps Grendel would wear a wide leather belt with this large pouch tucked into it.

In addition to his name, Grendel is called by other titles. He is referred to as the "bold demon," the "fiend from Hell," the "grim spirit," but also the "miserable man" (86–105). He is the "unholy creature," the "great ravager," and the "foe of mankind" (120–164). His titles tend to describe his murderous streak (like "evil marauder" [712]) or his moral evil (like "Shepherd of sins" [750] or "God's adversary" [786]). But the title most often used is the simplest: he is "æglæca," meaning the awesome one. He strikes fear and awe into everyone, and he is amazing to see. This title is morally neutral and is sometimes also used for heroes. However, Grendel is not seen as neutral. As the foe of mankind and the adversary of God, Grendel is portrayed as most definitely evil.

Grendel's motivation for raiding Hrothgar's hall is given in simple terms in lines 86–90: when he hears the poet in the hall praising God's act of Creation, he suffers. Miserably angry at the joy of Heorot's community, he must spy on them and take his private revenge for what seems not to be even his business. Why should Grendel, an unknown creature of the moor and swamp, take offense at Hrothgar's thanes drinking and hearing cheerful songs? Grendel's motivation, though stated clearly, raises more questions than it answers.

The answers lie in understanding the Germanic concept of monsters. This concept had deep roots in their earlier pagan beliefs, and a modified understanding of monsters continued long into the Christian era. It is hard for us to believe that the Germanic peoples, including the Christian English, completely believed in monsters. There is no doubt that the English believed in certain classes of beings just as firmly as they believed that lions existed in Africa, and perhaps more firmly, since they had "evidence" at times. England was scattered with mysterious arrowheads, called "elf-shot." Elves were known to cause sickness, and sufferers had to be cured by means of charms and spells. Trolls and dragons were less likely to trouble innocent people, as they stayed in remote places and kept to themselves, but there is no doubt that the English believed in them as well.

Monsters had an ancient place in the Germanic system. According to the pagan creation stories, in the beginning there were the gods and the giants. The gods included those still familiar to us: Odin/Woden, Thor, Freya, and many more. The giants were a cross between forces of nature and supernatural beings; they had control over storms, and most of them lived in the extreme north and were often called the Frost Giants. The gods and giants were perpetually and fundamentally at war, though some stories played on this tension by depicting temporary alliances or even marriages between gods and friendly giants. In the end, however, the giants were fated to attack and destroy the gods. The last battle of the gods, "Ragnarok," ended in their defeat, but the gods never gave up, battling like true Germanic heroes. The Northern Germanic concept of the gods was not a particularly moral one. The gods and the giants do not seem, by our light, to be very different. However, the gods stood for civilization and order and for upholding what men valued. The giants controlled destructive weather, while among the gods were forces of sunlight and growth.

Monsters fit into this system as the offspring and servants of the giants or Loki, the wicked god. In the battle of Ragnarok a giant serpent, a fierce, giant dog, and a deadly wolf would join the giants in their attack. While some magical creatures (like Odin's eight-legged horse) could serve the gods, the "monsters" (the misshapen, deformed, and threatening kind) were always against them. Monsters were on the side of the destruction of civilization, and as such their role in Ragnarok was to bring about the end of order.

When the English became Christians, they did not see any reason to stop believing in elves, trolls, dragons, and other monsters. In fact, many people at this time had such beliefs, because so much of the world was unexplored. From remote places came reports of huge creatures with long, white tusks and of giant ants that mined for gold. The English-produced *Liber Monstrorum* (*Book of Monsters*) includes dark-skinned people, Homer's one-eyed Cyclops, and humans with dog heads. Indeed, the manuscript group in which we find *Beowulf* includes *The Passion of St. Christopher*, the story of a dog-headed man who becomes a Christian missionary and is tortured for his faith. Some "monsters," such as scorpions and lions, were clearly part of ordinary animal life. But where did other monsters fit into the new Christian cosmology? If they were not the offspring and pets of the Frost Giants, then who were they?

Beowulf's poet explains these monsters' origin to his audience. In lines 102–114 we have Grendel's formal introduction, and we learn that he and other monsters are part of Cain's race. Cain was the first-born son of Adam, who killed his brother Abel in Genesis 4. After he killed him, he buried the body in secrecy, but God witnessed Cain's actions and punished him with banishment.

Kin-slaying held a special fascination for the Germanic people, as it was the ultimate betrayal of the most important bonds of blood loyalty. The Anglo-Saxons must have felt a keen interest in the story of Cain, his crime, and his banishment. They may have wondered why the feud ended with Cain, because in Germanic tradition the sons or brothers of the dead man would have to carry out revenge. The Bible does not list any son for Abel, but Adam had a third son named Seth. To Germanic minds, Seth would have the duty of continuing the feud.

The poet of *Beowulf* tells us that Cain and his descendants were in perpetual feud with God and man. In the medieval view, all living men were descended from Noah after the Flood, and Noah was descended from Seth; therefore, all living men were of the line of Seth. Given this lineage, wouldn't Cain's line continue to feud with the line of Seth, even today? Due to Cain's hideous evil, his descendants included giants and monsters. So in Cain's crime, subsequent feud, and deformed descendants, the English had a place to locate their monsters. If the descendants of Cain were at perpetual feud with God, then men, as the descendants of Seth, were at feud with the monsters. Moreover, because Cain was banished, the monsters were outlaws. An outlaw could be killed legally, and his family prevented from taking vengeance. An outlaw was literally outside the law, outside the protection of the community. The English did not see anything wrong with killing a monster; it was not like needlessly killing a useful beast, or immorally killing a man. Monsters were meant to be killed; they were outlaws. Monsters were at war, a terrorist guerilla war in which any and every man might be a target.

Grendel fits into this framework neatly. Like other giants and monsters, he is of the line of Cain, at feud with God and the descendants of Seth. When he heard the joyful songs of creation, he ground his teeth and swore to destroy Heorot. He is at war with Hrothgar's people, young and old. They can never strike back at him, but he remains at war with them for twelve years. Lines 154–155 tell us that he wanted no peace with any Dane, and lines 156–158 remind us that he never gave any compensation for these wrongful deaths. Lines 135–137 remind us that Grendel did not mourn over the destruction he caused, because he was "too fixed" in his feud. He is a one-monster, guerilla war machine.

Grendel's mode of attack is primitive. He comes at night, like an Icelandic zombie or ghost (several stories feature Grendel-like characters that must have their heads cut off). He does not use much intelligence but seems to walk in and kill someone instantly. He appears to work quietly, as he is often able to kill more than one person and even eat them on the spot. This way of fighting was disgusting to the Germanic peoples on several levels. It was cowardly, as the victims were always sleeping and could not fight back. It required no skill with weapons, and indeed Grendel uses none. Beowulf describes him as not knowing any "arts of war" (681–682) but as merely "brave / in his wicked deeds." Most importantly, his way of fighting was cannibalistic and revolting. Grendel drinks blood, which was disgusting and horrifying to the Christian English (who knew that Acts 15:29 forbade eating blood). Grendel's flamboyant blood drinking was guaranteed to turn stomachs and mark him as a particularly evil monster.

In the end, what kind of monster is Grendel? He has attributes of three different kinds, and without more description, no one can tell exactly what he was. Like a troll, he is large and lives in the wilderness, but he is also somewhat man-like. Like water monsters, he lives in a swampy lake. Like a ghost, he must have his head cut off. Perhaps the audience of the poem was willing to enlist all three kinds of creatures in their mental image of this fierce, evil monster.

THE ARRIVAL OF THE HERO (194–490)

With the scene set—the good king cornered by an evil monster—the hero begins to arrive. This is given in three stages: the sea crossing, the arrival at the coastline, and the arrival at Heorot.

The Sea Crossing

Lines 194–228 show us the voyage from Geatland to the Danish coast across an arm of the Baltic Sea. The hero is not named but is called only Hygelac's thane. A thane was a ranking member of the king's warrior band, a man of noble birth. Hygelac may have been known in legends. The *Liber Monstrorum* comments that Hygelac, "who ruled the Geats," was a giant that no horse could carry, and that his bones are preserved on an island in the Rhine River for all to see.

In lines 199–200 there are two good examples of the Germanic poetic diction technique, often called "kenning." This is a substitute phrase that leaves out the name of the actual item, but instead evokes it through its qualities. The hero wants his people to build a "wave-crosser," clearly a ship. He will take this vessel across the "swan's-riding," or the sea. The sea has many names in ancient poetic epics, since it was the most powerful natural object that coast-dwelling people faced. Vast, and both helpful and harmful, it was a force they could not forget. Here, the poet names it as the thing that the swan rides across; in another expression, it is the "whale's road." These substitute phrases evoke mental pictures and fit into the poetic

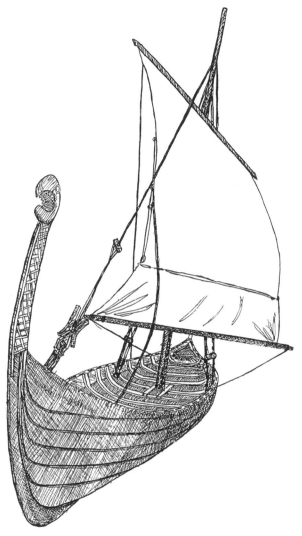

A seventh-century ship. A very small number of ships survived
through time to give us models to reconstruct ships of this period.
Steered at the back, they also used oars to supplement the wind.
(Figurehead based on a fifth-century one found at Appels, Belgium.)
(Illustration by L. D. Staver.)

line better than the single word. After calling the sea a "swan's-riding,"
the poet goes on to say that the ship flew like a bird, with its curved prow.
The image influences our mental picture of the ship: graceful and swift.

The short story of their crossing begins with the wish to go and challenge Grendel: the hero commands a ship to be built, consults wise men's

omens (presumably favorable), and selects a small band of strong war-riors. He chooses only fourteen companions. They board the ship with their war-gear, push off, and catch the wind for a flying start. Ships were one of the fastest ways to travel at this time. A ship running before the wind gave a sense of speed as the wind and drops of water blew in your face and the waves rushed past. A ship was slim and designed to cut through the waves; it was the race car or airplane of its time. The poet clearly admires ship travel and describes this journey with delight. On the second day, the war band arrives on the shores of Hrothgar's land.

Another item described in this passage is the armor. It is bright and finely polished, clearly an impressive sight to someone familiar with armor. On climbing out of the ship, the men shake out their mail-shirts. The armor description carries us into the second stage of their arrival, as the coast watchers see the brightness of their gear and sound the alarm.

The Arrival at the Coastline

Lines 229–319 describe the arrival of the hero in Denmark, and this scene takes place on the beach. The hero's reception by the Danish guard is not hostile; perhaps the smallness of the landing party reassures them that they are not under attack. The watchman can see that they are war-riors as they disembark, but because their manner does not suggest an attack, he is merely curious. However, he meets them with a martial flourish. Riding up, he shakes his spear and challenges them. He admits that he does not understand their purpose, coming openly under arms with one among them who is clearly a great lord. Are they spies of some sort? He cannot let them go without finding out. He wants to know their names, but more importantly, he wants to know their lineage, the names of their families.

Line 259 shows us a common Old English expression, one that seems stiff and strange to our ears. As the hero begins to answer, the narrator tells us he "unlocked his word-hoard." Speech, in this expression, is com-pared to a man who unlocks a treasure chest and begins to distribute the riches. Like the "swan's-riding," this description evokes a positive image of the hero's communication.

The hero answers, but at this stage of the poem he withholds his name. He repeats what we knew, that he is Hygelac's thane, but he adds the name of his father, Ecgtheow. He states that they are on a friendly mission and that he plans to give Hrothgar advice on how to rid himself of Grendel, if possible. If his advice does not work, then Hrothgar is doomed to endure his miserable situation forever.

Artist's conception of a warrior in full seventh-century armor.
His helmet bears a boar at the crest.
(Based on the Benty Grange boar-crest helmet.) (Illustration by L. D. Staver.)

The watchman responds first with a general observation. A warrior who wishes to think well, he says, must judge both words and deeds. This is his justification for the judgment he makes, which is to believe the stranger and let him proceed. He assures the hero of his help in guiding them and in guarding their abandoned ship.

This passage contains a detailed description of the armor that the Geats are wearing. In lines 303–306 we read that "boar-figures shone / over gold-plated cheek-guards, / gleaming, fire-hardened; they guarded the lives / of the grim battle-minded." The figure of the boar represented the god Frey, and was a common armor insignia. Archeologists have found several helmets with boar designs that are very similar to what the poem describes. As the strangers come within sight of Heorot, and the watchman leaves them to proceed alone, we learn more in lines 321–331 about the armor and weapons they carry. Below their boar-crested helmets, they have coats of chain mail. They carry shields (described as covered shields) and spears. Line 330 tells us that the spears were made of ash wood, and that the metal used in their gear was iron. (For more information, see "Weapons.")

The Arrival at Heorot

The arrival at Heorot is when Wulfgar, the doorkeeper, is first introduced. This position seems to have been a ceremonial post, rather than a menial job. Wulfgar is not a bellhop; he does not offer to carry their luggage. He is there to screen entrants to the hall, and he probably receives a measure of deference from the community. Wulfgar is called a prince of the Wendels, a neighboring Germanic tribe (also called the Vandals). Wulfgar has the right to walk up to Hrothgar and speak to him as a peer, if not quite an equal. Part of Wulfgar's job is to make sure that certain manners are enforced, and because the arriving hero follows these manners, he is reassured and pleased.

Wulfgar's first question is whether they are exiles. When there were struggles for dominance in one of the ruling families, survivors usually fled. If they fled to the court of a rival, they might be coming to ask for protection and eventual help. Much later in the poem, Beowulf will tell of a young king who helped an exile and found himself in over his head, and was killed. Taking in an exile was a risky decision. Beowulf has the look of an exile, coming with a small band of warriors, but his manner is more assured than an exile's. Wulfgar sees the swagger and consciousness of strength, and guesses that pride, not need, has brought them here.

Beowulf confirms that they are board companions of Hygelac. Every king had a group of warriors who ate at his table (board) and were expected to defend him to the death. This warrior band included young men who lived with the king and were trying to prove themselves so that they would win rewards of estates and wealth. The warrior band also included older men who already had estates, but who still spent part of their time with the king. Beowulf is one of the young men, and he seems to have chosen his companions from among the others. But they are not exiles; they are still the table-companions of Hygelac.

Now at last, in 343, the hero is ready to tell his own name: Beowulf. He asks permission to tell Hrothgar his errand, and Wulfgar politely reciprocates with the promise to quickly go and relay the message to Hrothgar. We are not to imagine Wulfgar leaving the door unguarded; rather, he would be in charge of a small troop, and Beowulf's band is not left standing outside. Just inside the hall's outer door there is an entry room, perhaps similar to the "mud rooms" of some modern houses. There are benches, and the Geats set down their shields and stand their spears against the wall. They sit or stand, watched by Wulfgar's men, while the thane himself goes into the hall to speak with the king.

Hrothgar is seated with his older men, the earls. These are the warriors who have survived battles, won rewards, and lived out their lives in loyalty. They are Hrothgar's power base and perhaps the fathers and uncles of many of his young men. The hall is a large rectangle, and the king's seat is located in the center of a long wall. Down the center there are fire pits for light and warmth. Tables and stools are on both sides of the king and across from him, on the other side of the fires. The earls sit nearest to the king, and the young men sit farther away, according to rank. From this position, Hrothgar can easily command attention for announcements.

Wulfgar speaks positively of Beowulf, of course. Hrothgar's reply shows the emphasis placed on family, on who your father was. Beowulf's father is well known, if not to us, at least to the Danes. We learn an important fact about Beowulf in this scene: he is not just a thane of Hygelac, he is also Hygelac's nephew. The father of Hygelac, Hrethel, married his only daughter to Ecgtheow: Beowulf's mother was the Geatish princess, and his father must have been a very powerful thane. This relationship between Hygelac and Beowulf is a critically important one, and we will explore this in more depth later.

Hrothgar has heard of Beowulf's strength, which by now has been defined as the strength of thirty men (specifically regarding the grip of his hands). Without hearing Beowulf's own words, he guesses the intent and says that God himself must have sent Beowulf at a time like this. Beowulf is invited to come in, and Wulfgar reminds him: leave your weapons here; helmets are welcome.

Speeches are rarely the most exciting part of epic poetry. But Beowulf and Hrothgar give formal speeches to each other, and there are notable and important parts of each speech. Beowulf's speech lays out in detail, for the first time, what he plans to do, while Hrothgar's speech explains why he feels free to accept the offer.

Beowulf's speech shocks a modern reader in several ways. First, a modern reader most likely would not find the boastful tone pleasing or even acceptable. Modern civilization values modesty, so that we may all live peacefully together without making others feel inferior. Those who have done great deeds are expected to downplay them and emphasize the group effort involved. But Beowulf does the opposite: he emphasizes that he does not need help when he does great deeds. He boasts that he single-handedly captured five enemies, and he implies that they were giants' kin. He boasts that he has single-handedly fought with sea monsters at night. He promises to work the same solo magic against Grendel. This sort of boasting may be acceptable in some areas of entertainment, such as professional wrestling, but it does not have a place in civilized life otherwise. In Beowulf's time, this behavior was clearly acceptable. He is not a boastful, self-assertive man in a negative sense. At each turn he has impressed the Danes with his perfect manners. It is clear that the Geats and Danes do not see anything wrong with Beowulf's boasting, as long as it is honest.

A modern reader finds Beowulf's speech shocking, too, in its casual acceptance of a fatal outcome for himself. He intends to fight to the death, and realizes that the death may be his. We shrink from death, but people in past times were surrounded by it and could more easily accept it. Beowulf goes a step further and even imagines his own death. He suggests that burial will not be necessary, since Grendel will eat him and then turn to eat his whole troop. He depicts the setting of the act as follows: Grendel is alone on the moor, with blood dripping over his lair as he dines on Beowulf's body. Beowulf asks only that survivors be sent home in honor, and that any surviving armor be sent back to Hygelac. This fatalistic, gory imagination strikes us as morbid; we would never speak that way. Beowulf, in context, seems not to be morbid at all. He fully intends to win this fight, but he wants the Danes to know that he fully accepts the consequences, too. He has accepted that this may be the end of his story, and he wants them to know that. The narrator allows him to play up his death, to heighten the sense of risk.

Beowulf also states his intention to fight Grendel without weapons. This statement was probably shocking to the audience of the poem, as well as to those characters who hear Beowulf utter the words. In science fiction movies, when the same outcome happens again and again (such as a time loop or a foe who destroys every weapon used again him), the characters stop and ask themselves, "What is the one thing we haven't tried?" They think of something that could not possibly work. Then a character says, "It is just crazy enough, it might work. It is the only thing we haven't tried before." Beowulf seems to be in this position. Many heroes have stood up to Grendel before, and, as Hrothgar says, many strong men have boasted that they would stand up to Grendel with swords. In the morning, however, the hall was filled with corpses. The poem implies that no one has ever tried to stand up to Grendel with muscle strength alone. No one has ever come into Heorot with the strength of thirty men, or even of three men, in his hand grip. Could this be just crazy enough to work?

Hrothgar's speech explains his public reason for accepting Beowulf's help. Of course, privately he is desperate enough to take help from anyone. But he has a prior link to Beowulf's father, and in that encounter he was the one granting a favor. Ecgtheow, we learn, had killed a man named Heatholaf. Heatholaf was certainly an important chief of the Wylfings, for the feud threatened war between the Wylfings and the Geats. The Geats must have felt outnumbered, so Ecgtheow fled. He was probably a young man, not yet married, and perhaps he arrived on the Danish shore in much the same manner as his son, with a small band of loyal, young friends. Hrothgar made the choice not only to shelter him but also to make peace. Rather than sending Ecgtheow with a war band against the Wylfings, he chose to pay the price in gold. Germanic custom allowed for a very large fine to settle a feud, and perhaps Ecgtheow, as a young man, did not have enough wealth to pay. Hrothgar chose to pay the fine, sending him back with ancient treasures, and in return, Ecgtheow swore loyalty to him. Was this loyalty ever called into active use during Ecgtheow's life? There is no evidence that it was. Ecgtheow seems to have returned home, received his estate from King Hrethel, and married Hrethel's daughter. It is only fitting that now, when Hrothgar is in need, the son of Ecgtheow would come and help him according to his father's oaths. The reader is left to wonder if Beowulf was aware of this oath before he set out, since he makes no mention of it.

THE FEAST (491–661)

The scene changes at line 489, when Hrothgar invites the fifteen Geats to sit with him at a feast and drink mead. Until line 661, the scene is a formal ritual feast; we are given no details about food, although there must have been something to eat, especially for the travelers. The focus is on the mead and the words that accompany it. The mead and the speeches signal a formal occasion and is similar to a modern wedding reception or awards banquet.

As previously described, the hall of Heorot would have been a large rectangle. The king sat at the center of a long wall, probably on a raised platform. The benches stretched out to his left and right, and directly in front of him were a series of fire pits. Across from this row of fire was another line of benches and tables. Servants roamed the hall, serving

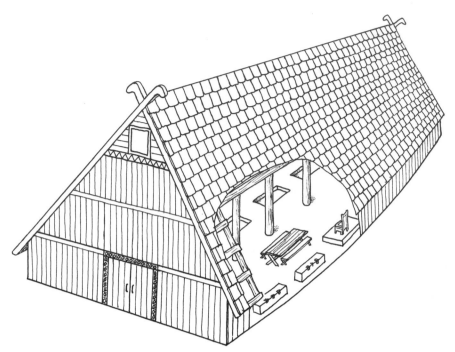

Artist's conception of the layout of Heorot: fire pits in the center,
king's elevated platform, movable table, and storage chests by the wall.
The construction is all wood, with wooden shingles.
(Illustration by Ellen J. McHenry.)

food and drinks that had been prepared in a kitchen. The kitchen was
probably an outbuilding: in every settlement, archeologists have found
many unattached, smaller buildings around the main building. We can
imagine loud talking and occasional singing among the seated men.

Two events probably brought a hush to the room, just as at a wedding reception when the guests' attention is claimed for a speech or a
toast. At every formal feast, there was a poet, or in Old English, a "scop"
(*shop*). The poet's job was to select stories and legends that would please
the company, perhaps by reflecting glory on their nation or by comparing their deeds with those of a hero. These stories may have been sung,
or they may have been recited to the accompaniment of a harp. (At times,
the same poet may have played the harp, and at other times he may have
used an accompanist.) Beowulf later recalls that Hrothgar himself sang at
the second feast, singing songs "both true and sad" (2109) and telling stories
of strange events while playing the harp to accompany himself.

The other event that would bring the room to a hush was the start of an important speech. At formal feasts, speeches seem to have been as important as the mead itself, and the two went together. While the narrator tells us nothing of the roast meats, honeyed sweets, or loaves of bread, he tells us in detail about three of the speeches in this first feast, which were given to welcome Beowulf and his men.

Unferth's Attack

A modern reader is jarred most by Unferth's speech. As soon as the Geats are seated, it seems, a man begins to attack and put down Beowulf. Unferth's name is given only four times; he is otherwise referred to as the "son of Ecglaf." He is called the "thyle" (*thee-lee*) of Hrothgar later in the poem, but scholars are not sure what this role was. Was a thyle the priest, the counselor, the spokesman, or the jester? There is support for any of these roles. When Beowulf began to speak to the coast watchman, he "unlocked his word-hoard," but when Unferth begins to speak, the narrator says he "unbound his battle-runes" (501). Runes, the early form of writing among the North Germanic tribes, were often involved in magic and were associated with the great god Woden. Is the narrator hinting that Unferth is the priest of Woden? On the other hand, he sits at the king's feet, which may be the position of a counselor—always on hand for discussion and advice. Hrothgar does not contradict him, so it is possible that Unferth is his spokesman, his press secretary. However, if Unferth is such a powerful man at court, even as a despised kin-slayer, it seems strange that he would engage in a public argument with Beowulf and lose humbly without further hostility. Perhaps he was an ignoble man, a sort of jester, who was tolerated because they could laugh at his foolishness and losses. From the evidence in the poem, we cannot be sure of his position, and scholars have argued for all of these possible roles.

Whoever he was, Unferth clearly had a personal reason to attack Beowulf. The narrator tells us that he did not want any man to gain more honor than himself. An alternate translation, suggested by Robinson (1974), has Unferth denying that anyone might care about honor more than he did. In either version, Unferth seems to be a narrow, judgmental man who is acting out of personal jealousy. He may also have been filling a political role. King Hrothgar might have appreciated Beowulf being questioned and hearing his answers, but to question Beowulf himself would have seemed impolite. Hrothgar and Unferth may have been acting in classic "good cop, bad cop" style, sharing the goal of putting Beowulf on the spot to see if he was a man to trust, but leaving the role of "bad cop" to Unferth.

There is no question that Unferth was filling a literary role. We can compare this scene in *Beowulf* with similar scenes in Icelandic and other

North Germanic stories and see a common pattern. While we feel that Unferth's attack on Beowulf is unprovoked and shocking, audiences of the time would have expected something like this. Many stories include a quarrel in a scene of feasting, and it generally follows the same outline: Speaker A, who may be trying to provoke a fight, or may be drunk and speaking idly, questions Speaker B's virtue as a warrior. Speaker A reminds Speaker B of something in his past that isn't admirable, and that calls into question his courage, strength, and/or honesty. Speaker B responds by admitting that the event occurred but puts a different interpretation on it. He challenges Speaker A with something in his own past. The quarrel may be the prelude to a physical fight, but more often it seems to be a verbal duel, while others in the room listen and perhaps cheer or laugh. Speakers A and B wish to say something so crushing that the other is silenced, but they do not resort to false charges. To succeed, each speaker must know the skeletons in the other's closet and must be able to zing the other one so hard that the pain stops him from replying.

Imagine that the year is 1960 and John F. Kennedy and Richard Nixon are at a mead hall feast. Instead of showing any civility to each other, or even sticking with relevant political issues, they behave exactly like Germanic warriors in Beowulf's time. Here is how it might sound:

> Kennedy: How much did that suit cost you, Dick? It doesn't fit quite right at the back of the neck, and I see where someone mended it; can't you afford a new one? Or aren't you used to buying anything new?

> Nixon: I certainly didn't grow up in the lap of luxury as you did! What were you doing while I was helping my father run a store and doing farm chores? Were you out playing tennis and expecting your servants to pick up after you? You didn't even know the Great Depression was happening, while I was studying law and living in a house without running water. The way you spend money, this country wouldn't last long; we don't all have "Daddy" to bail us out!

> Kennedy: It's true that I grew up in a rich family, but I don't vote for irresponsible spending. But I see you can't hold your liquor very well, or you wouldn't attack my father. I'd rather have my father helping me out in campaigns than what you've leaned on, a professional campaign manager who disgusts everyone with his cynical attitudes!

> Nixon: Right from the start I leaned on him, that's true. But another of his sayings was, "Truth is the best weapon we can use." Truth, you see, not cash. Maybe you'd like to tell the truth about your father's attitude toward Hitler? Wasn't he in favor of appeasement?

> Kennedy: There you go on my father again. What about me? I served in the Pacific on a PT boat and fought fascism. I was under fire when you were overseeing price controls back in California.

Nixon: I may have started out in the Office of Price Administration, that's true, but I served in the Pacific. And unlike you, I didn't have to deceive any medical boards to do it.

Kennedy: Now I know you've been drinking too much. What's so shameful about concealing a medical history in order to serve in the Navy? I was in constant pain, but I stuck it out and did my duty!

Note that in this imagined exchange, the two men accuse each other of things that are apparently true and quite personal. Each time an accusation is made, the victim must admit the truth of the charge. (They are not making false or sensational accusations.) Instead, the defender changes the focus, deflecting the negative. As we say today, each one tries to control the "spin" on the fact, and show how it has a positive side, too. The way to win this Germanic mead hall game is to turn an opponent's charge to your own advantage and especially to take advantage of a mistake. The winner is able to answer back in a manner that cannot admit of argument, or to bring an accusation that cannot be "spun" in a positive way. There is also a constant emphasis on the value of noble deeds, rather than empty talk or soft stay-at-home ways. Here, the fictitious Kennedy wins when the fictitious Nixon brings out a charge of deceiving the medical board, since the reason for Kennedy's deception was noble. Because Kennedy did not disclose his extensive history of illness in his teenager years, he was able to pilot a PT boat and become a hero. The fictitious Nixon would be embarrassed at his mistaken choice to bring out something so positive and would decide this was a good time to call for some more mead or warm his hands at the fire pit. The argument would be over.

Unferth's exchange with Beowulf is in this pattern: as a man, he wishes to see Beowulf's status fall; as a court politician, he wishes to question Beowulf's virtues; and as a literary partner in a Germanic debate, he begins with a story from Beowulf's past. Beowulf, he has heard, entered into a swimming contest with Breca, Prince of the Brondings. This contest was reckless, and (according to Unferth) Beowulf lost. Unferth suggests that Beowulf has a pattern of reckless boasting followed by losing, and that it will happen again at Heorot.

Beowulf's reply follows the pattern of Germanic insult-trading. He begins by suggesting that Unferth has had too much to drink, and that this has clouded his judgment. He offers an excuse for the recklessness of the exploit; that he and Breca were youths and were boasting to each other in their young enthusiasm. Then he retells the story and adds details that change the meaning. While Unferth had implied that Beowulf's arms clawed at the water helplessly, Beowulf carefully uses the word "row" to describe what he and Breca did, which opens the possibility that they set out on the sea in boats. While Unferth implied that Breca outlasted Beowulf and reached shore first, Beowulf explains that they were separated on the water, and that his real adventures began once Breca was out of sight. Breca reached shore while Beowulf was fighting sea monsters. If he did start out on a raft or boat, then the sea monsters quite certainly dragged him off and down into the depths. Then he fought for his life, swimming, and won. After a prolonged struggle he left several dead creatures to wash up on the beaches and was able to come to land himself. Beowulf's version takes all the shame out of losing.

Not content to retell his story in a more positive way, Beowulf then turns to Unferth. Has Unferth ever fought sea monsters? No. Has Unferth ever done such deeds with a sword in any battle? No. Beowulf turns to sarcasm and suggests that Unferth's great heroic deed was killing his own brothers, a fact that Unferth will not be able to put a positive "spin" on. But Beowulf continues: Has Unferth ever stood up to Grendel? No! He closes with a repeated boast that Grendel will find a very different hero waiting for him this time; one who has met monsters before, who knows pain, struggle, and victory, and who will come out on top. While Unferth had closed his speech with a taunt that Beowulf might not even dare to wait a whole night for Grendel, Beowulf closes with an imagined, glorious, Grendel-free future: When he has killed Grendel, Heorot will be safe for the Unferths of the world.

Unferth is silenced on all counts. As a jealous man, he finds that he cannot think of anything else to detract from Beowulf's personal qualities. As a court questioner, he finds that Beowulf has answered in full form, explaining the apparently negative story that had reached their ears (perhaps through Breca's people). As a literary figure engaged in a Germanic insult exchange, he cannot find a way to turn his cowardice before Grendel or his kin-slaying into positive accounts. He cannot say, "That may be so, I may have hidden from Grendel, but at least I . . . um . . . at least I spent the time killing my brothers! What were you doing when I was in a drunken fight with my family, were you off. . . . um . . . killing more monsters?" Unferth is silenced because he has been hit with two truly negative facts, and he is unable to turn them against Beowulf.

Queen Wealhtheow at the Feast

The result of the quarrel between Unferth and Beowulf is positive. Lines 907–910 tell us that King Hrothgar had been listening attentively

A horn-cup such as this was used for ritual drinking at a feast and
was carried instead of being set on a table.
(Based on the Taplow drinking horn.)
(Illustration by L. D. Staver.)

and was very pleased with Beowulf's answers. Beowulf had requested to
defend Heorot alone, with only his own troop of Geats to witness, and
Hrothgar had most likely been polite but doubtful. It was not easy for him
to withdraw his own men and give up possession of his hall to this band
of young, foreign teenagers. Regardless of Unferth's motives, for Hrothgar the insult-trading he witnessed was the last step of a job interview,
and we learn that he now has much more faith in Beowulf.

Queen Wealhtheow takes on a specific ceremonial role in this scene.
She carries, probably with help from several ladies who follow her, a special cup to each honored warrior. She begins with the king, and she tells
him that he should have a merry feast. She probably has a set phrase in
mind for each man. If the feast follows a battle, she may thank each man
for his courage to defend the hall. If it precedes a battle or raid, she may
command each man to do his best. Tacitus had noted that the Germanic
women stood on a hill above a battle, calling out to the men to fight harder
and protect them. By the time of *Beowulf*, it appears that most of the
women are not expected to do this, but the queen's progression of speeches
may be a ritualized version of this active encouragement.

Beowulf does not appear to be seated next to the king at this point.
He and his men are perhaps seated to the side, at their own set of benches.
The queen travels about the room and finally comes to Beowulf and his
men. When she gives the cup to him, we come to another function of
this ritual. When the queen approaches you with a cup of mead and offers
it with an exhortation to do your best and protect the hall, what do you

Germanic royal lady. Artist's concept of a noble lady in the
seventh century. Useful and decorative objects hang from her belt; she wears
a necklace of gold coins, as well as strings of amber beads.
(Illustration by L. D. Staver.)

say in reply? Most of the warriors probably made a short reply and promised they would indeed do their best. In pagan rituals, a cup of mead
may have been used in making oaths before a god. In this feast ritual, the
promises made before the mead-cup seem to have carried special force.
In the later, Viking Age poem known to us as the "Battle of Maldon,"
a group of warriors faces certain death before Viking invaders. They call

on each other to stand firm, and among these encouragements one says that they must remember the boasts they made in the hall over their mead. Perhaps, for a man trying to steel his courage or distinguish himself from his bench-mates, this was a moment to speak out loudly instead of murmuring, and to command the attention of the room in an extravagant boast. It would be up to him to remember his boast in the confusion and pain of the fight and stick to his resolution.

Beowulf responds in this manner. Wealhtheow gives him the cup, and as he takes it he makes a speech. The hall probably grew quiet when the Danes saw that the queen had reached the newcomers. Beowulf speaks out loud and makes his public promise to fight to the death. He has made this statement to the king before, but now he directs it to the queen, over the ritual cup of mead. He does not need to add the previous detail about being eaten; everyone knows that part, and this would not be the time. Now is the time to make his statement in a short, manly way for all to hear.

The only description of Wealhtheow in this passage is that she is "adorned with gold" (line 614) She may be wearing gold chains, hanging from shoulder to shoulder, across her chest. There are examples of burials in which women wore saucer-shaped brooches that pinned their clothing at the shoulder and were connected by strings of amber beads. Wealhtheow may be wearing an unusually spectacular version of these brooches and beads. The brooches may be pure gold, or they may be set with colored stones in the "cloisonné" technique. Between the beads, there may be sparkling gold coin-shaped pendants. From her belt would hang a gold chain or embroidered strip to hold fancy or ceremonial versions of tools (such as keys, a comb, or a knife). She may have a crown, a headband, or another golden head-covering of some sort. Damico (1984) argues that, in some circumstances, "gold adorned" may have referred to a special garment: a tunic of gold rings, perhaps including small gold shields, that may have covered a queen as ceremonial chain mail. If Heorot has gold wall-hangings, it is also possible that Wealhtheow's clothing has gold strands woven in to catch the firelight as she walks about.

IN DEPTH: GRENDEL, CAIN, AND "CHAM"

There was a flaw in the logic that Cain, the cursed kin-slayer, was the father of all monsters. Many generations after Cain, according to the Bible, there was a worldwide flood that wiped out all living things except for those in Noah's boat (the Ark). The descendants of Cain were killed in the Flood. So while they may have accounted for giants and monsters in the distant past, what about the monsters that existed in Beowulf's time? None of them should be alive, so where did the monsters, such as Grendel, come from?

The story of the Flood suggested an answer. After the Flood waters receded, Noah planted a vineyard and made wine. He drank the wine, became drunk, and fell asleep naked. One of his three sons, usually called "Ham" in modern translations but called "Cham" or "Cam" in Old English, saw Noah and thought he looked foolish. He told his brothers, Shem and Japheth, but they carefully covered their father without looking at him. When he woke up, Noah cursed Ham for making fun of his father (Genesis 9:18–27).

Medieval interpreters suggested that Noah's third son could be the father of more monsters. If he was wicked enough to laugh at his drunk father, they reasoned, then he must have been completely bad. They suggested that he had helped to preserve the black magic of Cain's line by carving spells and magic runes on stones and metal plates and then he recovered them after the Flood. The wicked Cam continued where Cain had left off, and because of this the line of Cam also became plagued with monsters. One medieval Irish text suggests that leprechauns, giants, and "horseheads," as well as all other deformed creatures, came from Cam (Orchard 1995, 70, 75).

In the minds of many, Cain and Cam began to be confused, and careless use could bring out the wrong name. In the *Beowulf* manuscript (line 107), Cain's name had to be corrected from a mistaken use of "Cam." Later in the poem (in line 1261), the scribe wrote the letters "camp" to identify who killed his brother. Some translators have suggested that this word means "strife," which is possible, but another possibility stems from this confusion about who fathered the monsters: Cain or Cam.

IN DEPTH: UNFERTH'S NAME

The spelling of Unferth's name is a point of uncertainty. It appeared in the official Old English editions of *Beowulf* as "Unferth," and all translators took this to be his name. Many speculated that it had a specific meaning, and that "ferth" was a spelling of "frith," which means "peace." Unferth, then, would mean "anti-peace," which seems to be Unferth's role in the story. Could his character have an allegorical meaning? Could he be the antagonist whom the hero must overcome? Could he be even parallel to Satan, because he is tempting God? Perhaps he symbolizes the constant strive for reward, the continual contest, that must have existed in halls like Heorot. These ideas can be found in older books and essays.

In more recent times, however, the actual *Beowulf* manuscript has drawn extra attention. Using photographic technology, its crumbling pages can be presented as images so that translators are not solely dependent on the printed editions. Unferth's name is written in the manuscript only four times, and each time it is clearly written as "Hunferth." One of the *H*s is enlarged and decorated, so it cannot be a mistake.

Why, then, do most books tell us his name is Unferth? Editors in the past changed it to Unferth because they assumed the *H* must be an error. The name does not alliterate with *H*-words, like "Heorot," but rather it alliterates with initial-vowel words, such as his father's name, "Ecglaf." It suggests that the poet may not have pronounced the *H* and alliterated it with words that sounded, rather than looked, the same. The name would be pronounced like our words "honest" and "herb."

If the name is truly "Hunferth," then it would not have meant "anti-peace," unless the poet intended the accidental resemblance as a kind of pun. "Hunferth" would be a rather common, pointless Germanic name: combining a root word that may have meant "bear" with the word for "peace," without any particular meaning. The poet may have realized, however, that it sounded like *Un-ferth* and enjoyed the pun.

FURTHER SUGGESTED READING

Bazelmans, Jos. *By Weapons Made Worthy: Lords, Retainers, and Their Relationship to Beowulf.* Amsterdam: Amsterdam University Press, 1999.

Bruce-Mitford, Rupert. *Aspects of Anglo-Saxon Archaeology: Sutton Hoo and Other Discoveries.* New York: Harper's Magazine Press, 1974.

———. *The Sutton Hoo Ship-Burial: A Handbook.* London: The Trustees of the British Museum, 1968.

Carver, Martin. *Sutton Hoo: Burial Ground of Kings?* Philadelphia: University of Pennsylvania Press, 1998.

Fjalldal, Magnus. *The Long Arm of Coincidence: The Frustrated Connection Between Beowulf and Grettis Saga.* Toronto: University of Toronto Press, 1998.

Green, Charles. *Sutton Hoo: The Excavation of a Royal Ship Burial.* Totowa, NJ: Barnes and Noble Books, 1963.

Grohskopf, Bernice. *The Treasure of Sutton Hoo.* New York: MacMillan, 1973.

Kendall, Calvin B. and Peter S. Wells, eds. *Voyage to the Other World: The Legacy of Sutton Hoo.* Minneapolis: University of Minnesota Press, 1992.

MacDowell, Simon. *Germanic Warrior: AD 236–568.* Botley, UK: Osprey Publishing, 1996. (This is an illustrated book.)

Newton, Sam. *The Origins of Beowulf and the Pre-Viking Kingdom of East Anglia.* Cambridge: D. S. Brewer, 1993.

Nicholson, Lewis E. "Hunlafing and the Point of the Sword." In *Anglo-Saxon Poetry: Essays in Appreciation for John C. McGalliard*, eds. Lewis E. Nicholson and Dolores Warwick Frese. Notre Dame: University of Notre Dame Press, 1975. (Discusses Unferth's identity.)

Orchard, Andy. *Pride and Prodigies: Studies in the Monsters of the Beowulf Manuscript.* Toronto: University of Toronto Press, 1995. (Includes *Liber Monstrorum.*)

Owen-Crocker, Gale R. *The Four Funerals of Beowulf, and the Structure of the Poem.* Manchester, UK: Manchester University Press, 2000.

Parks, Ward. *Verbal Dueling in Heroic Narrative: The Homeric and Old English Tradition.* Princeton: Princeton University Press, 1990.

Pollington, Stephen. *The English Warrior: From Earliest Times Till 1066.* Hockwold-cum-Wilton, UK: Anglo-Saxon Books, 1996.

———. *The Mead Hall: Feasting in Anglo-Saxon Tradition.* Hockwold-cum-Wilton, UK: Anglo-Saxon Books, 2003.

Puhvel, Martin. *Beowulf and the Celtic Tradition.* Waterloo, ON: Wilfrid Laurier

Williams, David. *Cain and Beowulf: A Study in Secular Allegory.* Toronto: University of Toronto Press, 1982.

4

Beowulf versus Grendel

THE FIGHT WITH GRENDEL (662–836)

IN LINE 662, Hrothgar and his men leave the hall in a procession. We can imagine the quiet and dark they left behind as the last door closed and only fifteen young men occupied a much larger hall than they had ever seen. It was customary for the fighting men to sleep in the hall. Benches were moved back and tables were set aside. At the side of a hall there were usually raised platforms, like window seats, running along the walls. Warriors were used to sleeping on the floor or on these platforms, and perhaps carried with them a cloak or blanket, as a cowboy would carry his bedroll. Line 688 suggests that the Danes provided pillows of some kind.

The narrator takes a moment to describe Beowulf getting ready for bed. For the feast, he has been wearing his full armor. Now, with the fires dying down and the scraps of food cleaned up by the last dogs, the feast is over and he can take his armor off. He gives his helmet and chain shirt to his servant. (The fifteen warriors may have traveled with a small number of servants, or the servant may have been a younger warrior acting as a squire.) We can almost see Beowulf stretch, perhaps comb the wind-blown tangles out of his hair, and prepare to sleep. Few of us would be able to sleep in these conditions, and Beowulf did not.

Beowulf has a last thought for his men. Perhaps he is responding to one of their comments; perhaps one of them has just asked him whether he thinks he'll get a wink of sleep tonight, or whether he thinks he will need any help. Perhaps one of them has asked if he should keep his sword nearby, rather than give it to his servant to put away. Beowulf replies that he isn't worried at all. He is sure that he is just as strong as Grendel, and he indicates that he is putting aside his sword out of a sense of fairness.

The narrator suggests a deep faith in God in this passage. Both Beowulf and the narrator's voice state that God rules over all and will give the victory as he wishes. In these lines we can probably hear the voice of the poet more than the voice of a historical Beowulf. Perhaps the poet does not want Beowulf to be accused of pride, so he is careful to remind the audience that although Beowulf trusts in his own strength, he has a greater reason to be confident. Surely God will not let down the champion who pursues the feud of Seth against Cain! All of the Geats fall asleep after their journey and are fast asleep when the moment comes.

The camera's eye swings outside the hall, as though we are watching a movie. We have watched the Geats fall asleep and caught one glimpse (702–703) of Grendel's slow creep in the dark. The camera moves back into the hall to check on the men, and as they are motionless, the camera moves outside again, and now it follows Grendel's point of view. We see him progress from the moor's mist to where he recognizes the immediate neighborhood of the hall, where he stops, feeling hungry. The narrator again reminds us that the hall is gold-adorned, as if to contrast with Grendel's low creep from a place in the wilderness. Grendel arrives at the hall (720), and with a flick of his wrist, he pulls the locked door wide open. The creature from the black mere now steps onto the paved floor of civilization.

The camera shows us the hall through Grendel's eyes, as "he saw in the hall many a soldier" (728). These are the same men we had just left, chatting, stretching, pulling bolsters under their heads, and falling asleep, but through Grendel's eyes they look different. To Grendel, this scene is like a smorgasbord, and he intends to fill several plates with the juicy fresh meat he sees under the heat lamps. If this were a Looney Tunes show, we might see the sleeping Geats turn into roast turkeys for a moment.

A reader who sees this poem as a primitive, random affair must fully appreciate the dramatic care taken in this scene. Both sides are represented now, and we know the thoughts of each. Grendel's thoughts are plain, and we can see him standing near a cooling fire pit, looking from side to side, trying to decide where to start. No one has moved yet, but the narrator reminds us of a pair of open eyes in the hall. Beowulf is watching Grendel's every move (736–738), although he is not moving a hair himself. He intends to measure Grendel's movements and find the best way to come at him. Two are awake in the hall, but only one is aware of both. All that remains now is for the narrator to bring them into contact.

The contact is sudden and violent. Perhaps Beowulf had intended to wait until Grendel turned his back, but Grendel makes a lightning strike before Beowulf is ready. In one move, Grendel kills and eats one of the Geats. Like a film in slow-motion, we see Grendel in gory detail as he slits, drinks, bites, and swallows the last pieces. Grendel, as a large creature, must take very big bites indeed. Beowulf has not even had time to react. Perhaps he instantly realizes that it is too late to save his friend, and that he can only make use of the short time, while the monster was distracted, to make his own plans. Grendel hardly pauses for breath. His next victim is a large, meaty looking fellow who appears to be asleep: Beowulf himself.

The fight is over almost as soon as begins. Grendel's shock at meeting someone as strong as himself, ends any real struggle for mastery. Grendel's reeling semi-intelligence can only think of escape from a situation he had considered impossible. Beowulf is immediately master of the hall, and the only question is whether Grendel will be able to pull away. As we know, he finds that he cannot.

Beowulf, with the grip of thirty men, is able to hold onto him as he thrashes about. Grendel probably picks up anything he can find to try to hit Beowulf and loosen his grip. Beowulf, on his side, recalls his boasts and focuses solely on not letting go, although his fingers feel like they are breaking (760). We have a brief picture of the flight-pursuit dance, as Grendel moves back, Beowulf steps forward, Grendel steps outward, and Beowulf turns inward (761). The town around Heorot is woken up by the noise, and we can imagine the Geats pressed back into the corners of the hall in an attempt to avoid the flying benches. The narrator gives comic-book style details of every blow, but wants us to understand that the struggle was so violent that any other hall would have collapsed from the shock. Perhaps the inner pillars have collapsed, splintered from Grendel's weight suddenly thrown back, to catch Beowulf off balance. Heorot, fortunately, was built with iron reinforcements. The circle of reaction to the fight spreads until the entire neighborhood of the Danes is wakened by Grendel's horrible screams. Beowulf is trying to crush the life out of Grendel and has pinned him fast.

The Geats, who knew that Beowulf intended to fight alone, finally begin to draw their swords and take shots at Grendel. Although they are not able to make any dent in Grendel, due to his magic curse against weapons, it is important to realize that Beowulf's men are not going to stand by and see him get hurt. Beowulf may have vowed to fight Grendel alone, but his men vowed to back him up in any fight. They would not be fulfilling their vows if they let him manage alone. This is important to remember when later, in a third fight, Beowulf will need help from his thanes in spite of his vow to fight alone.

The end comes suddenly, as Beowulf and Grendel's very souls are matched against each other—hate for hate, life for life—and it seems that it cannot go on any longer. In a desperate move, Grendel pulls away and leaves his arm behind. Perhaps he has been slowly crushed and wounded; he probably bears internal injuries and several broken bones. His shoulder may have been dislocated earlier in the struggle. In any case, in one last screaming tear, his shoulder comes apart. Either Beowulf was only holding his arm at that point, or the sudden severing throws Beowulf off balance. Grendel, howling into the night, runs free to his home in the wilderness.

The fight ends with an event that seems particularly savage to us. Beowulf's men gather around, and as Beowulf appears to be essentially unhurt and is rejoicing, they take from him the arm he still holds. Perhaps we are to imagine that this arm is about six feet long. It is thick and its fingers are claws. The narrative suggests that they saw it "under the curved roof" (836), and this may indicate that it was hoisted up with rope so that all could see it without pushing or shoving.

THE AFTERMATH OF THE FIGHT WITH GRENDEL (837–990)

In line 837, the sun comes up and it is morning. The town is already awake, but no one has dared to come out. Who knows if the monster may flee and take one last victim as he passes? But they heard his dying screams as he faded into the distance, and in the morning quiet they may be able to hear the Geats talking and calling out the news. Many people around the Heorot neighborhood come to see what had happened. Not only that, but from far away, land-owning earls arrive on horseback to see what had happened. Grendel's footprints and arm are the talk of the countryside. In fact, many people set out to follow the tracks in search of the dead troll. The tracks lead them to a pool of water that is welling and boiling with blood.

Three separate events stand out in the Danes' exuberant daytime celebration of Grendel's defeat: first, they create an impromptu race; second, a poet sings for them; and third, the king arrives to speak his words of triumph and thanks.

The horse race seems to stem from the field trip to follow Grendel's tracks to the end. How many of these warriors would have dared to take this path only the day before? While any gathering of fighting men on horses must have quickly included a competitive, drag-racing element, this race has a different feel. They are taking back ownership of their land from the monster that terrified them. Like the people of Oz when they realize the wicked witch is dead, the Danes want to swarm over the paths Grendel used and set their horses' hooves directly into his footprints as a symbol of triumph.

The poet's song is a moment that tantalizes historians. The author did not choose to give us the exact words of the songs that were sung in celebration of Beowulf's victory, but instead summarized the songs. Perhaps they were well-known stories.

The most that historians can say is that the singing poet chooses to remind the Danes of two warriors: one who was great like Beowulf, and another who was strong but ended badly. One is to serve as a point of praise, and the other is perhaps an example of what not to do. Sigemund and Fitela (called "Sinfiotli" in Norse), uncle and nephew in the Volsunga Saga, are cited first. After doing many great deeds and traveling about together, the most glorious battle for Sigemund arrived without Fitela at his side. Sigemund was able to kill a dragon by pinning him to the wall to melt in his own heat, and then he loaded his ship with the dragon's treasure. Sigemund was a legendary warrior, and to be compared to him was as honorable as an American president being compared to George Washington. It is clear that the singing poet has selected this song for the occasion, in order to imply that now, in their own time, they have found Sigemund's equal.

The second song is very difficult to understand. While we have the stories of Sigemund in full form in other Germanic literature, the story of Heremod is difficult to piece together. Heremod appears to have been an earlier king of the Danes. He may have been a relative, or he may have been the king who was in power before Scyld arrived; perhaps his downfall left the Danes ready to accept the miraculous baby in a boat as their next king, since their royal house had come to disaster. The song of the poet in lines 898–915 tell a fractured, confusing story that implies Heremod's downfall was the result of his own flaws. He struggled to keep his throne, but he finally lost and went into exile. Among a foreign people, probably the nearby Jutes, he was betrayed and met death at the hands of his enemies; perhaps they were the relatives of people whom he had killed. The rest of the song expresses the disappointment of his people at his downfall, for he had come to power at a young age, and they had hoped he would turn out well. While the story is hard to understand, the moral is clear: Beowulf became a friend to all mankind by ridding them of a monster, but sin possessed Heremod and he came to a bad end. So, all young men take warning: don't be like Heremod.

The third event of the immediate aftermath comes about when the thanes on their horses return, some racing, some listening to the songs. Now the king pays a formal visit, arrives in a parade with all his surviving thanes, and the queen with all her maidens. Hrothgar, looking on the bloodied arm of Grendel, gives a heartfelt speech. First, he simply states that he can't quite believe his eyes. Is it real? They never thought this day would come, and now a man has conquered Grendel. He blesses Beowulf's mother, if she is still alive, for if so she can celebrate having such a son. But what reward can Hrothgar give for this immense deed? Hrothgar proposes to adopt Beowulf, at least "in my heart" and perhaps more formally. He will give him great riches, having given treasures for much lesser deeds. Where can he find anything great enough for such a hero? May God himself be the ultimate giver of rewards!

Like a true warrior, Beowulf still seems to be too full of the fight for ceremonial words. Telling Hrothgar that he took on the challenge for free, he breaks out in enthusiasm: "I wish you could have seen him yourself! He was covered in blood! I tried to pin him, but he got away!"

Looking at the torn arm with its immense claws, Unferth is silent. (Some translations may follow the Old English text and call him the "son of Ecglaf.") Confronted with the wrecked hall, a torn, bloodied Beowulf, and the awesome claws of the monster, he faces the stark differences between words and deeds. The last words of the episode are from the viewpoint of the watching thanes, as they gaze for the first time at the dreadful, steel-like claws that killed so many of their friends.

THE GIFT-THRONE (991–1250)

A second feast begins, first with the cleanup from Grendel's struggle. The servants of Hrothgar mop up the blood, cover the splintered pillars, repair the benches, and sand the claw-marks off the walls before covering them with tapestries. The narrator isn't specific about this repair effort, so we can imagine what we will: tiles replaced in the floor, temporary hinges installed for the great doors, and new boards brought for the tables. This second feast is a more momentous occasion than the first, as it is a formal celebration marked by ceremonial gift-giving.

The first duty of a Germanic king was to give gifts wisely. All of the loot from any raid belonged to the king, and from this hoard he handed out rewards in accordance with each man's effort and standing. The formal feast was his gift-giving occasion, and his chair was generally called the "gift-stool." The queen, too, handed out rewards as she walked around the room with the official mead-cup.

The rewards fell into roughly three categories. The most common was the ring (probably an arm-ring), as well as other treasures of a non-weapon nature. The more gold and jewels on these treasures, the higher they stood as a reward. The next category of reward-gifts was weaponry, including swords, shields, chain mail and helmets, and perhaps also the more common spears and bows. Horses or ships were less common, but they would also be in this weapons category. The greatest reward category, which was also the least common, was land itself. The young men, after they had proven their worth and were in their twenties, could one day expect to receive a grant of an estate from the king; such a reward would probably be announced at a formal feast like this one.

All three kinds of rewards are mentioned at different points in *Beowulf*. Much later in the poem, when he is back home in Geatland, Beowulf will recall that at these feasts in Heorot both the queen and her daughter were giving out rings to the warriors. In Geatland, Beowulf will receive an estate from his king at a formal feast of welcome. Here, at this second feast at Heorot, the main point is to reward the hero with the richest weapons-gifts. The poet takes delight in describing these gifts to us: a golden banner, a helmet, a "byrnie" (or chain-mail shirt), and a sword. The banner has the insignia of a boar on it (the sign of the pagan god Frey) and a common totem for battle. The helmet, perhaps also decorated with boar pictures, has a feature so interesting to the teller that he takes five lines to describe it. To help strengthen the ridge of the helmet's top, it is wound with wire; this feature may have been useful as a guard against sword blows that could shatter the joints of the helmet plates. The chain-mail shirt is made of tiny, forged iron rings. Beowulf later explains that it had belonged to Hrothgar's brother and nephew, who are presumably both deceased by this time.

The sword is called a "treasure-sword." It is possible that, depending on the meaning of a doubtful phrase. (It may be the sword of Healfdene, Hrothgar's father, but the manuscript may also mean that the son of Healfdene gave the sword. Translations will vary.) This treasure-sword is almost certainly decorated in golden designs and inlaid with jewels. The Germanic peoples of this time knew the art of cloisonné, which produces an effect similar to stained glass. Some sword hilts have survived in the great royal burials such as the one at Sutton Hoo. They are so magnificent that it is hard to imagine using them in the dust, dirt, and blood of a real battle. This sword would be a large reward for any hero, but Beowulf has done something more magnificent than usual. Hrothgar might be considered stingy if he did not offer Beowulf more for a reward; so, after all these, into the feast-hall come eight horses, one wearing a priceless jeweled saddle. We are told that this is Hrothgar's own horse, and that he is giving all of the horses to Beowulf.

Lesser treasures are not named, but Hrothgar also gives rewards to Beowulf's men, as well as a sum of gold to be returned to the dead man's family as blood-money. The Geats, especially Beowulf, are fully satisfied with their pay for the risks they ran.

TWO QUEENS: HILDEBURH AND WEALHTHEOW

At the feast, unusual prominence is given to two women; they are both queens with ties to the Scyldings. One queen, Hildeburh, is the subject of a song, but the other, Wealhtheow, is Hrothgar's queen, who comes to offer a celebratory mead cup. There are parallels between the two women, and without doubt, *Beowulf* intends for us to see their differences and their similarities. The scop's song is about a fight at the royal seat of Finn of the Frisians, but the story told in *Beowulf* differs from the one fragment of this song that survives. The change in focus casts the queen as the main figure, allowing us to ponder the roles of these two women.

Hildeburh

Lines 1071–1159 tell the sad story of Hildeburh. It is not easy to discern what is actually taking place in this passage. As background, let us consider the proposal of J. R. R. Tolkien, who thoroughly studied this passage in conjunction with a fragment of poetry on the same topic, usually called the "Finnsburgh fragment." Tolkien compared this fragment and the story of Finn in our text and created a summary of what may have happened. This summary was his best guess and may be very close to the truth.

Hoc, King of the Scyldings, married his daughter, Hildeburh, to Finn, King of the Frisians. Frisia was south of the Danish lands, and it was located along the coast, just to the north of the Rhine River. Today it is part of the Netherlands. Tolkien speculated that the Jutes were being pushed out of their lands in Denmark by the Scyldings, and that Finn of the Frisians allowed some disaffected Jutes to stay in Frisia and be represented in his royal hall. Although the Danes and Jutes at this time were rivals for the same lands, Finn hoped that he could maintain peace for himself among these quarreling neighbors. Finn and Hildeburh had a son, who is not named. According to Tolkien, this son was probably sent to live with Hildeburh's brother, Hnaef, who was now the Scylding king. (Around the ages of seven or eight, boys were usually sent to live with their mother's brothers, who took over their education.) The event that precipitated the fight was probably the official homecoming of the young prince of Frisia. The boy might have been about fifteen, and had completed his education as a warrior and future king. Hnaef and his retinue arrived at Finn's hall for a fairly long visit. Apparently they came after the autumn harvest, although they knew that during the winter they would find it difficult to return to Denmark.

With Hnaef was a warrior named Hengest. Hengest is the name of one of the Jutish chiefs in early English histories, who was the first to come to the island of Britain and begin its conquest. Tolkien considered them to be the same person, as the timeline and setting are about correct. The presence of Hengest was perhaps the key to the fight, for as a Jute who was loyal to the Scyldings, he was at odds with other Jutes who were rivals of the Danes. These Jutes, at Finn's hall, saw Hengest and his Jutish followers, and immediately the scene was set for a feud.

There are two stages to the feud. First, there is an attack on Finn's hall, where Finn's role seems to be the hopeless bystander who is caught in a tragic situation. Finn allows Hnaef and his men to defend the hall, and the fight, according to the fragment, lasts five days. Hnaef, the "young king" of the fragment, falls, as does the Frisian prince he may have been fostering for his sister. The fight ends in a stalemate, as the defenders and attackers set out terms for peace. Some of Hnaef's followers head home, but some of them stay. Finn gives them a hall to live in, in return for vows of loyalty to him. They then become temporary residents of Finnsburg.

Hengest, however, not only survived the fight but became de facto leader of the Danish remnant. It was very hard for him to stay on at Finnsburg, as he had to watch Hnaef's killers come and go. As winter drew to a close, one of his warriors put a sword in his lap (perhaps Hnaef's sword) as a reminder of his duty to avenge. Hengest reopened the feud, in conjunction with a fresh attack by the Danes, and this time Finn was killed, his hall was burned, and Hildeburh was taken back to her Danish homeland. The *Beowulf* manuscript calls this story of disaster and tragedy the "Freswael" (the Frisian tragedy). It may have been a well-known event, just as today many people continue to talk about the major battles and attacks of the world wars; especially those wars involving betrayal and/or the loss of civilian life.

With Tolkien's scholarly help, the song of the scop at Heorot becomes clearer. However, unlike the fragment, the story in *Beowulf* does not focus as much on the brave fighting men. The fragment tells its story from the viewpoint of the men inside the hall, who see the gables burning and call to each other to stand firm. The scop at Heorot opens with the name "Hildeburh," the thrice-bereaved queen. In an ironic under-statement, he forecasts that the tragedy of the tale hangs on the bad faith of the Jutes. The burden of his next fifty lines is that Finn did his best to make peace. Not only did he stop the fighting, but he offered a home to the survivors; he promised them material support, food, and shelter; he promised them payment, rings of gold and ancient treasures, to close the feud; and he swore oaths to support Hengest and the survivors and to promote nothing but peace. Hengest swore oaths of loyalty to Finn, and all appeared well.

The sorrow of Hildeburh, as a human being and a woman, is the focus of the funeral scene. This scene is foreign and grisly to a modern reader, as we cannot conceive of burning our dead. This scene is made worse by the graphic detail the poet supplies, since most of us have probably never given much thought to what a burning body looks like. But the focus of the passage is on Hildeburh's loss. Her brother, Hnaef, is dead, and is placed on a pyre and surrounded by gold. At the last minute, Hildeburh decides that her son will be burned next to his uncle, who was probably his foster-father and closer to him than his own father. Hildeburh must look on to see her son and brother burned together, and perhaps the graphic detail is intended to evoke the same emotions that she must have felt as she watched those two dear faces melt in the heat. Women lamented as pyres burned, weeping and screaming as the flames finally died out. Hildeburh was perhaps the only mourner for the Danes, who may not have brought any women with them on their voyage. We read that Hildeburh sang a sad lament, and here we must join the historians in wishing that the poet had told us what she sang.

The final thirty lines of the scop's song tell about Hengest's reopening of the feud and do not focus on Hildeburh's role in the same way. Hilde-burh becomes a passive victim, as the remains of her family are swept away in fire and battle. Her home is destroyed, and her husband (and possibly younger children) are killed. The final lines tell us that the queen is taken back to "her people," but we wonder if she could ever feel at home there again.

Anglo-Saxon battle poetry did not portray fighting as being without cost. Rather, there was always a consciousness of the high human cost, and of the limited gains of a victory. In the story of Hildeburh, the ulti-mate Danish victory over the Frisians and the full vengeance for the death of Hnaef are not told with pride. It is a story of betrayal, hate, and sorrow. It is tragic in every sense, as it involves the downfall of a royal house through a fatal flaw (Finn is too easily persuaded that all will be well) and he does not fully consider the possibility of treachery.

The story of Hildeburh also illustrates the dual loyalty of a Germanic queen. Hildeburh is typical in her role as "peace-weaver," the princess married to an ally to preserve the peace. This role could be especially difficult when an ally was new and had recently been an enemy. The princess-bride was expected to remain fully loyal to her father's house, but at the same time she was expected to be a loyal and permanent member of her husband's family. She was expected to step into a public role as well as a private one. Her job was not unlike an American First Lady, who must look just right in public, speak well to general audiences, "connect" with the voters, and give good, private advice to her husband. In addition, the Germanic queen might even find herself in command of the war band, especially if her husband suddenly died. It was not an easy job, and it required the right sort of upbringing and character.

Wealhtheow

When the poem returns us to the noise and light of the feast at Heorot and the scop lays down his harp, Queen Wealhtheow immediately appears. The contrast is most likely intentional, as we turn from the sorrowful, homeless Hildeburh to the gold-crowned, secure Wealhtheow. Wealhtheow's name means something like "foreign servant" or "foreign captive," and it is a reminder both of Hildeburh's capture by her own people and of the difficult role of the foreign bride-queen.

The first requirement of the foreign queen's role was tact. The queen must be careful not to bring her own people into disfavor by acting foolish; she must not play favorites and meddle in politics so as to create factions for or against her native land. Her position was that of an ambassador as well as a queen. Further, the peril in which Hildeburh found herself is a reminder of how any royal house could fall through invasion or treachery. The queen could perhaps help to support alliances by showing wise favor to the strong, by smoothing over quarrels and giving gifts to create loyalty. There is evidence that most Germanic queens had some independent power to give these gifts; perhaps they stored treasures that had been given to them, so that they could in turn give them out. Germanic brides were not given toasters or towels; they were given weapons to pass to their sons, and if they were royalty, then the weapons were valuable heirlooms. Their husbands paid them gold at betrothal, and very likely this gold remained theirs for personal wealth. Using their gift-giving power wisely was the first task of a royal "foreign captive."

In the second feast, we see Wealhtheow in this gift-giving role. She appears in the hall wearing her gold and goes first to where Hrothgar and Hrothulf are seated. She then proceeds to where Beowulf now sits with the young Scylding warriors. It is likely that he has been promoted from a far-off bench to a place very close to Hrothgar. Her visit to these seats has a purpose, and at both stopping-points she makes a careful speech that may be clearly heard throughout the room. Wealhtheow may have waited to enter until the scop finished his song of Finn, and then as the noise rose again, put a stop to it with her formal parade. Behind her, her servants carry a treasure as an official, ceremonial gift.

Wealhtheow wants to thank, praise, and honor Beowulf, and the ancient treasure-gift is for him. It is a fabulous necklace with its own story attached. However, her speeches do not focus on Beowulf and the death of Grendel, as we would expect. Instead, she appears to be pursuing a political agenda. The purpose of her two speeches, to Hrothgar and to Beowulf, appears to be the promotion of Hrothulf as the successor to Hrothgar.

The reader may wonder why she is trying to promote Hrothulf, the nephew, when she clearly has sons of her own. As with other gray areas in the poem's narrative, we do not know enough about the family, or about its history, to answer this question. There is no reliable history of Denmark in this period, but all accounts agree that Hrothulf did become king, and some medieval stories suggest that he was a very powerful king. The narrator of *Beowulf* seems to be working within this historical framework. He plays up the tension between the children and the nephew, by means of Wealhtheow's speech that favors the nephew. Why would the queen take this position?

It is clear that she senses the tension at court over who will succeed the aging Hrothgar. Is the tension caused by Beowulf's presence, or was it pre-existing? If it was pre-existing, it may be because of the difference in age between the young people. Wealhtheow's sons sit with the young warriors, next to Beowulf, but they may be no older than Hildeburh's young son. As Hildeburh's son was not able to withstand the treacherous attack of the Jutes on his father's hall, perhaps Wealhtheow's sons, Hrethric and Hrothmund, will not be able to stand up against treachery at Heorot. Wealhtheow may perceive that the nephew, Hrothulf, is older and stronger, and has the support of the earls. She may be uneasy about Hrothulf's intentions and is attempting to stave off future strife. She may fear that a faction will form around Hrothulf, to kill off her sons and place him in power. She may even fear that if Hrothulf is chosen as a successor, a faction will form around her sons and result in a tragic civil war like the one at Finnsburg.

As a "peace-weaver," Wealhtheow must do her best to pour oil on troubled waters. Her speech suggests that Hrothulf is especially dear to her, and that she trusts his intentions fully. She states that she knows he will be kind to her boys if he becomes king. Her speech to Beowulf echoes her trust that here at Heorot, loyalty will carry the day, and the earls will be united. She may be asking Beowulf to exert his influence in the future to make sure things stay quiet.

The poem appears to support the idea that Wealhtheow fears discord, through hints that foreshadow future trouble. Lines 1164–1167 tell us that "their peace was still whole then, each true to the other," and that Unferth is also true. Perhaps the poet is suggesting a story, not known to us, in which Unferth had played a role in the discord that would soon engulf Heorot. Wealhtheow's assurances that all hearts at Heorot are united, and all intentions true, may also be ironic foreshadowing of future grief and betrayal. Another Old English poem, called "Widsith," speaks of Hrothgar and also hints at trouble. This poem is the song of a traveling scop, who lists the kings before whom he sang. Among his listed kings are Hrothgar and Hrothulf, and the singer tells us that Hrothgar and Hrothulf were at peace for long time. This peace, says "Widsith," lasted until after the feud with Ingeld.

But it may not be necessary to reach so far into the future to understand the passage. Damico (1984) argues for another interpretation, in a careful study of the character of Wealhtheow. Wealhtheow may be doing nothing more than quelling rumors that are flying around the community that Hrothgar intends to adopt Beowulf as his legal heir. She refers to this in 1175–1180, saying that she has heard that Hrothgar is calling Beowulf his new son. In this public setting, she tells her husband that he should be leaving his estate only to his kinsmen. She may be reminding him that in his gratitude for the death of Grendel, he is going a step too far. Her statements of dependence on the good Hrothulf and the other earls may be to remind this community that they are not forgotten, and that there is a common interest in finding a peaceful solution to the succession.

Wealhtheow's gift to Beowulf is an ancient necklace, along with other treasures that include rings and clothing of some kind. The necklace, or "neck-ring," is not described. We can be certain that it was opulent and large, for subtlety in gold decoration was not admired among these nations. It appears to have been acceptable for either a man or a woman to wear, for we read that this particular neck-ring was worn by Beowulf, his uncle Hygelac, and Hygelac's wife, Hygd, and it may have been worn by Wealhtheow before that. Instead of describing this neck-ring, the poet tells us that it was just as magnificent as the "Brosinga necklace," an ornament of pagan legend. This necklace had belonged to the goddess Freya, but the brief digression discusses a later phase of its history. It became the property of Eormanric (also spelled Ermenrich), King of the Goths, another Germanic people. A man named Hama stole it, fleeing from some kind of treachery. Hama was a celebrated figure in the legends of the Goths, but it is not clear if he was an exile or a mercenary. "[H]e chose eternal counsel" (1201) is an interpretation that suggests Hama's end was to enter a monastery. This particular interpretation is from a medieval Norse source, but its accuracy cannot be verified. It is clear that the story of Hama and the gold was known at the time, but all scholars today consider it to be lost and beyond comprehension. In any case, we can imagine the most impressive, opulent neck-ring this side of Valhalla, and that is the kind that Wealhtheow gives to Beowulf.

The other detail given to us about the necklace seems out of place: Hygelac, Beowulf's uncle and King of the Geats, will wear this same neck-ring on his last raid. In search of treasure, he begins an aggressive war against the Frisians and the Franks and falls in battle. We read that fate struck down Hygelac "when in his pride he went looking for woe" (1206), and from this line it is evident that the poet does not approve of this raid. The focus in this brief mention of Hygelac's death is on the neck-ring, as it passes, verbally, through many characters' hands in a few short lines: Wealhtheow, Beowulf, Hygelac, and the victorious Franks. Treasure has a life history of its own, like the Brosinga neck-ring that passed from Freya through many greedy hands to Hama, who perhaps lost it in the end. Weahltheow's beautiful neck-ring, too, is doomed to pass into another gold-hoard and out of Norse history.

The second feast closes shortly after Wealhtheow's speech. Men continue to drink for some time, but the hall is converted into a sleeping-room once again. This was the general custom, but in the opening lines we learned that warriors were becoming afraid to sleep at Heorot. Now, with relief that Grendel is dead, they flock back into the hall and set out their bedding. There are, however, two notable exceptions. Hrothgar does not sleep in the hall; perhaps because he is old, he goes to his own house. (This may be a smaller building nearby.) Beowulf, too, is given "guest of honor" chambers in a separate building, along with his men.

Through line 1250, there is every reason to assume that the story is over, with the exception of one ominous line: "Wyrd," the Old English word for "fate," enters the room in line 1233. There is something unpleasant looming in the near future, which brings a "cruel fate" to many an earl, and waits until "evening came, / and Hrothgar departed to his own dwelling" (1234–1236). What presence is out there in the dark?

★

★ ★

IN DEPTH: THE FINNSBURG FRAGMENT

The Finnsburg fragment reminds us of the fragile state of Old English literature, as we have already seen in the perilous history of the *Beowulf* manuscript. The fragment was discovered around 1700 by a clergyman who was in hiding. (He was in hiding because he rejected the new King William and Queen Mary, who had been chosen by England's Protestant Parliament to replace the Catholic James II.) This clergyman, George Hickes, discovered a volume of old manuscripts in the library of the Archbishop of Canterbury, in Kent. Kent was the main area where the ancient Jutes from the Danish peninsula had settled. In the volume, Hickes found a single leaf and copied its contents for later printing. The original leaf is missing from the volume; perhaps Hickes never returned it or it was lost in some other way, but we still have the copy he made. The story presented on this single sheet of writing was a section of a war story, very similar to Old English poems such as "The Battle of Maldon" or "The Battle of Brunanburh," and it was similar in style to *Beowulf*. Because it was only one page of the story, it begins and ends abruptly, even mid-sentence. It describes a battle in a royal hall, in which Hnaef and his warriors fight in a place called Finnsburg. It is so similar to the story in *Beowulf* that it must be another version of the same event.

IN DEPTH: WEALHTHEOW, "FOREIGN CAPTIVE"

In her careful study of Hrothgar's queen, Damico (1984) argues that Wealhtheow could be the mother of all three young princes. We know that Hrothulf is the son of the dead Halga. Could Wealhtheow have been Halga's widow and Hrothulf's mother? It was not unheard of for a widow to marry the next surviving brother. Halga might have been the older brother, killed in battle, and survived by a young wife and baby son. In this light, Wealhtheow's affection for Hrothulf, and dependence on his kindness to her younger sons, would be perfectly natural.

Scandinavian legends, such as the "Saga of Hrolf Kraki," say that Halga (called "Helgi" in Norse) was the greater Danish king, and they portray Hrothgar as the younger brother. Helgi's son was called "Hrolf," a Norse version of Hrothulf. Hrolf's mother, Yrsa, was well-known in legend, and some of her personal attributes are shared by Wealhtheow. While Yrsa's story did not include a remarriage to Helgi's brother, Damico sug-

gests that the author of *Beowulf* chose to model Hrothgar's queen after
Yrsa so closely that much of the audience would automatically connect
them. "Wealhtheow" is a very unusual name for a woman in Old English,
but Yrsa, who was a cattle maid in her youth and was twice captured by
kings and twice made queen, was indeed a "foreign servant" or "foreign
captive." Perhaps by naming Hrothgar's queen in a way that would remind
the poem's audience of Hrolf's mother, the poet of *Beowulf* wished to
suggest that there was more to the family story than met the eye.

If Wealhtheow is intended to be Hrothulf's mother, her words at the
second feast are fitting. Perhaps Wealhtheow, like Hildeburh, would eventually suffer bereavement by seeing one of her sons kill the others. However, the idea that Wealhtheow was the widow of Halga and mother of
Hrothulf cannot be supported without extensive connections to other
texts outside of the Old English corpus. Most of these texts were written
several centuries after the manuscript of *Beowulf* became known. It must
remain an interesting and attractive hypothesis, one that is unable to be
conclusively proven or ruled out.

FURTHER SUGGESTED READING

Bonjour, Adrien. *The Digressions in Beowulf.* Oxford: Society for the Study of Mediaeval
    Languages and Literature, 1950.
Chambers, R. W. *Beowulf: An Introduction to the Study of the Poem with a Discussion of the
    Stories of Offa and Finn.* Cambridge: Cambridge University Press, 1958.
Chance, Jane. *Woman as Hero in Old English Literature.* Syracuse, NY: Syracuse Univer-
    sity Press, 1986.
Damico, Helen. *Beowulf's Wealhtheow and the Valkyrie Tradition.* Madison: The Univer-
    sity of Wisconsin Press, 1984.
Horner, Shari. *The Discourse of Enclosure: Representing Women in Old English Literature.*
    Albany: State University of New York Press, 2001.
Stitt, J. Michael. *Beowulf and the Bear's Son: Epic, Saga and Fairytale in Northern Germanic
    Tradition.* New York: Garland, 1992.
Tolkien, J. R. R. *Finn and Hengest: the Fragment and the Episode,* ed. Alan Bliss. Boston:
    Houghton Mifflin, 1983.
Wrenn, C. L. *Beowulf with the Finnsburg Fragment.* New York: St. Martin's Press, 1973.

5

Beowulf versus Grendel's Mother

GRENDEL'S MOTHER (1251–1306)

Grendel was given little physical description in the poem, and the same is true for his mother. The narrative of the poem assumes that either we know what she looks like or that her appearance doesn't really matter. She is called three words as soon as she is introduced: "modor" (mother), "ides" (lady), and "aglæca-wif" (as Grendel had been "aglæca"). The three concepts seem hard to integrate, at first. We know she is the mother of Grendel, although Hrothgar says there was no father, and the narrative says that both sprang from Cain, so calling her a "mother" is only natural. The term "lady," as applied to this slime-covered fen monster, seems startling; the word "ides" has only been used to describe the royal (human) women up to this point. That the she-monster is called a "terrible female," the approximate meaning of "aglæca-wif," seems appropriate. The three terms together are hard to see as a unity. Is Grendel's mother a bestial female, like a she-bear robbed of her cub, or is she a regal figure demanding justice for her feud?

While Grendel's feud with Beowulf is accepted as simply being part of his monstrous nature, the episode with Grendel's mother demands more explanation and raises more questions. It is portrayed less as an outcome of monstrosity and more in the terms of a specific feud. The mother is an "avenger" (1256), who remembers "her misery" (1258) and must take a "sorrowful journey" to "avenge her son's death" (1278). These words might describe a less passive Hildeburh, a Hildeburh who decided not to weep at Finnsburg but instead to go to Hengest herself and ask him to avenge her son's death against the other Jutes. Germanic heroines of legend give us examples of the role of women in vengeance. In the story of the Volsungs, Signy puts avenging the death of her father and brothers above the lives of her own children, and she urges her surviving brother to complete the vengeance. In the same tale, but a generation later, Gudrun forces her sons to swear to kill her daughter's murderer. In two tales from Iceland, another Gudrun goads her husband to kill a man who slighted her, and a mother scolds her son Bardi for not avenging his brother's death. Women frequently vented their grief by demanding vengeance, even when the men considered that it was better to maintain a truce. In this tradition is Grendel's mother justified in taking vengeance herself when she has no one to send? Many readers feel that her revenge comes from grief, which is a human emotion and seems justified.

On the other hand, the monsters are already outlaws. They may operate in the spirit of revenge, but they are not taking legal vengeance. A victim's family could demand a life for a life; however, by the time of Christianity, the payment of blood-money was legally preferred. But Grendel had already demonstrated that he never played by these rules. He took life after life and offered no recompense. The rules of the blood feud recognized that all players were of equal moral stature, and that every man should be held accountable for his actions. Grendel was only partly human and refused to be held accountable, dying the undignified death of a wounded animal. Was it legally permissible for his mother to demand payment for his death?

For the audience of *Beowulf*, the two possible perceptions of Grendel's mother were probably both present. On the one hand, she is grieving and has just come from the scene of her son's death. The poem comments that there was no good exchange; that "both sides" had to bargain with "the lives of friends" (1305–1306). This comment seems to make a moral equation between the losses. On the other hand, Grendel and his mother are outlaws, monsters, cursed by God and half-bestial. The heart can allow that she would desire revenge, but the law cannot. Grendel's death was a legal execution, in a way, and the law did not allow for the family of a man hung for murder or theft to seek vengeance against the king who condemned him." Grendel's mother has merely continued the feud for the lowest reason, to kill and kill alike, and it will only be settled with her own death unless more relatives come forward.

The poem makes a point that is confusing: it sets us up to believe that the mother is less strong than the son. When Grendel's mother struck the hall, "The horror was less / by as much as a maiden's strength, / a woman's warfare, is less than an armed man's" (1282–1284). It seems to suggest that Grendel's mother is less frightening and may be weaker physically." But will this prove to be the case? Perhaps the men in the hall underestimated the strength of the mother, which caused their sense of fear to be less. Perhaps the mother did not cause as much destruction, and so for the moment, made her strength appear to be minimal. Unfortunately for Beowulf, her strength will not be any less than her son's.

Grendel's mother follows a different strategy than her son. Grendel became accustomed to the hall, and in his pride, not only did he carry victims away, but often he ate them on the spot. The mother has never been seen in Heorot; only her extremes of anger and sorrow are enough to drive her into the dwellings of men. She takes no risks and makes a lightning strike. With an instantly killed victim in hand, she takes a life for a life and leaves as quickly as she can.

THE PURSUIT OF THE MOTHER TO THE FENS
(1306–1441)

The pursuit begins with the discovery of the victim; the men in the hall must awaken the king. There is great emphasis on the status of the victim; he was no young man, but was one of the King's oldest friends. He is a nobleman, and we learn that his name is Aeschere. Beowulf also awakens, and both he and the king arrive in the hall around dawn to find disorder, uproar, and fear. The narrative is careful in detailing the time-order of this day. We are to understand that the attack took place in the wee hours of the night, before the sun rose, and that in the gray dawn's twilight the leading men arrived on the scene.

In one of the poem's few humorous touches, Beowulf appears not to notice what has happened; there is at least dramatic irony in his question. Given that he has been urgently woken at an earlier hour than he expected, he fails to notice the signs of tragedy and asks Hrothgar if he had a pleasant night's rest. Hrothgar's reply is heartfelt, but it also reveals the hierarchy of the society. Hrothgar mourns the mother's revenge, but he feels that she has gone too far in that she took the highest-ranking man after the king himself. Like the king, Aeschere had the authority to give treasures, and his men will miss their lord.

Hrothgar gives a vivid description of the "mere," a word for a small lake, where the water-trolls live. Its chief features include a threatening landscape, stormy weather, solitary and fearsome animals, and unnatural fire on the water. It has high cliffs, waterfalls, and a cold forest. Its head-lands are windy, and its storms are so violent that the waves climb as high as the sky. We learn that wolves haunt the hills surrounding it and that sea monsters (1425–1441) live in the water. These characteristics may seem to be part of the natural order, such as the harsh weather that one might find in Patagonia, but there is something more. The fire on the water at night is enough to deter even hunted stags from swimming in the water to escape hunters. Animals are as afraid of the haunted mere as the Danes themselves!

Beowulf's response to Aeschere's death is at once familiar and strange. To the sorrowing Hrothgar, he offers a platitude about death. "Each of us shall abide the end / of this world's life," (1386-1387) he says, echoing the narrator's sentiment that death will eventually catch up to everyone. In other words, it doesn't make any sense to grieve too much, since death is inevitable. But Beowulf offers a comfort that sounds strange to modern ears. He promises vengeance, so that Hrothgar may not grieve, and so that he himself may seek glory before his own death. His statement, "It is always better / to avenge one's friend than to mourn overmuch" (1384–1385), is given in the tone of the obvious. It is a statement to which he expects no disagreement.

The idea that vengeance is the best comfort after a murder makes a great deal of sense in a culture of feud but not in a culture of restitution, such as the later Anglo-Saxons encouraged. Paying the "wer-gild" (the "man-money") meant settling a feud without any vengeance. In a modern culture of social restraint, we find even less to agree with when Beowulf makes this pronouncement. There are occasions when a murderer is sentenced to death, and the victim's family appeals to the judge to spare his life. "His death won't bring back my son," they say. "It will only bring about more death. Two wrongs don't make a right." It is difficult for many modern readers to understand a culture in which vengeance is so critical, but we must accept Beowulf's culture as consistent, and one that many ancient people would have agreed with. There are some cultures in the modern world where the values of Beowulf's society are still in operation. Tit-for-tat killings are not restricted to the ancient past.

Beowulf's trip to the haunted mere is made in a full state parade. Hrothgar's second-best horse arrives; it is possible that Beowulf is now riding the gift horse of the previous night's feast. With all of the Geats and many of the leading Danes, the procession follows the footprints of Grendel's mother. Beowulf scouts ahead at one point: he may be impatient with the slow pace of the horses and foot soldiers. The most startling discovery is the discarded head of Aeschere, which may have been spat out like a seed as the mother passed by. It is implied that the body of Aeschere went into the water with the murderer, for the water "boiled" with blood.

There are three places in the poem where this same mere is said to bubble with blood. There is definitely something magical about this detail, as it does not seem realistic. In the first instance, Grendel's torn arm had bled for several miles before he reached the mere, and yet the mere is said to be welling up with blood when the Danes scout it a few hours later. The same is true for Aeschere, who would have been bleeding while he was carried over the path to the mere. Also, water would quickly diffuse the color of blood. The descriptions of blood seem to be statements about morality, for blood has always symbolized the crime and the life taken. The poem has already cited Cain's murder of his brother, Abel, in Genesis 4. In that passage, God tells Cain that Abel's blood cries out from the ground. Approximately 600 years after the *Beowulf* manuscript was written, Shakespeare's Lady Macbeth feels that the stain of blood is on her hands from the murder. Blood is the sign of life as it leaves the body, and it stains the murderer or the murder site, or in this case, it is in the water of the mere.

Unable to attack the mother, the Geats make one small inroad on the haunted mere. A Geat lets fly an arrow against one sea monster, and its wound causes it to be hooked and brought to shore. We have no description of the "wave-roamer," so we cannot know if we should picture a shark, the Loch Ness monster, or a mythical creature combining the body of a whale, the teeth of a lion, and the tusks of an elephant.

BEOWULF IN THE HAUNTED MERE (1441–1622)

Beowulf's preparations for the fight are explained in detail. An audience familiar with war and weapons would be interested in this section. Did he wear his helmet, which would make swimming difficult? Yes, he did, and he also wore his chain-mail shirt. Although swimming is much harder with heavy metal armor, it was important to Beowulf to wear some protective covering as he sank past the sea monsters. When he fought against Grendel, Beowulf had used no sword, since he knew that Grendel was charmed against iron. In this instance, he accepts the ceremonial presentation of a sword, "Hrunting," from the shame-faced Unferth. Unferth's probable high status at Hrothgar's court is reinforced by his ownership of this weapon. If he was not a famous warrior himself, then perhaps his father had been, because the sword is said to be an ancient treasure that never fails its owner. Now, armed with a sword and dressed in his chain mail and helmet, Beowulf is ready to go.

Beowulf is now in a position to ask more of Hrothgar. In his first challenge, he had asked only that Hrothgar send home any surviving armor with his companions. Now he asks that Hrothgar do more. Having publicly adopted Beowulf as his son, Hrothgar should protect the Geat warriors and possibly take them into his own household. He should send the treasures of last night's feast to Hygelac, to show Hygelac that Beowulf did his duty and that Hrothgar had honored it. Finally, he should let Unferth have his own sword as a trade if Beowulf does not bring the borrowed sword back.

Beowulf is a glorious hero, but like any mortal man he calculates by probabilities and is unable to see into the future. He predicts that, because he has "Hrunting," he will either gain victory or die. Neither outcome will prove to be true, and one wonders if he would have bothered to take a sword with him had Unferth not made a show of giving him this treasure-sword. Perhaps Beowulf wonders if Grendel's mother will be just as impervious to iron as her son. Perhaps he is showing optimism so as not to shame an important man who has already suffered a downfall of pride. On the other hand, perhaps he would actually prefer go into the water with a sword, just in case it does work. The sword may also be useful to fend off sea monsters!

Many surprises are revealed in the fight with Grendel's mother. The first surprise is where Beowulf decides to go to find her: straight down to the bottom of the mere. We might expect that she lives in a cave along the side of the mere, but Beowulf knows better, and he knows he must dive directly into the water. The details of his swim are somewhat contested, and most translations suggest that it took him a day to reach the bottom. We wonder how he could have held his breath and how an inland mere, or sea loch, could have been so deep. Robinson (1974) suggests that it was full daylight when Beowulf reached the bottom. The phrase usually translated as "a day's time" could also mean "during daylight." Recall that Beowulf had come into Heorot just before dawn that same day. Some time passed while they saddled the horses and prepared to leave, and the journey of several miles to the edge of the water took maybe an hour at the least. The mere, ringed with trees, would not receive direct light from a slanting morning sun. As Beowulf dives in, however, the sun is fairly high and there is full daylight.

Robinson's translation that it was daylight would explain another detail. Almost as soon as Beowulf is past the point where the waiting men cannot see him, Grendel's mother, who is indeed on the bottom, looks up through the water and sees him. We have all seen underwater footage of sharks or men swimming at a higher, more sun-filled level than the cameraman: the water shines in the sun, and the body is clearly outlined. The mere must be murkier than the ocean water we see on film, but still, it is through the sunlit background that the mother is able to see the intruder long before he sees her. In the end, being seen immediately by the mother actually saves Beowulf some time, for rather than searching the mere's bottom looking for her hidden lair, he is dragged very rapidly into it, perhaps before his breath has run out. Beowulf's high-speed trip downward is fearfully dangerous; sea monsters are clawing at him, tearing at him with tusks. He is bruised, but his chain-mail shirt protects him from getting seriously wounded.

The second surprise of this conflict comes at the bottom of the mere. We expect Beowulf to drown, as he would if a giant squid or a shark dragged him under the ocean waves. Instead, just as we are aware that his lungs are ready to burst, he finds himself in an air-filled underwater cave. It is more than an underwater cave, however: it is a hall. The hall is not only air-filled, it is a real hall with a central fire. On the walls hang treasure-weapons, as perhaps there were at the hall of Heorot. Now the tables have turned, and Beowulf the avenger is in the enemy's hall, as Grendel's mother had been in Heorot.

The fight follows four quick steps. First, Beowulf gets his bearings and wrenches free to take a stab at the mother with Unferth's sword. Second, the sword failing, he flings it aside and tries to wrestle as he had grappled with Grendel, but he trips and falls. Third, Grendel's mother does not play by the rules and pulls a knife on him, which his chain-mail shirt turns away. Fourth, Beowulf tries a new approach: he takes a sword from the wall and brings it down on her neck, beheading her. This fourth step ends the fight, with her death.

Why did the second sword succeed where Unferth's sword did not? The poem tells us that the second sword is older and larger. The sword is not only older, it is more supernatural, fit to kill a supernatural being. Unferth's sword is meant for fighting humans. An ancient sword might also be made of bronze, not iron, and if Grendel's mother is charmed against only iron, then she would suddenly be helpless. The sword Hrunting apparently bounced off her head, while this one slices right into the bone. It is a giant's sword, and one that only Beowulf could lift (although apparently Grendel was able to mount it on the wall for his mother). These are not the Frost Giants of Norse legend, but the human giants of early Genesis who lived before the flood. The sword may have some power of its own; perhaps it was made to kill Cain's kin but failed to work because its original owner perished. Having waited patiently on the wall for many years for a hero to come, the sword fulfills its purpose. The poem does not directly suggest such a story, but in evoking the age of heroes and giants before the Flood, it suggests a magical past.

The magical giant's sword is able to do one more task before it fails. Beowulf now cuts off the head of Grendel, although Grendel is already dead. As previously noted concerning the nature of Grendel, this was an important step. If Beowulf had not found Grendel and taken the chance to cut off his head, perhaps Grendel's undead body may have been able to roam the land again, causing ruin and death. Icelandic stories of such zombies, called "draugrs," make it clear that the only way to stop them is to cut off their heads. Another reason for beheading is that many people survive all sorts of wounds, but the loss of a head is sufficient proof of death. In the Bible there are examples of trophy heads, like the stories of Goliath and of John the Baptist. In the same manuscript-binding with *Beowulf* is the story of Judith, a courageous widow who beheads Holofernes, the Babylonian commander. Clearly, there is no better death certificate than a severed head.

Two beheadings in the underwater hall create a new upwelling of supernatural blood. Like a water jet in a hot tub, the blood bubbles up to the surface. Hrothgar's counselors see it, and these wise old men, who know too well the ways of the world, unanimously conclude that the blood can only be that of Beowulf. In a world where men meet death, and where fate is known to bring about sudden reversals of fortune, their "wisdom" is understandable. Perhaps Hrothgar is growing tired, for the decision is made to abandon the mere and go home. Only the Geats, Beowulf's companions, remain. They are sick at heart but retain some remote hope that makes them stay until they are sure of the outcome.

The magical natures of both the sword and the blood come together in the vivid image of the sword blade melting. Like "battle-icicles," the sword melts "like ice / when the Father loosens the frost's fetters, / unwraps the water's bonds" (1606–1610). The poem states that the heat is from the monsters' blood, which the metal cannot stand, but clearly there is a supernatural principle at work. The sword has done its duty and the blade now melts; the monster's blood takes a last revenge on the blade that spilled it. Beowulf would be well within his rights to take other things from the hall, but, perhaps unnerved by the melting sword, he decides not to touch the remaining weapons and treasures. With three possessions, Hrunting, the giant sword hilt, and Grendel's head, Beowulf is ready to swim to the surface.

SECOND FEAST AT HEOROT (1623–1887)

As Beowulf emerges from the water, dripping and covered with slime, the focus quickly shifts to the trophy head of Grendel. Exactly how large was Grendel? Although Beowulf is able to swim upward with the head, it now requires four normal men and two long poles to transport it. Grendel's head is the size of a boulder! The Geats are able to make an unexpected, dramatic entrance when they drag the head into the hall by its hair.

Beowulf's short speech summarizing the fight emphasizes the danger he was in and then focuses on the finality of this victory. After his fight with Grendel, his speech to Hrothgar had resembled an instant replay, describing the wrestling, the wound, and the pain he inflicted. This speech omits the details of the fight but tells about the swords, which is a point sure to interest everyone in the hall. Beowulf, having been to the lair of the water-trolls, can now assure everyone that there are no more of them lurking about. Heorot can finally rest in peace, at least until the next human assault or raid.

The magical giant's sword is again the focus of attention. As Hrothgar examines the hilt, the narrative tells us more about it. The hilt is decorated with snake-like designs and fancy scrolls, but more than that, there are runes cut into it. Runes were ancient letters, modeled after the Roman alphabet, and they were also magic symbols. To cut or carve runes was to cast a spell, and the owner of a stick or weapon with runes possessed that magic power. In this Christian-era poem, there is little use made of these magic runes (there are no incantations to the gods and no indication of the types of spells they were), but we learn that they tell a story. Runic writing could tell a story, although it was more often used for simple inscriptions. The monks favored Latin script, but there are some poems in runic writing. By Anglo-Saxon times, runes formed a full alphabet. The narrative of *Beowulf* envisions a sword with more than just an inscription of the owner's name. The owner's name is included, but the runes (or perhaps pictures) also tell the story of the ancient struggle with evil in the days of Genesis.

The inclusion of the runes is one of the most colorful and successful fusions of old and new religious beliefs in the poem. In pagan times, the runes might have told about an ancient struggle between the god Tyr and a Frost Giant, or about the defeat of the gods in the last battle. Runes were associated with Woden ("Odin" in Norse) and were part of his magic spells. But in this Christian epic, the runes are brought into the service of biblical history. Their magic is part of the magic of writing, as it connects us with the past. The writing on the ancient weapon is a direct testament of the pre-history time periods. Surely the original audience of *Beowulf* felt the same thrill that we might feel on seeing prehistoric cave paintings, or the original Declaration of Independence, or even the burnt, cracked manuscript of *Beowulf* itself. Writing connects us to the

Artist's conception of an ancient sword hilt with a runic inscription.
(Based on the sixth-century sword found at Snartemo, Norway.)
(Illustration by Andrew McHenry.)

past by telling the forgotten story, and if we can see the actual writing itself, the connection is so much stronger. The sword's inscription describes the ancient struggle with giants (the Christian version) and how "Frea" (the Lord) set out to subdue them. In the Anglo-Saxon poem "Genesis" (in the passage dealing with the giants), the chosen word for "Lord" is the same word as the name of the pagan Norse god, whose sign was the boar. On the sword hilt there is an almost perfect synthesis of pagan and Christian beliefs.

Hrothgar's "Sermon"

As Hrothgar holds the sword hilt in his hand, he ponders the history of the blade. Either in pictures or in runes, the story is told of a great race of mankind that was wiped out by the Flood. In the poem, Hrothgar appears to know the story, but a true historical Hrothgar could not have read Genesis to know about Noah's Flood. He ponders the wickedness that led to their downfall and sees the reversal of fortune for the sword's owner. A great earl, he reasons, owned this sword and then fell either to the monsters descended from Cain or to the Flood itself. He sees the name of the original owner written in runes and thinks of this story as though he himself, or a lord of a Germanic tribe, had been the "earl" who owned the sword. It stirs his thoughts, and he begins one of the longest speeches in the poem.

This speech is often referred to as "Hrothgar's Sermon" because of its formal structure and moralizing tone. Hrothgar does not quote the Bible, but his conclusions are the same peculiar blend of Germanic values and biblical morals that the whole poem presents. He "preaches" against pride, but it is important to note that the pride he speaks of is not necessarily pride as we think of it. In developing his topic, he uses a formal, four-part structure. First, he considers a particular example of a king who was overthrown in a sudden reversal of fate; second, he considers a general case of the psychology behind kingly pride; third, he warns Beowulf personally to take heed; and finally, he uses his own situation as an example for all.

Hrothgar begins with a general proposition that if an earl (or a king) acts in truth on behalf of his people and does not exhibit the fateful forgetfulness of pride, then he is a better man. It is possible that he is speaking of Beowulf at this point, as he turns immediately to him and tells him to temper his strength and glory with wisdom. He may already be praising Beowulf for taking care of the people and being born a better man. He may also be thinking of the sword's original owner, and how it would have been better for that man if he had been virtuous and escaped the wrath of his fate. In any case, Hrothgar predicts that Beowulf will become the better sort of hero.

Immediate to his mind is an example of a man who did not pass this test. Scholars believe that Heremod may have been an earlier king of the Danes. In the myth of the infant Scyld arriving by boat, the implication is that the Danes did not have a king when the child arrived. If there is any historical basis to the stories, then perhaps a sudden vacancy in the royal family allowed for a change in dynasty, which resulted in the myth of the child who came over the waves. The story of Heremod seems to fit the slot: he is called the King of the Scyldings, and he seems to have been betrayed or cast out on account of his being unfit to rule. Perhaps this created the vacancy that the miracle child filled.

We do not know the full story of Heremod. In lines 901–915 (the song of the poet as they celebrated the death of Grendel at dawn) Heremod is called headstrong, crippled by cares, and a burden. He was betrayed among the "Eotens," and this word is ambiguous in itself. It could mean either the neighboring Jutes or the giants. If Heremod was a historical figure, then betrayal among the Jutes (possibly a generation before the sad story of Hildeburh and Hnaef) would make sense. If Heremod was a mythical figure, then perhaps he was betrayed in the land of the Norse giants, to the far north. Most scholars consider the Jutes a more likely option, fitting Heremod into history rather than myth.

Hrothgar does not give a more detailed account of Heremod's downfall, but he does fill in Heremod's psychological background. Heremod was greedy, and he betrayed the bonds of the hall-loyalty. He "cut down his table-companions" (1713). We can imagine the king and his band of warriors at a feast, and as they became drunk, the king lashed out and killed someone. He did it again and again, and each killing was under different circumstances but each time showed the same intolerance and impulsiveness. The first few times, the men were saddened but assumed it would not happen again. As Heremod began to make a pattern of it, however, their loyalty faded and they were afraid to keep him in power any longer. Heremod's other fault was that he did not give gifts. This flaw, in the Germanic system, was unpardonable. All spoils of battle belonged to the king, and from that hoard he doled out rewards. These rewards may well have been the main income for each warrior, and they were theirs to keep or sell. The warriors were dependent on gifts of estates to support their families. A king who failed to give gifts was like a nation that does not send paychecks to its army.

The mind of Heremod is depicted in colorful terms. In his heart, he nurses a "blood-ravenous breast-hoard" (1719). This description brings to mind a different picture; perhaps he not only had a hot temper, but he also killed his table companions in order to avoid sharing. We can imagine him looking over the hoard of spoils that technically were his property but, as everyone knew, were his to give away. He knew that the incredibly intricate helmet taken off the Frankish king should go to Herewulf, the hero who killed the king's bodyguard, but he wanted it for himself. What better way to keep it than to make sure Herewulf would not recover from his wounds? A blow on the head in a fit of drunken rage would ensure that Herewulf's fragile condition would worsen and that the helmet would remain in his hoard. So greed and betrayal worked together, and Heremod's men grew more and more dissatisfied with their king. The earlier story suggested that the older men, who had known his father, watched in dismay as he failed to live up to his earlier promise and squandered all of the solid ties of loyalty. A revolution in the hall may have forced him into exile, and, wandering friendless into the land of the Jutes, he may have met a violent death. Heremod's memory continues to serve as a warning to the Danes: a man born into good circumstances may forget his duties and come to a bad end.

At line 1724, Hrothgar transitions to discussing the nature of man in a more general sense. How does this happen? How is it that a man can be gifted with strength, honor, and success and throw it all away? He paints a picture of a man with many advantages over his fellow men, who enjoys every kind of success and freedom. This man (in line 1740) at last comes to the turning point, the beginning of downfall. Pride awakens, his conscience sleeps, and he becomes greedy. He stops giving gifts. In the end, he is mortal, he dies, and all of his treasure is given to another. Not only is he unable to "take it with him," but after his death, another gives his treasure away, as he should have done.

This portion of Hrothgar's message is the closest to a sermon. The conscience is the soul's shepherd, and it falls asleep. The tempter comes, either sin or the Devil, and shoots an arrow. This figure of the evil one who shoots an arrow of sin into the heart is a familiar figure from the Bible: Paul's *Epistle to the Ephesians* warns the believers to wear the armor of faith to ward off the flaming darts of the evil one. The figure is also familiar in a culture that used bows as daily tools for shooting birds and rabbits as well as enemy warriors. Hrothgar's picture is both from the Bible, and at the same time from his own culture, and it is believable as something a pagan king might say. For the audience of *Beowulf*, it was a word-picture that they might expect to hear on any Sunday in church.

The sin that Hrothgar's imaginary king falls into is derived from Germanic values, not from the Bible. Feeling greedy, he fails to give gold rings to those who boast. The loyalty of the hall was built around these gifts. The warrior would promise to defend the hall or die, and the king would give him a ring as a pledge of this promise. Failing to give the rings was a way of dishonoring the promise of loyalty, so greed was the worst possible sin for a king. In the Christian culture of the audience, greed had other meanings. They knew that God required giving to the poor, but here Hrothgar makes no mention of alms-giving. They knew that supporting the church through gifts was also required by God, but Hrothgar makes no mention of this role in the duties of his imagined king. According to Hrothgar, his imaginary king fails in just one aspect: he does not uphold the bonds of the Germanic war band.

In line 1758, Hrothgar brings the point of his message home to Beowulf. He tells him not to be like the unhappy owner of the sword hilt, not to be like Heremod, and not to be like any other figure of pride and subsequent downfall. He tells him to learn wisdom while he is young, and that he should give gifts and pay attention not to his own riches and glory, but to strengthening the bonds of communal loyalty. This has been the message of his "sermon," yet in closing he returns again to biblical language. He tells Beowulf that by choosing wisdom, he can choose "eternal counsel" (a term generally used to mean spiritual wisdom and salvation). In lines 1763–1768, Hrothgar lists the terrors that may attack Beowulf in his lifetime. This short passage is compelling in its efficiency and poetry; it achieves rhetorical power through its relentless list and is followed by the conclusion, "in one fell swoop / death, o warrior, will overwhelm you."

Hrothgar's last point is about his own situation. It does not fit into this scheme directly, but it is an example of how evil reversal can come to any king. He states how he brought peace to the Danes through fifty years of firm rule, but in the end even he suffered from an enemy that he could not placate or defeat. This statement seems less like a moral and more like a transition and compliment. He has been warning Beowulf not to kill his friends and not to become piggish and suspicious. Now, he brings his hearers back to the present occasion. He could not rid himself of the monsters, but look! Beowulf has done it! Let's all sit down and drink! His last moral point is that just as he had to wait for God's hand of freedom from the monsters, so Beowulf and all kings must remember their Creator and avoid sinful pride.

This last feast is told in few words. The Danes were preparing themselves for a funeral rather than a victory feast, so this sudden reversal (the incredible return of Beowulf) has left Hrothgar unprepared. It is late, and Beowulf is tired. Hrothgar does not have time for more than an ordinary feast, and there are no gifts laid out. After Grendel's death, he had the day to look over his hoard and make selections, but this time he is apologetic that the gift-giving will have to wait until morning. Clearly, Beowulf is too tired to care. The feast probably wraps up earlier than usual, and all men sleep in the hall without fear. One detail stands out, because it is unusual in a heroic story for any mundane parts of life to be recorded: as Beowulf retires, a servant goes with him to attend to whatever needs he may have. The poem does not tell us what these needs may be, but we can assume that cleaning his cuts and poulticing his bruises are probably included. Beowulf may also want the mere-slime washed out of his hair and his clothes washed and sewed. This detail is a small reminder that even in heroic days, a bevy of hired men and women took care of these constant needs of all mankind.

TRANSITION BETWEEN DENMARK AND GEATLAND (1887–1962)

A modern story might choose to skip the transition time when Beowulf is traveling home, or it might choose to feature an important conversation or detail from the journey. The ancient poet creates a passage that can appear abrupt, disorganized, and slow-moving to a modern reader. Three main objectives appear in this passage: wrapping up unfinished business in Denmark, savoring the sea voyage, and setting the scene at home.

As morning comes, Beowulf's mind turns first to packing up and going home. He returns the sword Hrunting to Unferth, with a polite speech about how it was not Unferth's fault that the sword failed. The poet wishes to show some of Beowulf's character, having him go out of his way to give honor to a man who tried to dishonor him. With the gear ready to move, Beowulf seeks out his host for a farewell speech, and he may also remember that he was promised further gifts.

Hrothgar calls the speech of Beowulf the shrewdest speech he has ever heard from a young man, so it is well to look at what Beowulf says. Beowulf's main point, that the ties of alliance between the Danes and Geats should be strengthened, seems to be that of a political ambassador. Beowulf may not be much older than twenty-two, and he has just fought two tremendous battles, so Hrothgar is surprised that he thinks about politics.

Beowulf makes three points. First, he suggests that he would be glad to do more for the Danes in order to merit more affection. Second, he promises to bring help in the form of a large army of warriors if the Danes are threatened by enemies. He seems to realize that he does not truly have the authority to make this promise, but he states his confidence that his uncle will back up any promise he makes. Third, he suggests that Hrothgar's son, Hrethric, might like to travel to Geatland and strengthen the alliance further. All of his attention is given to strengthening the alliance and helping their two nations cooperate.

Hrothgar's response suggests that most young warriors did not think this way. This may be his moment of greatest regret, because he cannot actually adopt Beowulf and keep him as a successor. Hrothgar, like most old men of that time, knows that the strength of a people is in its alliances as much as in its war band. Most young men undervalue alliances and are impatient with courting approval, preferring to try their own abilities. Hrothgar may feel that his nephew, Hrothulf, is not attentive enough to alliances, and that his own sons are still so young that they focus mostly on building their muscles and learning to shoot. The fervency of his farewell to Beowulf, the tears he weeps as he embraces him for the last time, may be a sign that he wishes he could, indeed, keep Beowulf as his successor.

Hrothgar predicts that if anything puts an end to Hygelac, either by sword or sickness, then the Geats will choose Beowulf as their next king. Germanic tribes had a tradition of selecting a king from among the royal family, or from a new dynasty if the old one had ended (as in the case of Heremod). Hygelac may not have had children at this time, so Beowulf, as the nephew, would be a natural choice. But even after Hygelac's sons are born, as we will see, the Geats had some choice in the matter of selecting a grown man over a child. Times were too dangerous not to allow for some flexibility in the matter of kingship.

Hrothgar's parting gifts for killing Grendel's mother are twelve treasures. We expect to learn more about them, but nothing more is said. Perhaps, with the ship preparing to leave and the other treasures bundled up to carry, Hrothgar selects smaller treasures such as rings, jeweled brooches, or golden cups. Nothing could be more troublesome to carry than the eight horses already being led down to the sea! The ship is piled high with treasures, although the poet assures us that the ship's mast is still high above the heap. For a final exchange of gifts, Beowulf pulls out a gilt sword, perhaps part of his hoard from Hrothgar, and passes it to the coast guard. The coast guard's respect in the mead hall, says the poet, increases after that.

As before, the poet loves to describe a sea voyage. The ship is "ring-necked" with a "sea-curved prow," and it "sliced through the deep water" (1896, 1904). In just a few lines, the poet packs in details: the great sail, the creaking timbers, the straining rigging, and the prow wet with waves. The ship pushes forward with the wind, and in a short time the cliffs of Geatland are visible. Again, the ship is spotted by a coast guard and quickly tied up at the beach. The cargo is unloaded quickly, as we can imagine, for it contains not only live horses but also treasures to tempt any thief.

Beowulf's re-entry to his homeland does not read smoothly. Perhaps it worked better as a live recitation and to an audience who loved the side stories that feel more like digressions to us. The poem mentions the first view of Hygelac's hall, right by the sea, and is then immediately sidetracked by a story about a legendary queen. Hygelac's young queen, Hygd, is probably a teenager. Like Beowulf, she is wiser than her age suggests, and she is good at that most important of all skills, gift-giving. By contrast, says the poet, think of a queen who was terrible! The suggestion seems to be that at least Hygd was better than that, but to a modern mind it seems that she could hardly have helped being better.

The digression about this legendary queen, like many of the side stories, raises more questions than we can answer. Is her name Modthryth or is it Thryth? Because of an ambiguity in the original language, both names are used by editors and translators. R. M. Liuzza (2000) prefers a reading in which the element "Mod" is part of the sentence rather than part of her name, and the meaning of the word would be that Hygd herself considered the legendary queen Thryth to be an example of how not to act. The story states that Thryth married Offa, King of the Angles, in southern Denmark, but it does not tell us where Thryth lived as a wicked princess. Was she a Geat, and thus a local example to Hygd? Were Hygd and Thryth supposed to be relatives? Is it possible that they were both from some other neighboring people?

The story is straightforward enough. Thryth was so proud and so disrespectful of the bonds of the war band that if any man, except one related to her by blood or marriage, dared to look at her eyes, she would cry out, "Off with his head!" If we modern readers were projecting a role of ceremonial power (instead of real power) onto the royal ladies of *Beowulf,* then perhaps the story of Thryth should make us pause and reconsider. Thryth apparently had the power to put innocent men to death, although onlookers found it wrong and shocking. She destroyed the bonds of hall loyalty. Perhaps her father found it expedient to shuffle her out of his hall as soon as possible, so she was gold-laden and sent to Anglia for Offa to deal with. It seems that Offa was able to teach her new ways, and under his roof she took up the approved role of ring-giver.

The praise given to Offa, a legendary King of Anglia, also raises questions. The Anglo-Saxon royal houses claimed descent from the legendary kings of the continental tribes; specifically, the later King Offa of Mercia claimed descent from this earlier Offa. Could the poem's lengthy praise of Offa of Anglia be intended as a compliment to Offa of Mercia? Since no one knows where or when the poem was composed, this has often been seen as a telltale clue that it may have been written in Mercia, during King Offa's reign, around the year AD 780. On the other hand, the much earlier King Offa of Anglia was a tall figure in legend. As a young teenager, he was said to have single-handedly fought back an army to restore the borders of Anglia. In a poem that spends time praising the exploits of great men, it is not so surprising to find another legendary giant singled out for attention.

The second part of the poem, then, ends with the first sight of Hygelac's hall. The hero has come home.

★

★　　★

IN DEPTH: THE HAUNTED MERE AS HELL

Scholars have noted the similarity between the description of Grendel's mere and the description of hell in a tenth-century sermon. "Blickling Homily 17" describes hell in terms very different from the way modern culture depicts it. Most people today are familiar with cartoons that depict hell as a cave full of fires and smoke and devils with pointy beards, horns, and evil smiles, prodding the damned with pitchforks. The Blickling preacher had a very different vision of hell; one that is instantly familiar to careful readers of *Beowulf*. It is worth quoting in its entirety (translated here by Liuzza, 2000):

> As Saint Paul was looking toward the northern part of this world, where all waters descend, he also saw over the waters a gray stone. And north of the stone had grown very frosty groves, and there were gloomy mists, and under the stone was the dwelling-place of sea-monsters and evil spirits. And he saw that on the cliff many black souls were hanging in the icy groves, bound by their hands, and devils in the shape of sea-monsters were clutching at them like greedy wolves. And the water was black under the cliff below, and from the cliff to the water was about twelve miles. And when the boughs broke, the souls that hung on the twigs fell down, and the sea-monsters seized them.

What a horrifying vision! It has all the elements of nightmare: cold, helplessness against the pursuit of monsters, and a terrifying fall into water from which there is no escape. If we allow ourselves to believe in this image for a few moments, rather than remaining distanced by the antiquity and quaintness of the vision, it becomes a terrifying idea. Imagine the horror of Anglo-Saxon audiences to find that Grendel and his mother lived, literally, in a miniature hell. The banks are haunted by wolves, and the water is haunted by sea monsters who hunt victims like wolves. The overhanging trees are frosty, even in summer; the cliffs are high and a torrent of water falls from them. Where the "Blickling Homily 17" left out the fires of hell, *Beowulf* supplies them, in the fires that burn on the water at night.

IN DEPTH: BIBLE PARALLELS TO HROTHGAR'S "SERMON"

Hrothgar's speech is often called a sermon, although the poem never specifically states that Hrothgar is a man who believes in the Bible, and it certainly does not say that the speech is given in a church. Part of the reason it is called a sermon is because of the message, which reminds Beowulf that he, too, will die. At least one passage seems directly comparable to well-known Bible passages. Hrothgar cites a list of things that may overcome the strong man and bring him to death. "Sickness or the sword will shatter your strength, / or the grip of fire, or the surging flood, / or the cut of a sword, or the flight of a spear, / or terrible old age, or the light of your eyes / will fail and flicker out; in one fell swoop / death, o warrior, will overwhelm you" (1763–1768).

There are at least three similar passages in the Bible. Psalm 91 lists the terrors that the one who trusts in God will not need to fear: the terror of the night, the arrow that flies by day, the plague that wastes in darkness, and the destruction that wastes at noonday. In Ecclesiastes 12, Solomon describes old age and death with images of decay and broken mechanisms: the doors on the street are shut, the silver cord is snapped, the golden bowl is smashed, and the wheel at the cistern is broken. In Romans 8, Paul describes the many terrors that cannot separate a believer from Christ: tribulation, distress, persecution, famine, nakedness, peril, or sword. These well-known passages were probably familiar to the poet of *Beowulf*, especially if he was a scholar or monk. Hrothgar's "sermon" imitates the rhetoric of these lists and evokes a biblical intensity, and at the same time it does not injure the portrayal of a pagan king through direct quotation.

FURTHER SUGGESTED READING

Chambers, R. W. *Beowulf: An Introduction to the Study of the Poem with a Discussion of the Stories of Offa and Finn.* Cambridge: Cambridge University Press, 1958.

Chance, Jane. *Woman as Hero in Old English Literature.* Syracuse, NY: Syracuse University Press, 1986.

Lerer, Seth. *Literacy and Power in Anglo-Saxon Literature.* Lincoln: University of Nebraska Press, 1991. (This includes a chapter on Hrothgar and the sword hilt.)

6

Beowulf versus the Dragon

MAIN CHARACTER INTRODUCTIONS

Beowulf: First the returning hero of the earlier poem, then the aging King of the Geats. In the later part of the poem, he is as old as seventy, and although he is still strong, age has robbed him of his strength, as it had robbed Hrothgar. Beowulf has no sons; perhaps he did not marry, or perhaps his wife and children have not survived. His nearest kinsman appears to be the young Wiglaf.

Hygelac: King of the Geats, maternal uncle of Beowulf. He has been ruling the Geats for a few years and has not been married long when Beowulf returns. He is, or will be, father to one daughter and one son, Heardred. He will die in a raid on the Franks, far from home, in the territory of the modern Netherlands.

Hygd: Queen of the Geats, wife of Hygelac. Hygd has no speaking lines, and only appears briefly. She is said to be young, perhaps still in her teens. Hygd may be the mother of Hygelac's daughter and son (Heardred), or she may be their stepmother. (If the chronology of Geatish history is taken seriously, Hygelac could already have a daughter of marriageable age.)

Wiglaf: Young kinsman of old King Beowulf, son of Weohstan. He appears to be part Swedish, perhaps an outcome of fluid loyalties and intermarriages. He is loyal to Beowulf, however, and is named Beowulf's personal heir after aiding him in his fight with the dragon.

THE MESSENGER: This character is unnamed but gives a long and significant speech about the fate of the Geats.

THE DRAGON: The dragon has no name. He is not a character who speaks, and he is the least human of Beowulf's foes. He is at least several hundred years old and has occupied the treasure-barrow for a very long time before being disturbed.

THE LAST SURVIVOR: This character is not part of the story itself but appears in the narrative. He was part of a more ancient tribe that died out, and he undertook to bury the accumulated treasure before his own death. This barrow later became the lair of the dragon. His viewpoint is elegantly portrayed in the poem's narrative.

HRETHEL, HEREBEALD, HAETHCYN, AND HEARDRED: Kings and princes of the Geats, members of Beowulf's family. Their tragic feuds brought Beowulf to power but also laid the groundwork for future disaster.

ONGENTHEOW, OHTHERE, ONELA, EANMUND, AND EADGILS: Kings and princes of the Swedes, who live to the north of the Geats. Their dynastic struggles embroil the Geats in constant controversy and war.

BEOWULF'S RETURN (1963–2199)

The first thing Beowulf does upon returning to his homeland is sit at a feast with his uncle, King Hygelac, and narrate the story we have just read. On first glance, it seems like his story only reiterates the familiar and can be skipped. However, Beowulf's tale changes the emphasis and adds details. It also may have functioned as a refresher for a story that was too long to tell in one sitting. This part of the poem might typically have been told to an audience that had changed since the first lines were sung or over the course of two days.

A few of the new details clash with the previous story in ways that we cannot completely explain. Hygelac, in asking for the story, says that he tried hard to dissuade his nephew from going (1992–1997), but the early lines had assured us that "wise men did not dissuade him" (202). Does this change imply that Hygelac is not wise? Did the other wise men encourage Beowulf, while Hygelac was the only negative voice? Similarly, later (in lines 2183–2189) the narrator tells us that Beowulf was considered a weakling and a loser when he was young and had to prove himself. This jars with the early narrative, in which Beowulf was clearly always the young, strong man, who spawned tales of his feats of strength and courage. While there are some athletes who are born with and overcome physical problems (like O. J. Simpson, who wore leg braces as a child but grew up to be a football legend), this scenario does not seem likely in Beowulf's case. Many scholars believe that at least two authors (and perhaps many more) had a hand in creating the poem, and these two discordant notes may be evidence.

Most of the new details only expand on the original narrative. We learn that the name of Grendel's last victim was Hondscio, whose name literally means "Hand-shoe," or glove. We learn also that Grendel wore a victims-collection-bag on his belt (called a "glof" in Old English), and from these details one may wonder if the poet intended irony that Hondscio (meaning glove) was put into the "glof." This bag sounds like a mythical (or even magical) item, as it is made of dragon-skins and has some sort of amazing clasp.

Beowulf gives some details of personal observation, which focus more on Heorot and its inhabitants than on the slaying of the monsters. We learn that Wealhtheow was distributing gold rings at the first feast (not just at the second feast), and that Hrothgar's daughter Freawaru helped her. We hear about the harp-playing at the feasts, and it might be suggested that even Hrothgar himself played the harp. Beowulf clearly indicates that he told long stories from his store of old wisdom, although the narrator has only given us one such story directly (the story in which Hrothgar uses Heremod as an example of how not to govern).

A very large part of Beowulf's commentary on Hrothgar's family centers on his own speculations about what he saw. Freawaru, who was not even named in the early text, is promised in marriage the king of a neighboring tribe, the Heathobards. The Heathobards appear to live south of the Danes, perhaps in the neck of the Danish peninsula or on the coast of modern Germany. Beowulf alludes to the history between the Danes and the Heathobards and predicts trouble.

Apparently, there was once a feud between Hrothgar and Froda of the Heathobards. At least one hero of the Heathobards, Withergyld, is said to have died in this war. Hrothgar wants to preserve peace on his borders, so Freawaru is to marry Froda's son, Ingeld. This common tactic often worked, but at times, as we saw in the story of Finn and Hildeburh, it could also be disastrous. In this case, Beowulf predicts that the feud is too recent and the need for revenge is too strong. Just coming to Heorot for the bridal feast will be enough to provoke old memories of the war, since Heorot will be decked out in its finest and trophy weapons will be on the walls. The sight of these old weapons will remind the Heathobards of the deaths of their fathers, and as the mead flows, eventually one of them will stand up and slug a Dane and pandemonium will break loose. Beowulf is sure that Ingeld's infatuation with the bride he has just met will not be as strong as his desire to avenge his father's feud, and Freawaru's bridal feast will end with funeral pyres. From the poem "Widsith," we know that Hrothulf and Hrothgar "humbled Ingeld's battle-array, hacked down at Heorot the pride of the Heathobards" (Widsith 48–49). Beowulf suggests that Ingeld cannot be trusted and that the Heathobards are only laying a trap for the Danes; but in the end, it would clearly have been better for Ingeld to keep his men quiet and take his bride home.

Beowulf does not add new information to the account of his fights, apart from his personal comment that it was a burden for the Danes not to be able to build a funeral pyre for the honored counselor Aeschere, the last victim of Grendel's mother. He retells the stories in much the same way that we heard them already, and they are even less vivid. One of the oddities of this narration is that the character Beowulf shows much more interest in the way a feud with the Heathobards might reopen than in his own exploits. He expends a good bit of narrative energy imagining the scene and dialogue at the bridal feast, but waves off his own fight with the comment, "It is too long to tell how I handed back payment / to the people's enemy for all his evils" (2093–2094). About Grendel's mother, he laconically explains, "There for a while, we fought hand to hand" (2137). He does reiterate the main points (such as injuring Grendel, and finding the "mighty sword" on the cave wall) but does not elaborate on them.

When it comes to treasure, Beowulf has more to say. He can also play "show and tell," bringing the items out so that he may give them in his turn. His main points about his treasure, however, have to do with political relationships. He wants to make two points very clear: he thinks Hrothgar did the noble thing and really treated him right; but, in spite of how he was treated, he never intended to stay in Denmark and always kept his loyalty to home. His clear statement, "Still all my joys are fixed on you alone; I have few close kinsmen, my Hygelac, except for you" (2149–2151), seems to serve the same purpose as Wealhtheow's speech stating that *of course* Hrothgar's throne would go to his own nephew or sons. It suggests that Hrothgar really did try to adopt Beowulf and was genuinely sad and sorry that he could not. Beowulf may have been tempted to stay, since his own people were much less powerful, but in his own words he said he never considered it at all. Beowulf as a man, rather than a hero, is very bonded to the family that raised him, the family of King Hrethel.

Only the first round of Danish treasures is brought out. These are the treasures that Beowulf received after killing Grendel. Almost all of these become gifts for Hygelac's family. Of the eight horses (1035), four go to Hygelac and three go to Hygd, which leaves one for Beowulf (probably the one wearing Hrothgar's best saddle). The war-gear of Heorogar, Healfdene's son (1020, 2158), goes to Hygelac, and the shining necklace from Wealhtheow goes to Hygd. After he killed Grendel's mother, Beowulf received twelve unnamed treasures, which he apparently is able to keep without giving offense. His men, too, apparently take home their rings and other prizes.

Why does Beowulf give the best treasures to Hygelac? It is because they are "kings' treasures" and Hygelac is the King. If Beowulf kept them, it would look like disloyalty as he would be placing himself higher than his uncle. Beowulf would look like he was hoping to make himself greater and take over the power. On the other hand, Beowulf is Hygelac's "thane," a sworn retainer. The economic exchange of the thane and his king was that any booty won in a war belonged to the king, and from that hoard the king gave out rewards. Although Beowulf has not been in any ordinary battle, he considers himself just as much Hygelac's thane in his fight against Grendel, as in any other fight. He won treasures, and they must go to his king. He gives them with no strings attached, confident that an exchange will be made.

Hygelac, in his turn, gives Beowulf another treasure-sword, the sword of Hrethel, and a huge area of their territory to rule over. The text tells us that it was 7,000 "hides," but "hide" actually has nothing to do with animal skins. A "hide" was an ancient measurement in Anglo-Saxon England that was roughly equal to the amount of land that was necessary for a large family to live off, including their dependents. This may have been roughly 120 acres, but the size of an acre varied from place to place. The ancient rule of thumb was that a "hide" was about as much land that a yoke of oxen could plow in one day. A modern acre is 4,840 square yards; about 200 feet by 200 feet. A modern square mile contains 640 acres. Assuming modern measurements (probably do not correspond to the measurements of Beowulf's time), Beowulf's new territory amounted to approximately 1,300 square miles. (Most likely it was a bit larger since less fertile lands tended to count as larger acres.) This area is approximately the size of Rhode Island or Yosemite National Park; similar to a large U.S. or English county. In modern Sweden, the lands of the Geats, in the south, are divided into provinces. The two southernmost provinces, Skåne and Blekinge, are about 4,258 and 967 square miles, so Beowulf's lands were probably somewhere between these two sizes. In a time when all travel was by water or foot, these lands were fairly large princedoms. If Beowulf were subject to the expectations of the Anglo-Saxon Midlands region, he would be required to raise an army of 1,400 foot soldiers from the population he now ruled.

HYGELAC'S LIFE AND DEATH
(2200–2210, AND OTHER REFERENCES)

Perhaps the most compressed transition in literature is the set of ten lines between 2200 and 2210. In the space of these lines, Hygelac dies, and Beowulf not only takes charge but ages fifty years. Kiernen (1981) has speculated that the transition was composed during the process of joining together two separate manuscripts: one tells about the youthful hero, and one tells about the aging hero's last fight. Two scribes wrote the manuscript as we have it. The second scribe, who copied out the last section and then edited the entire manuscript for errors, may have been working on a set of dwindling parchment books. Kiernan shows how there are many signs that the second scribe squeezed in extra words and extra lines in this area of the manuscript. If this is the case, then perhaps the time transition was summarized because there was not much parchment left to write on. In any case, there is so little warning of a time shift that a dozing reader can miss it.

Hygelac's death is discussed in detail, but it is scattered over many groups of lines. In the first section of the poem, there is foreshadowing of Hygelac's last battle in the history of the wonderful Brosing necklace (1202–1213): Hygelac will wear the necklace into battle in Frisia (on his last raid against the Franks), and the Franks will loot it and carry it away. The actual moment of death, however, passes by in just a few words of this transition section: "after Hygelac lay dead" (2202). Fifty years pass by quickly, and the rest of the details of Hygelac's death come out in recollections. Beowulf tells some of it, as part of a memoir of his life and his family's history; the Geatish messenger who tells of Beowulf's death fills in some details; and the narrative voice of the poem fills in a few more points.

In summary, the story is that Hygelac took Beowulf with him on a raid against the Franks. The Franks, a Germanic tribe that had long been in contact with the Roman Empire, were civilized, Christian, and rich. Some of the grave goods that archeologists find confirm Franks' craftsmanship and wealth in gold and jewels, and the Geats would have been well aware of their skill. The land of the Franks was naturally fertile and the climate was warmer. Frankia might be a very desirable target for northern raids; certainly, the later Franks suffered at the hands of the Vikings who raided them just as Hygelac had.

Hygelac, however, was unsuccessful. The poem tells us little, but the account of Gregory of Tours, a Frank, tells that the warships had loaded with treasure and captives and set out to sea to return to Geatland. Hygelac remained behind, intending to follow them after a short time. However, when the Frankish king, Theudericus, heard of this raid, he sent his son Theudebert with an army. In a land battle against both Hetware (local inhabitants) and Franks, Hygelac was killed. (Some medieval sources stated that his bones, the bones of a giant, were kept as a curiosity on an island in the Rhine River.) His body was looted, although the Geats may not have been totally routed (lines 1213–1214 suggest that the Geats had some success). Beowulf survived and killed quite a few Frankish heroes, including Day-Raven ("Daeghrefn") of the Hugas, and possibly as many as thirty others. In his own memoir, he says that he carried the armor of thirty men when he escaped from the battle and returned alone.

Did he return completely alone, or did he return alone without Hygelac but with some men to sail his ship? Did he swim home or simply travel by water (2360)? Robinson (1974) argues that we know only that he returned home over the water, and because the journey would have been about 500 miles, swimming is unlikely. The setting is not one of magic and marvel, like the cave of the monsters, but it is a seemingly factual account of a real battle of men. Some translations, however, will state that he swam home alone.

When Beowulf arrived home, the Geats faced a problem. Hygelac's son, Heardred, was not full-grown, and even Heardred's mother, the widow Hygd, preferred that Beowulf inherit the throne. Beowulf's own account is that he resisted this proposal and felt he owed it to Hygelac to see his son become king. Instead, he probably acted as a counselor and regent to the boy. Eventually, upon Heardred's death without an heir, Beowulf becomes the last of Hrethel's family to inherit power.

Beowulf's memoir includes another chapter, which explains how Hygelac came to be king in the first place (see family tree on page 27). King Hrethel's first child was a daughter (who married the possibly Swedish nobleman Ecgtheow), and his following three children were sons. When young Beowulf left his father's house at age seven and came to live with his grandfather Hrethel, he met Hrethel's sons: Herebeald, Haethcyn, and Hygelac. Hygelac may have been only ten years older than him, or even less, and they may have done many things as companions. But Hrethel's family eventually suffered a reversal of fortune. On a hunting trip, Haethcyn's arrow went off course and struck his older brother, Herebeald. At the death of his oldest son, Hrethel's grief was endless. Normally, he would have vented it in seeing the killer put to death, but in this case, that would have eliminated one more son from an already dwindling number. Hrethel died of grief, and Haethcyn became King.

In a parallel story of Norse mythology, Odin's son Balder was killed by a dart thrown by his blind brother, Hod. The dart was not supposed to injure Balder, as all things on earth had taken an oath not to harm him. However, the evil god Loki knew that the mistletoe had not taken the oath, and so he made a dart out of this "harmless" plant, and gave it to Hod. Hod, blind and tricked, was just as much a victim as Balder, but in spite of this, another son of Odin eventually killed him in revenge. The duty to vengeance was very great in pagan Norse culture, and so Beowulf portrays Hrethel's chief sorrow as being unable to fulfill this duty.

Beowulf's story goes one step further, however, and creates one of the most vivid images in Anglo-Saxon literature. This is the mini-story of the old man who sees his son hanged on a gallows and cannot offer him any help. The old man's grief is called forth every morning, and his bitter despair is shown in every line. He sees the empty house his son used to live in, and he hears the desolate silence in his hall. Eventually, he takes to his bed and weeps, and "all too vast to him seem the fields and townships" (2461–2462). Hrethel's grief is depicted as being like this old man's, as he wastes away to death. (See "In Depth: Odin worship," at chapter's end, for more thoughts on Hrethel and his son's death.)

The story of Hrethel's family troubles blends into the accounts of feuds between the Geats and their northern neighbors, the Swedes. We will learn later how Haethcyn died in battle and Hygelac succeeded him. These matters are covered separately in a later section about the political struggles between Geats and Swedes.

THE DRAGON BATTLE (2210–3182)

The final section takes far longer to relate the battle against the dragon than the earlier sections took to relate the other monster battles. This is primarily because the main story is punctuated and interrupted by memoirs and side stories. Some of these stories are covered previously (concerning the inheritance and death of Hygelac), and some are covered later (concerning the feud between the Geats and the Swedes). First, we will consider the elements of the conflict with the dragon itself.

The Last Survivor

Fifty years pass by in one line: Beowulf held the kingdom for fifty winters. In line 2210, he is the "old guardian of his homeland" and no longer the young hero. With no further prologue, the monster of the last conflict is introduced. The fight against the dragon is difficult to follow, because interspersed with it are details (given in the previous and following text) concerning the political affairs of the Geats. The following summary and explanation of the fight with the dragon skips over these sections and treats the battle as a single continuous story.

The first section introduces the dragon and answers some questions about how the conflict came about. It retells the discovery and provocation of the dragon three times, each time adding more detail. The general outline of the dragon's discovery is that a runaway slave stumbled upon the hidden entrance to the barrow and took a golden cup out of the hoard (2214, 2225, 2280). The barrow had been there for over 300 years, undisturbed, and its pathway to narrow entrances was hidden from view. The door, however, was open. Why?

In lines 2231–2277 there is an embedded story of how the hoard of treasures came to be buried and then discovered by the dragon. The treasures had never belonged to the Geats or Swedes, but to a forgotten people who had occupied the same land before them. Some catastrophe, perhaps a plague, had wiped out this tribe and left one lingering man in charge of all of their possessions. This man set about building or completing a barrow (an underground burial chamber). He built it to be concealed and kept its doors and passages very narrow, perhaps through crevices in the rock. Piece by piece, he carried in the wealth of his nation and then sat down to look it over.

The man's words are reported in what is generally called "The Lay of the Last Survivor" (lines 2231–2270). The tone is sad and is the first we see of the prevailing literary tone of the last section of *Beowulf*. The word most commonly used to describe this Lay, and this entire section, is "elegiac" (the tone of an elegy). An elegy is a poem or song composed to mourn someone who has died, or a poem that conveys the tone of pensive sorrow. The Last Survivor knows that he is only counting off the days until he also dies; therefore, his story will have no happy ending. He is doomed. Recall the youthful Beowulf's words (572–573) as he told about his contest with Breca: "Wyrd [Fate] often spares an undoomed man, when his courage endures!" Courage alone is not enough, but without it, doom is sure. Even with courage, sometimes Fate will bring about a man's death, because it is his time to die. The Last Survivor is doomed; he cannot survive.

His elegy is mourning the deaths of his people and his own death. It takes the form of him looking at the many treasures and weapons that surround him and mourning that no one can use them. "Here is a cup," he thinks, "with no one to polish or use it; here is a helm and chain-mail shirt, with no one to keep them bright or wear them in battle; here is a harp, with no one to play it; here is the gear of falcons and horses, with no one to train or use the noble animals." Sitting in the underground room of the hoard, he grows weaker and eventually dies. He has forgotten to complete one critical task: he never shut the door.

Men may have deserted the southern coast of Sweden for now, and they may be long in finding the open door, but it does not take long for a treasure-hunting dragon to find it. Why? Because it is his nature to do so (2275). Fish swim, birds fly, and dragons sniff out gold hoards. The dragon is only doing what dragons do.

Dragons

How do we know what dragons do? Ancient sources from all around the world (but chiefly in Europe and China) speak of dragons, those rare creatures that are combinations of serpent and lizard. Little detail is provided, however, in old sources. Chinese dragons are peaceful and wise, the totems of the Imperial dynasties. They only want to do good for the people and are worshipped. They have beards and tusks, and they do not have wings, although in some stories they can fly. European dragons, in contrast, are rotten to the core. They have wings, and usually they can spout flames. They eat livestock, and in later stories they eat young girls. Having a dragon in the neighborhood is a disaster, and it is imperative to kill the dragon as soon as possible.

The oldest European stories and the most local legends give few details beyond these. Most other details have been created in modern dragon stories, as they turned into the creatures of fairy tales and fantasy games. Most, if not all, of these modern stories are based on *Beowulf*'s dragon, simply because it is one of the more detailed dragon accounts. Some other references in Old English literature speak of dragons, but with far less detail. According to some obscure lines in the Old English poem "Solomon and Saturn," a hero killed twenty-five dragons in a remote plain, and that since that time, no one can find the place, but all dragons come from there. A short section in *The Wonders of the East*, discussed previously concerning the kin of Cain, alleges that dragons are all born on an island somewhere in the Indian Ocean (where headless men also live). These dragons are 150 feet long and as thick as pillars. There isn't any more detail, although the *Liber Monstrorum* describes serpents that contain some of the traits of mythical dragons. Some are 120 feet long, some have poisonous breath, some are studded with emeralds, and some are born in cold lands and roam the rocky land looking for hiding places and food. If a dragon is a type of serpent, then here might be some details; and yet, they are never called dragons ("draca").

The dragon of Beowulf, then, is one of the earliest detailed portraits of a European dragon. It is clearly an animal: it acts by nature, not by intelligent thought. It does not appear to talk; at least, there is no reported speech. It is long (fifty feet) and thin, and it can crawl on the ground, perhaps smelling for the trail of the thief. Its chief trait is its fond attachment to its treasure, almost an obsession. We do not know what this dragon eats, but we do know precisely its animal reaction on finding its cup missing. When it cannot find the exact thief, it takes to the air (although wings are not described, the dragon can fly). It breathes fire, and thus burns up towns and halls. Fire is the dragon's chief weapon, but it has also sharp teeth and jaws large enough to bite a man's neck. Beyond that, its bite is poisonous, like a snake's. The most surprisingly animal trait of the dragon is that it is shy; until now, it has never sought out mankind, and it is shocked and frightened at seeing Beowulf.

The Geats, and the Anglo-Saxon audience, were sympathetic to the motive of revenge, but not if it was a dragon's. Why was the dragon's passion for burning towns in payment of his missing cup not a sympathetic emotion? Think back over the many actions and stories throughout this poem. One of the morals that the characters and the narrator are always voicing is that treasure is for giving. No one who hoards treasure will find sympathy. Revenge is for someone's death, but it is not for the loss of treasure. Treasure is to be used to create bonds of loyalty, although in itself it is lovely and precious. Hoarding it is just plain and, in their view, the dragon's anger is no excuse for its destructiveness.

Any mental picture of the dragon, created from images of fantasy dragons, is probably correct enough for the story. Just as Grendel's appearance was not described, neither is the dragon's. Does it have horns or ridges on his back? Perhaps. Does it have claws? Is it brightly colored? Probably. The closing lines suggest color (3040). Does it have a beard, like a Chinese dragon? It might. All we know for sure is that it has teeth, wings, and flames.

Beowulf Enters the Dragon-Feud

Beowulf, King of the Geats, is now about seventy-five years old. He becomes entangled with the dragon by means of the dragon's flight of vengeance. Among other buildings, Beowulf's royal hall is burnt to the ground. We are not told of loss of life, but it can be assumed that a large wooden hall cannot be suddenly burnt without casualties. Beowulf was apparently not at home; maybe he was visiting one of his earls. His hall burnt and some of his people killed, Beowulf is cut to the core by the sudden reversal of fate. Long ago, Hrothgar had warned him that even the good king who ruled well might be subject to sudden tricks of fate in his old age. It happened to Hrothgar, and now it is Beowulf's turn. Unlike Hrothgar, Beowulf is sure he can avenge himself. Is there any young hero on the scene to take his place? Apparently not.

Beowulf's mindset is explained briefly but with care (2327–2332). His first thought may be to recall Hrothgar's words, and he wonders if he has offended God, the Ruler of All. These painful, dark thoughts are completely unlike his usual mental state. He knows (2342) that he is doomed to die. Like the Last Survivor, he has only to spin out the days with the appropriate actions, and the end will come. There is no good outcome, only a possibly successful one. The Old English word for someone who was doomed to die, "fey," survives as an antique word. "Fey" means not just doomed to die, but also having the mindset that comes with knowing that you are going to die. Nothing matters if you know you will die in battle. Fey can also imply a touch of madness and an other-world, fairy state of being. Beowulf is doomed to die, and so now he has a fey mindset. He is not mad or impractical, but he sets out to make sure his last battle is at least successful. It is clear that he has to avenge himself, which means he must make a successful attack on the dragon.

First he commands that a special iron shield be made. All Germanic nations, from Tacitus' Teutons, to the civilized English of the late Anglo-Saxon period, to the fiercest Swedish Vikings, used wooden shields. The center "boss" was metal, but the shield itself was always wooden (see Chapter 11, "Anglo-Saxon Culture," for more detail). An iron shield will be unusually heavy, but it will not catch fire. Next, after this is finished, he chooses companions. This is probably a mix of his youthful and experienced retainers, which add up to twelve including Beowulf himself. The thirteenth man is their guide, and he is the runaway slave: the thief.

At first, Beowulf's frame of mind on setting out is reported as carefree and confident. With his new iron shield, he remembers his many victories and does not feel afraid. But when they reach the cape on the seashore, where the dragon's barrow is located, Beowulf's mindset changes. Now he truly feels fey; deep in his heart he knows that this is his last battle. He is "restless and ripe for death" (2420). It is in this state of mind that he takes time out to rest and tell one last story. Many of the details we have of Hrethel's family and some of the details of the Swedish feud

come from Beowulf as he lingers. Recall his eagerness to attack Grendel's mother, when he would not linger on the shore of the haunted
mere. Now, on this shore, he lingers and speaks to his companions. The
tone of his speech is elegiac; he speaks of death and loss. It is in this frame
of mind that he tells about Hrethel's loss of his son and how an old man
grieves when he loses his oldest son. Like Hrothgar long ago, an old man
with many memories, Beowulf wants to tell it one more time. Through
remembering the grief of Hrethel, he wants to mourn his own coming
death. Perhaps he wishes to cheer himself with a memory of past victory
when he tells about defeating Day-Raven in a crushing blow. Beowulf
knows he is no longer as strong as thirty men, but he hopes he still has
enough strength for his last task. After a last formal boast, he gets up and
is ready for the fight.

Beowulf's last instructions almost bring about defeat, and they represent the first action that brings any hint of criticism from the narrative
voice. Although he is there with eleven companions (the runaway slave,
presumably, has been allowed to leave), he wishes to fight alone. He
instructs his men not to help him but to stand back and watch, waiting
in safety. His men must have heard this instruction with a mixture of
relief and discomfort. They now have a conflicting loyalty. They need
to obey their king, but on the other hand, their normal duty is always
to come to his aid. For him to command them not to help is a contradiction; it releases them from their oaths to help him, without releasing
them from their oaths to obey him. At the same time, they have no
desire to fight the dragon. Their shields are wooden, and they have never
fought any supernatural or inhuman creature. In their minds, fighting
monsters is Beowulf's specialty, even if he is now seventy-five. Is Beowulf
right, however, to command his men to leave him alone? According to
the Germanic traditions, there is no "fine print" that states if a king is
attacked by a supernatural beast, then everyone is allowed to run away.

The fight begins in an unpromising way. Beowulf, finding that the
door into the cavern is steaming with the dragon's heat, decides to call
him out. The dragon, hearing a human voice, hopes to find the thief and
rushes out. Both of them are still for a moment and stare. Who is this?
But then the dragon answers with its usual weapon: a stream of fire.
Beowulf's iron shield does not burn, but it cannot stop the flames and
intense heat, and Beowulf is overcome. First, he quickly strikes a blow
with his sword, not enough to kill the dragon, but enough to wound
and astonish it. This wound only makes the dragon's fire hotter, and
with his sword not strong enough to pierce the dragon's scales, Beowulf
must do something he never thought he would do: he runs away.

"Wyrd" (fate) is against Beowulf this time. When Grendel's mother attacked him with her knife (while he was still catching his breath), fate had been with him and had denied her victory. Fate is not with Beowulf now, but is it with the dragon? It is not long until Beowulf steps forward again to fight the dragon, and the wounded beast and burned man begin a battle to the death.

Wiglaf Enters the Dragon Feud

Among the waiting eleven men, who can all see the progress of the fight, one is a kinsman of Beowulf. We do not know the exact relationship they have: Wiglaf is not of Hrethel's family, but he is related to Beowulf. He could be two generations younger and related on the side of Beowulf's father. Perhaps he is a grandnephew, the grandson of a sister or brother. In Germanic culture, the sons of a sister had a special relationship to their uncle, so it is possible that Beowulf helped to raise and educate Wiglaf.

Out of all the fighting men, Wiglaf feels the greatest responsibility toward Beowulf; therefore, although Beowulf's parting instructions have been enough to keep him sidelined at first, now he stands up to fight. He tells the men around him that they had all taken mead together and all promised to uphold their king. It was for their extra-hardy loyalty that they were chosen for this last journey! Wiglaf scolds the others for bearing gift-weapons and forgetting, in their panic, the oaths that occasioned the gifts. "I would much prefer," he says, "that the flames should enfold / my body alongside my gift-giving lord" (2651–2652). It seems wrong to go home carrying the weapons he gave them, no matter what he said! The words are no sooner out of his mouth than the other ten have fled to the woods in hopes to hide from the dragon's eventual wrath. Like the Danes, who saw blood in the water and assumed Beowulf's death, the Geats see him stumbling and assume that he will fail.

Wiglaf is very young, or else the Geats have been at peace for many years, for we learn that this is the first time he has stood up beside his king in battle. In spite of his inexperience, he draws his sword and walks down toward the dragon. His wooden shield is quickly burned up, and his chain-mail is useless (in fact, it is probably worse than useless, becoming very hot). Wiglaf's main help to Beowulf seems to be in supporting the shield that he is becoming to weak to hold. Now Beowulf, who is encouraged and perhaps physically supported, is able to stand up and deliver the final blow, sending his sword into the dragon's skull. The dying dragon, however, is able to bite Beowulf's exposed neck. In spite of their reciprocal wounds, they continue to fight for the final last blows. Wiglaf is able to strike lower, into the dragon's abdomen, which begins to drain the dragon's firepower. Beowulf, weakened from blood loss but still focusing all his energy and concentration on the fight, is able to stab the dying dragon again, and at last the dragon falls and is still.

Beowulf's Death

The worst part of Beowulf's neck wound turns out to be a serpent-like poison that immediately makes the wound burn and swell. Beowulf knows that death will come in only a matter of minutes, and he is able to sit down by the wall so that he may die in peace. Wiglaf is able to fetch water (perhaps they carried water-skins that were left on the cape) and wash the blood and some of the poison away. Beowulf's last minutes are spent partly communicating with Wiglaf and partly viewing some of the hoard that he never even got to see.

The last act of a noble father was to give his war-gear to his son. Beowulf says that he has no son, although the story does not explain this. It would be unusual for a king not to marry, but it would not be unusual for his wife or children to die from disease. Although we are not told that any family members died in the dragon-fire of the hall, it is possible that some did. Wiglaf appears to be his nearest relation and will be his personal heir, although there is no guarantee that the Geats will select him as the next king.

At Beowulf's request, Wiglaf runs quickly into the deserted barrow, so that Beowulf may look at the treasures as his life fades. Wiglaf, although he is in a hurry, is stopped by the sight of the treasure. The barrow is dark, but there is a magical light coming from the ancient king's banner that is still hanging high, where the Last Survivor had set it up. In this light, he can see the gleaming of gold and jewels, as well as many iron objects that have rusted and leather fittings that have molded. After a stunned glance around, Wiglaf loads everything he can carry into his arms and runs out of the barrow, hoping he is not too late.

After Wiglaf once again revives him with water, Beowulf is just alive enough to look weakly on the treasures. His last words are filled with dramatic irony. He sees the treasure as being destined to belong to his people; perhaps to form the core of a new royal hoard, or perhaps for a new King Wiglaf to give out and form new bonds of loyalty in the younger generation. He envisions his warriors, the "brave in battle," building him a new barrow right here on the cape, where passing ships may see it. Could this cape be one near where he had returned home from Denmark or Frisia? It may not be unfamiliar land, far from home, but rather a place he has walked on many times without knowing a dragon slept beneath his feet. Beowulf's words convey an ironic meaning to his audience. We know that the treasure was never used by his people, and that instead of a peaceful future in which sailors steer past his lonely barrow, the likely future of his people involves war, burnt towns, and a flight from their homeland.

Beowulf's last act is to give his necklace and war-gear to Wiglaf, as promised, and his last words are, "I must follow them" (2816). Although he is not descended from Scyld Scefing, whose funeral opened the poem, he appears to be following this great king of the ancient past (along with Hygelac and Hrethel, and perhaps even Ongentheow) into the land of the dead.

Last Words about Beowulf's Death

Apart from the narrator, three voices have the last say about the death of Beowulf. Wiglaf is trying to revive the old king with water a third time when the other ten warriors come. They are probably drawn by the silence and peek over the hill to see if the dragon is dead or alive. Wiglaf repeats his previous sentiments: when Beowulf gave out war-gear, he completely threw away his treasures. No one stood by him when he needed it, and he himself, a young man, was barely able to help kill the dragon. Wiglaf's speech makes it clear that the warriors all knew that when the king needed them, his instructions to stay back were not supposed to be followed. When given the dual duty to support and to obey, obeying was a lesser duty when compared to giving him defensive support.

Wiglaf commands a messenger (probably one of the shame-faced warriors) to go and tell the rest of the earls, who have stayed back even further, waiting on a hill. The messenger's speech is largely covered in the following section, as it deals with Geatish political matters. His meaning is clear, however: the death of the king is nothing short of a disaster to the people. A modern audience, accustomed to smooth changes of power, would wonder why. But Beowulf is leaving no firm power structure behind him, since he has no son. Wiglaf is clearly very young, perhaps even too young to rule, and while his status as dragon-slayer may help him, in the end he may not have either the solid, loyal support or the actual fighting prowess to carry it off. If another earl begins to rule, then there may be divisions and rivalries until a dynasty is established. In the meantime, surrounding enemies will want to take advantage of this

weakness. It is very likely that the Geatish people have not been growing in importance, and their main asset has been the personal strength of
Beowulf. With him gone, they now face a future with no certainties but
those of war on every side.

The messenger's second theme focuses on the plan for the funeral.
Beowulf will be burned, of course, as befits a noble warrior. But with
him will go most or all of the dragon-hoard, which is indirectly a cause
of his death. Beowulf had intended to give the treasure to his people,
but the messenger here expresses what may be a universal sentiment:
Beowulf's people cannot bear to own and wear these things. The messenger even implies that it would be best if they put all of their gold (the
things they already own) into the fire with the king. After all, what awaits
them but slavery for the women and death for the men? His last image
is grim, as he describes the raven, eagle, and wolf dividing the Geatish
corpses in shares.

The assembled Geatish earls return to the scene of battle. It is all as we
left it, only now we see it through their eyes. Beowulf—mangled, black-
ened, pale, and covered with blood—is propped against a wall. The dragon
lies where it fell, all hacked and twisted. There is a hasty pile of treasures
next to the old king, and Wiglaf still sits nearby. Wiglaf explains what
happened and begins to give directions. It is possible that Wiglaf's clear
ownership of Beowulf's war-gear, in addition to his near kinship, has
indicated to them that he is the heir apparent. As young as he is, he tells
them what to do and how to carry out treasures and build the king's
pyre. He appoints specific warriors to go into the barrow, and he sends
others to find dry wood. Some of the treasure will be burnt with Beowulf,
and some will be piled into his new barrow.

The last voices speaking about the death of Beowulf are those of an
old woman and twelve earls. The old woman stands up as the flames leap
up to consume the king's body, and she sings a song of lament about the
coming defeat. She predicts the twin fates of men and women: harm and
captivity. After the flames die out, and the barrow is built (which may
take a day or two), twelve noble earls ride slowly in a circle around it
and sing a song of lament. They praise Beowulf's deeds over his lifetime.
Beowulf's final epitaph is not, as he had predicted, that he refrained
from killing his kinsmen; rather, it is that he was gentle and kind and that
he earnestly sought for fame. To yearn for fame was a good thing; it did
not mean wishing for "fifteen minutes of fame" in a cheap way. It meant
wanting to be so great that fame would naturally follow. Beowulf
wanted to be praised, and he tried hard to be the kind of man that would
merit it.

GEATS AND SWEDES

Throughout the last section of *Beowulf*, small pieces of a story emerge. This story is one that has nothing to do with fighting monsters. In six increasingly detailed installments, the narrator tells us about the wars between the Geats and their northern neighbors, the Swedes. These wars, at the time of the dragon fight, are at least forty years past. They took place not long after Beowulf returned from Denmark; perhaps within ten years. Two questions come out of their inclusion in the narrative: what happened, and why is it being used in this way (in a story about fighting monsters)?

The first of the six entries is at line 1968, where Hygelac is named the slayer of Ongentheow. Beowulf is returning, and it is the formal introduction of Hygelac, but nothing more is said. After Beowulf's report on his trip to Heorot, the narrator explains (2202–2206) why Beowulf later became king: the Scylfings (Swedes) killed Hygelac's son, Heardred. As Beowulf readies his attack on the dragon, in lines 2379–2396 the narrator explains more about Heardred's death and how Beowulf was chosen. After Beowulf arrives at the dragon's home, he speaks his last formal words to his men and recounts the story of strife between Geats and Swedes well before the death of Heardred, including the story of how Hygelac succeeded to the kingship of the Geats (2425–2489). He explains, at last, the actual death of Ongentheow that had been credited to Hygelac in the opening lines. More detail is added in lines 2602–2620, just as Wiglaf readies himself to fight and pulls the sword that his father won in those same feuds. Finally, the messenger who carries the news of Beowulf's death to the Geats pauses, in lines 2922–3000, to consider the most vicious side of the feuds and predict that even fifty years will not have been long enough for the Swedes to forgive and forget.

The story of the feud can be straightened out and retold in a cleaner narrative for our understanding. First, consider the family trees of the two generations in question. Beginning with the earliest details, provided by Beowulf as he sits by the dragon's barrow, the story begins with Hrethel and his three sons. One day, while hunting, Haethcyn kills Herebeald with a stray arrow. Hrethel's grief is tremendous, but he cannot vent it in revenge on the killer, because the killer is next in line to rule. Dying of grief, he leaves the Geats in the care of Haethcyn. The Swedes to the north (perhaps always eyeing the more fertile lands that the Geats occupy, or perhaps recalling some previous feud) choose this moment of Geatish vulnerability to attack. In a raid, they win a significant victory on a hill in Geatland called the "Hill of Sorrows" ("Hreosnabeorh" in Old English).

Young King Haethcyn decides to retaliate and attacks the Swedes with a large war band. At first he is successful and captures a Swedish stronghold that includes the queen, wife of Ongentheow. Ongentheow may have been away hunting or raiding, because he comes back quickly and counterattacks; he rescues his wife and retakes his hall. The Geats, outnumbered, are pressed back into a wood called "Ravenswood." In this battle, Haethcyn dies. Night falls and the battle ends, but Ongentheow calls out to the Geats and tells them that with the first rays of dawn, he will come after them. He says that he will take all of them, slit them open, and hang them out for the birds to eat. For the war band, Ongentheow's threat is a fate worse than death, and they pass, according to the Geatish messenger's account, a wretched night trapped in the wood.

At dawn, however, new hope comes as Hygelac appears with another party of Geatish warriors. Their arrival breaks the siege of the wood, and the Swedes are now surrounded. In the battle, Ongentheow finds himself under attack by a pair of brothers, Eofor and Wulf (meaning "Boar" and "Wolf"), and they fight fiercely. In spite of his own head wound, Ongentheow manages to wound Wulf severely, but Eofor presses in to take revenge, and Ongentheow dies. Wulf is rescued, and, after the battle is over, Hygelac (the new King of the Geats) rewards Eofor and Wulf. Eofor, now the avenger of Haethcyn, marries Hygelac's daughter, and both men receive estates.

Following Ongentheow's death, his older son, Ohthere, becomes King of the Swedes. Ohthere has two sons: Eanmund and Eadgils (see family tree on page 27). But at Ohthere's death (maybe ten years later), his brother Onela seizes the throne.

We met Onela briefly, in the opening lines of the poem, as the husband of Hrothgar's sister. By now, Hygelac has died in a raid on the Franks. Hygelac's son, Heardred, is King of the Geats, but it is implied that he is not old enough to handle the task. He is not experienced or strong, and his main source of support is the unfailing loyalty of his older cousin, Beowulf. Heardred is faced with a decision that is beyond him: the sons of Ohthere are on the run from their uncle, Onela, and they come as exiles to Geatland.

Either the two young men, Eanmund and Eadgils, are looking for a new home or they are looking for military support. Heardred, who may be as young as fifteen years old, must decide whether to shelter them or suggest that they pass on to Denmark or Frankia instead. Perhaps Heardred, recalling the feud between the Geats and the Swedes, sees here a chance to make his mark. If he supports Eanmund, who has probably arrived with his own loyal band of exiled warriors, then he could strike back at Ongentheow's son while at the same time forming ties of loyalty and gratitude for his support. It is possible that he is thinking there may be a share of the fabled treasure of Uppsala as a reward. Heardred chooses to shelter and support Eanmund and Eadgils, most likely with Beowulf's approval.

Onela proves to be much harder to unseat than they calculated. He strikes first and comes right into Geatish territory to find his nephews. In the battle, both Eanmund and young King Heardred are killed. Eanmund is killed by a Swedish warrior named Weohstan, and Onela gives him Eanmund's war-gear: helmet, chain mail, and sword. Eadgils presumably escapes and is not seen again for a safe period of time. Onela's victory is complete, and the Geats are cowed. The wording of Beowulf's accession to the throne of the Geats suggests that he only became king through Onela's approval; Onela had probably heard of his famous exploits in Denmark and was more pleased to shake his hand than to split his skull. Onela and Beowulf both share ties to Denmark, one through marriage and the other through his father's treasure-debt and his own vows. Onela travels back to Uppsala in the secure knowledge that the Geats have been crushed.

There is one last strike in the feud, however. Some time later, Eadgils reappears in the land of the Geats. Beowulf has not forgotten the death of his favorite cousin. In a move to avenge Heardred, Beowulf supports Eadgils once again, and this time Onela is overthrown. Perhaps it is at this time that Weohstan crosses over to the Geatish side. He marries into Beowulf's family (the Waegmundings) and has at least one son, Wiglaf. Wiglaf inherits Eanmund's war-gear and uses these same weapons in his battle to aid Beowulf against the dragon.

We will never know exactly why this complex story is laid out in pieces throughout the last section of the poem. There are a few things that can be said with certainty, and there are a few less certain suggestions. First, it is clear that the poet found the story highly interesting and expected his audience to appreciate it. The *Beowulf* poet's strong interest in stories of treasure, weapons, and revenge could be likened to a modern author's interest in stories about love or psychological development. Taken as a story in itself, the feud between the Geats and the Swedes has many elements of tragedy and suspense. One by one, the family of Hrethel is cut down by accident and pride until Beowulf, the last heir, dies. When the Geats were trapped in the wood and threatened with shameful deaths without warriors' burials, who could have known that Hygelac was about to appear at dawn with Beowulf at his side?

Second, it seems that the poet used the complex insertions both to slow down the dragon-fight and to explain just how high the stakes were in Beowulf's last battle. In the early insertions, we learn that Hygelac's brothers and his only son are dead. In the later digression, we learn that the feud with the Swedes was so bitter and so personal that they are also likely to have kept it alive in song and story. They will not forget Ravenswood, and although Eadgils is now King of Sweden and presumably grateful to Beowulf, his warriors may seek an opportunity to reopen old wounds. Without knowing the background of Geatish politics, we would not understand what a shocking loss Beowulf's death is to his people.

Third, the poet may have borne in mind the differences between feuds and struggles among men and fights with the ancient evils (the kin of Cain and the monsters born of the earth). Feuds among men toss back and forth, as one and then the other gains the upper hand. Ongentheow is a glorious king; he is a hardy old graybeard and not an evil man, let alone a monster. Haethcyn and Heardred, in their errors of pride and confidence, are not like Grendel in his bestial arrogance. Beowulf has been a good king to his people, but he, too, has made mistakes and taken risks. He supported his weaker cousin, Heardred, in his disastrous decision to meddle in Swedish politics, and then he tried the same himself. There is no weight of evil on one side, and the balance of power is not supernatural but an accident of arithmetic. Who has more men? Is it Haethcyn, Ongentheow, or Hygelac coming at dawn? If Eofor alone had attacked Ongentheow, would he have prevailed? What if Ongentheow's son had helped him attack Eofor, and Eofor's brother Wulf had been far away? Men only have the advantage over each other through accident, often they are literally stumbling in the dark, and through the pride that cannot hear a mistake or an enemy approaching, because it is so busy shouting out threats.

IN DEPTH: ODIN WORSHIP

H. M. Chadwick's 1899 classic book, *The Cult of Othin*, examines the sparse literature of the Germanic tribes to determine when the worship of Odin (also called "Othin" or "Woden") began and how it was carried out. When the Romans first knew the Germanic tribes of the North, the sparse evidence suggests that they were not yet worshipping Odin. Odin's cult focused on war and death and became dominant in the centuries between Tacitus (around AD 100) and *Beowulf* (set and possibly

composed around AD 600). There are points in the poem's third section
that imply this Odin worship and can provide a context for the meaning
of some passages.

There is a minor point of overlap between Beowulf's report to Hygelac
and the Danish history by Saxo Grammaticus (written in Latin in the thirteenth century). Saxo reports that the warrior who incited the slaughter
of Ingeld at Freawaru's wedding was a legendary man named "Starkathr."
This warrior is connected, in Saxo's tales, with the worship of Odin. It
is from some of these tales that we learn how human sacrifice was part
of Odin's rites. In one story, Starkathr must help the Swedish king, who
has been chosen by lot as a human sacrifice to Odin. He constructs a harmless gallows (made of a tiny pine tree and the stretchy intestines of an animal) and finds a marsh reed as a mock spear. Odin, says the story, turned it
all into the real items at the last minute: Starkathr's marsh reed became
a spear, and the pine tree became a strong gallows. The Swedish king was
sacrificed to Odin through stabbing and hanging. While Saxo's stories cannot be taken seriously as history, they report the traditions of the region.

There is indirect evidence (from many other tales out of all parts of the
Germanic world) that both of these modes of death were part of Odin
sacrifice. Odin was the ruler over death in battle; a warrior's death in
battle ensured entrance into Valhalla. Warriors might also devote their
enemies to Odin by promising to slaughter any captives. This intention
was signaled by shooting a javelin over the enemy army's heads. Many
of the people found in Danish bogs are thought to be war captives, and
the bogs have preserved them with ropes still around their necks. Hanging seems to have been a typical method for offering captives to Odin,
so it is possible that these Danish "bog people" were Odin's victims,
although this theory cannot be proven. According to the tales, Odin
himself hung on the central world-supporting Tree for nine nights and
found knowledge of secret, magical runes through this experience.

After Haethcyn's death, the Geatish army was hiding in the woods in
Swedish territory. Ongentheow and his men called out to them and
informed them that at dawn they would be captured. Some would be
gutted (a mode of Odin-worship also attested in other Germanic tales),
and many would be hung. The cult of Odin provides the context of
these threats. The wood where they were hiding was called Ravenswood;
the raven was sacred to Odin. Only the coming of Hygelac at dawn,
blowing his horns, saved them from final devotion to the god that both
sides worshiped. While the text itself does not make the connection to
Odin clear, the general evidence of other tales clearly provides a context
for Ongentheow's threats.

Finally, there is a very provocative connection to the story of Hrethel and his sons. After Herebeald is killed by a chance arrow, Hrethel dies of grief. Between the accidental death and the father's death from grief, Beowulf's narrative describes an old man's sharp grief for a son on the gallows. This description appears to be a metaphor, showing how the fathers' feelings of grief are similar, and it asks us to imagine how terrible it would be to see a son on the gallows. However, the passage has always jarred careful readers. Is it really meant as a metaphor? Why was the son hanged? Hanging implies criminal execution to us, but there is no suggestion of this meaning in the text. There is no suggestion of the hanged man being a war captive, either.

Chadwick's reconstruction of Odin's rites opens the possibility that the hanged man is Herebeald and the grieving father is Hrethel. Herebeald, part of a royal warrior family, had already been stabbed with a javelin, albeit accidentally. Considering that the death was not really an honorable warrior's death, the family may have completed further Odin rites to ensure his entrance to Valhalla. His dead body may have been hanged and probably later burned on a pyre. If the son on the gallows is Herebeald himself, and the grieving father is Hrethel, then the meaning of the passage slightly changes. Now, rather than an elegant metaphor, we are given an extended insight into the king's mind. He can see Herebeald's wooden hall, empty and in mourning, in a nearby compound. The lands he fought to rule and had hoped to pass to his oldest son are too extensive. He turns his face to the wall, as he is unable to look outside with any composure while his son's body hangs. The passage suggests that the body remained on the gallows many days. They could conceivably have acted out Odin's nine-day hanging feat. Ravens, the birds sacred to Odin, are also mentioned in this passage.

None of these connections can be proven, due to the scarcity and unreliable nature of early Germanic literature. They remain, like so much else in *Beowulf*, as mysteries and possibilities.

FURTHER SUGGESTED READING

Bonjour, Adrien. *The Digressions in Beowulf.* Oxford: Society for the Study of Mediaeval Languages and Literature, 1950.

Lionarons, Joyce Tally. *Medieval Dragon: The Nature of the Beast in Germanic Literature.* Enfield Lock, UK: Hislarik Press, 1998.

Owen-Crocker, Gale R. *The Four Funerals of Beowulf, and the Structure of the Poem.* Manchester, UK: Manchester University Press, 2000.

Rauer, Christine. *Beowulf and the Dragon: Parallels and Analogues.* Cambridge: D. S. Brewer, 2000.

7

Literary Techniques

To correspond with the three parts of the poem, this analysis of literary techniques breaks down the poem into these three parts: the fight with Grendel (including the hero's arrival), the fight with Grendel's mother, and the fight with the dragon. These parts play different roles in developing the character of Beowulf and in changing the tone of the work.

PART ONE: GRENDEL

The fight against Grendel, with its lead-up and aftermath, is the largest part of the poem. It is a complex story created with literary techniques common to modern literature, although these techniques are often developed in ways that are hard to recognize. The conventions of storytelling have changed a great deal since *Beowulf*'s time, but the human mind and its perceptions have not.

Contrast

The tool most often used by the *Beowulf* poet, and the one used to achieve the most effects, is contrast. Contrast is used in setting, characters, and plot; it helps to create the tone. Most often the contrast is very high, as it pits dark against light or good against evil.

The setting of the fight at Heorot is laid out with great care. By the time the fight takes place, the reader knows a fair amount about the court at Heorot, with its ornamented appearance and its manners. Heorot is to be taken as the height of Germanic civilization; even the floors are tiled and the roads are paved. Everything is done according to custom and rule, from the seacoast to the gift-stool. The hall is built on a high place, where the sea winds blow and the morning sun shines. By contrast, Grendel is the enemy of civilization, mankind, custom, and light. He lives on a misty moor and only comes by dark. He respects no customs of man, not even paying blood-money for murder. He does not build; he breaks. The careful setting of the Danish hall provides a way to understand Grendel by contrast. The poet of *Beowulf* uses the light-filled depiction of Heorot to make the darkness of Grendel stand out.

In showing us his characters, the narrator most often uses contrast, rather than the modern method of describing appearance and state of mind. Beowulf's character is first developed in contrast to Unferth. Unferth's insecurity and low motives provide a dark background against which we can see Beowulf's confidence and generosity. This mode of definition through contrast may have been more effective with contemporary audiences than with modern ones. We can imagine many sorts of men between the extremes of Unferth and Beowulf, and we are left still wondering about the particulars of Beowulf's personality. For now, the narrator has no more to say about Beowulf's character; and for audiences of the time, there may have been no need. A mark of modern literature is the careful exploration of a character's mind, giving motives for action and inaction, and even motives for other motives. But an ancient hero was a man of action, and he was defined by his deeds. For Beowulf to contrast with Unferth (Beowulf being more confident, more intelligent, more generous, and even more humorous) was perhaps enough information and more than legends usually gave.

Unferth, however, is not an entirely mean man. The poem is careful to show that he was honored, too; in his time, he had received treasures from Hrothgar. He may have been reasonably good at fighting and even better with wise counsel. He may have come from a noble family. Beowulf and Unferth are not as opposite as, say, Beowulf and Grendel. Each man shows us possibilities for the other. Could Unferth have been heroic like Beowulf? Could Beowulf, in the failing strength of middle age, ever become mean-spirited and regret that a younger, stronger hero would take everyone's attention? The poem does not develop these possibilities, but inherent in many of the contrasts is a sense of risk. No one is secure in his present state. His present honor (entailing comfort, wealth, and happiness) depends on his own actions, the actions of others, and the decrees of Fate ("Wyrd" in Old English). Every man is a warning and a lesson to every other.

Wealhtheow is also developed in contrast to Hildeburh. Hildeburh's tragic story directly precedes Wealhtheow's main entrance, and it seems deliberately placed for a comparison. Hildeburh, who was last seen going into tragic exile from a ruined home, contrasts with Wealhtheow, who still wears her golden treasures and sits securely in her own seat. Did Hildeburh behave in any way different from Wealhtheow or contribute to her own downfall? Did she fail to speak Wealhtheow's wise words of strategic peace? Did she fail to see the cracks in the temporary alliance with the Jutes or notice the threat hanging over the presence of Hengest? Will Wealhtheow ever come to a fate like Hildeburh's, taken back to her family home with no reason to remain?

A more indirect contrast develops Hrothgar's possibilities, as the horse-back "scop" sings of Sigemund and Heremod. Sigemund took gold from a dragon that had hoarded it, and Heremod fell from honor among his people. Later we learn that part of Heremod's downfall was a failure to give gifts. Hrothgar now has a chance to prove whether he is like Heremod and the dragon when it comes to hoarding his treasures. Will he use this opportunity to avoid Heremod's fate? Every man is a lesson and a warning to every other.

Irony

Irony makes use of contrast, and it also uses understatement to achieve a dramatic effect. With irony, we look for a disjunction between what is expected or seems appropriate and what is stated literally. It is impossible to know if the author of *Beowulf* felt the irony as we do, but we can appreciate the verbal contrast in our own way.

The narrator uses understatement when speaking of Grendel's part in the fight. First, the narrator states that in coming to Heorot that one last time, Grendel never found worse luck (716–719). Considering that Grendel had scored at least one victim on every previous trip and was now up for defeat, that statement seems like an overly safe summary. This last trip is an unhappy journey (765). Beowulf, too, uses irony in speaking of Grendel's defeat: Grendel forfeited his arm but made a poor bargain and got little comfort from this (970–975). Considering that Grendel's arm tore amid agonizing screams and a spray of blood, that statement also seems understated for the occasion. Beowulf had previously understated, with clear ironic intent, the possible reverse outcome: no Danes will need to cover his head (445–447) because Grendel's teeth will handle that job. Grendel is a thorough undertaker, and no scraps will be left (apart from the chain mail that he will spit out like fish bones). The contrast between the reverent ritual of covering a dead man's face and the irreverent devouring of anything edible creates irony. We would expect a hero's death, not a steak's.

The narrative voice can be ironic in its understatement at the feast, too. Beowulf, heaped with expensive gifts in embarrassing plenty, "felt no shame" over the gifts he received (1025). Since he received a huge fortune, it is clear that he was very far from any cause for shame, as if that had ever been in question. Unferth, we learn, was not merciful to his kinsmen (1165–1168), although he appears peaceful now. Given that Beowulf already accused Unferth of killing his brothers, this comment seems too placid. It is impossible to know if the poet who worked in Old English felt the irony of these understatements.

Finally, there is a dramatic irony in the last scene of this section. The Danish warriors, at last secure in a peaceful night's rest, are careful to have their armor and weapons handy. However unlikely it may be for enemies to attack them this night, when all the countryside is abuzz that a great hero is at Heorot, they must still, like firefighters, have all gear ready to step into at a moment's notice. Ironically, this preparation will not help them at all. They are about to be attacked by a foe who does not care about armor and weapons.

Foreshadowing

The narrator frequently hints at what is about to come, either in the course of the poem's events or in the future lives of the characters. These hints often come at moments of contrast and either remind the audience of a good outcome at times of fear, or suggest a dark outcome in times of joy.

When the fearful, nervous Geats are going to sleep in the dark, echoing hall, they are not sure if they will live through the night. The narrator assures the audience that God will give victory to them (696–700). As noted above, Grendel's last journey to Heorot is labeled an unlucky one, in case anyone still wondered what the outcome would be. Why not leave the audience in suspense? The narrator appears to use suspense as one of his tools, but not as the only one. When he tells the outcome, he reserves the means as a surprise.

As the new hall of Hrothgar comes into use, the narrator suggests that one day it will be destroyed by fire (82–85), although at this point no one has imagined it. He gives many dark hints about the future of Hrothgar's hall and the treachery that may lie ahead. Just as no one thought of the new hall in a burnt, broken condition, no one at the feast thinks of treachery (1017–1019). We realize that "wyrd" may be bringing more tragedy to the Danes, but the narrator does no more than foreshadow it.

The section closes with sudden, strong hints that death is again around the corner. "Wyrd" has decreed more tragedy (1233–1235) and one man is "ripe for death" (1240). There is an abrupt contrast with the happiness, peace, and safety of the previous scene. To a first-time reader of *Beowulf*, the hints are startling indeed. Grendel is dead, so what more can happen? Are the Frisians going to attack? Why is only one man going to die?

The other kind of foreshadowing is less subtle. Sometimes the narrator casts ahead in time and tells us some details about the future of the characters. This method is clearly done in the history of the necklace, when we learn that Hygelac (whom we have not even met yet) will die in a raid on the Frisians. The narrator often casts ahead this way, perhaps as a way of tying together different time periods in his plot. Perhaps he wishes to remind us that every man's character is a warning and a lesson to the rest.

Narrative Voice

The narrator's voice is usually submerged beneath the voices of his characters as they speak for themselves, or in the direct tale of events. At times, however, distinct traits of this narrative personality come through. Two such times have been addressed above: the ironical use of understatement, and the use of hints as foreshadowing.

Another mark of this voice is the desire to be understood as telling a received tale. This is perhaps a hallmark of the "scop," as we read that the singer on horseback wanted to tell all the tales he had heard (875) of Sigemund. To hear something meant that the teller had not invented it; rather, it was the mark of truth. Today, we may insist that something must be true because we really did read it, especially if it appears in an authoritative work such as an encyclopedia. The narrator of *Beowulf* begins with the authoritative voice of tradition: "we have heard of the glory in bygone days / of the folk-kings of the Spear-Dane" (lines 1–2). This same verb, "heard," is repeated at other times: the narrator has heard of Healfdene's daughter's marriage (62), the fame of Heorot (74), and the wide reporting of Grendel's death (838); he has never heard of a greater ship (38), assembly (1011), treasure gift (1027), or golden neckring (1197). When something cannot be heard, it cannot be known; men do not know what happened to the ship of Scyld Scefing (50).

The narrative voice also makes some moral pronouncements. Several themes emerge, which are used again and again in the story. It is well for

a young ruler to give gifts and create loyalties (20–25), just as the glorious Scyld did. Certainly, as the story goes on, we see and hear of examples of those who do this (Hrothgar) and those who do not (Heremod,
though little is said). God's rule is another theme that reappears: It is well
known that God rules the world (700–702), and that he ruled in past
times as he does now (1057–1058). Just as Beowulf expresses contempt
for death (450–451, 793–794), the narrator agrees that Death comes for
all (1002–1008). One proverb acts as a summary for many that came
before it, when the narrator closes the first gift-giving by saying that
"understanding is always best, spiritual foresight—he must face much,
both love and hate, who long here endures this world in these days of
strife" (1059–1062).

Dramatic Timing

Far from being a simple tale with a straightforward plot, *Beowulf* uses
dramatic pacing to introduce characters and create tension. In the first
section, there are two sequences of approach and entrance into the hall.
First, Beowulf comes nameless to the shores, and with each stage more
of his company's size and appearance is revealed. We learn his name
only in the third challenge and introduction, and we learn a little bit of
his biography after that. The poet could have chosen to introduce him
as he prepared to leave Geatland by saying, "Then Beowulf, sister's son
to Hygelac, stated his wishes to try his strength with Grendel. Beowulf
had killed monsters before, in particular in a contest at sea with Breca,
now King of the Brondings, when they were boys. Beowulf's strength
was greater than any man's, and so he decided to set out." Instead, the
poem uses a dramatic approach in stages to tell us all of this information.

Grendel also approaches by stages, but in a different way. As part of
the setting, we learned about Grendel's history. His approach is the
physical stalking of the hall. Here is fear of all kinds: the fear of the monster in the night, the fear of the helpless victim who is not able to see the
attacker's entrance, the fear of the nonhuman and undead. His arrival is
not unexpected, but in his steps toward the hall there are all the elements
of a horror movie.

The timing of Wealhtheow's entrance, contrasted with the song of
Hildeburh's tragedy, is also deliberate. When she first entered the feast,
she was a stereotyped character; a cardboard queen with a cup. In her
second entrance, the tragedy of the song opens our minds to the political
possibilities of her situation and her speech. What tragedy, we wonder,
is she trying to prevent?

Finally, of course, the transition from the first section to the second has dramatic timing. Unlike the heavily foreshadowed entrance of Grendel, the next episode has no foreshadowing until the last ten lines before it happens. Just as we have come to assume that the narrator will always build things up before they happen, he lets us down and sets us up for a surprise.

Psychological Development

There is one notable exception to the lack of psychological development in the characters. Within the story of the Freswael, the tragedy of the Frisians, there is a fairly lengthy psychological portrait of Hengest. This is the first of several small but significant portraits of states of mind.

Hengest is the defeated second-in-command of the Scyldings, perhaps a Jute betrayed by enemy Jutes. He is sitting out a long, dull winter, far from his own family and farms and deserted by many of his friends. Possibly victimized further by a language barrier that makes it difficult for him to understand his hosts, he is very lonely. The passage shows us his state of mind. He is unwilling and desolate (1129). He dreams of home in his frustration at having missed his chance to return before the winter storms came. Perhaps Hengest was wounded and needed to recover his strength before traveling. He has a long time to ponder the ice and storms. The descriptions of the weather create a mood that reflects his mindset: cold, stormy, and fixated. The coming of spring brings change to the earth (1135), and it also brings a change of heart for Hengest. As the ice thaws, so do his inaction and indecision. The seasons mirror his mind.

It is a short passage, but in its direct portrayal of a state of mind, not action or words, it foreshadows the modern role of fiction. Only a narrator can enter into a man's mind and describe what he is not saying. That is the unique role of fiction, for it shows us what we cannot know. No one in Finnsburg knew what Hengest had in his mind, and how he dreamed of home. No one knew how the winter hung heavily on him, and meanwhile they were most likely occupied with sliding on the icy rivers and ponds or carving ornaments on their tools. Only a narrator, looking back, can say with certainty what dreams the angry Jute suffered from and what temptations came into his heart to break his vows.

PART TWO: GRENDEL'S MOTHER

The story of Beowulf and Grendel's mother is only about 700 lines long. It is the shortest section of the poem. Its main literary focus is to develop the character of Beowulf through his actions and through more speaking lines. It also begins to use symbolic meaning through setting and through the mysterious sword hilt.

The Character of Beowulf

In the first part of the poem, we knew little of Beowulf other than his boasting and his strength. Apart from his description of the battle with Grendel, in which the eager but tired voice of a young wrestler came through, there was little to distinguish his personality from his physical presence. In the second section, we learn much more about him. He still does not rise in complexity to the level of a modern psychological hero, but he begins to have a few personal attributes.

He Is Brave. We knew that Beowulf was brave from the first fight, in which he did not seem nervous about meeting Grendel but continued, right up to bedtime, to boast that they were at least equal in strength. In this section, he astonishes us more by diving straight into the mere without any hesitation. Fear of water is a normal human instinct. We admire, with a sense of shock, the pearl divers of the Pacific Ocean, who dive to painful depths without breathing equipment and remain in the water long to retrieve the pearls. But even a fearless pearl diver might hesitate to dive into Grendel's murky mere, which is filled with toothed and aggressive creatures. Beowulf, on the other hand, is eager to dive in. Even a pearl diver knows approximately where he is going, but Beowulf does not know where Grendel's mother might be. A pearl diver might wisely decide to dive on a different day because a man-eating shark had just gone by with the taste of blood in its nose. Beowulf dives in knowing that Grendel's mother could still be eating Aeschere's headless body and be ready for dessert.

He Is Modest. After the hall boasting, it is surprising that Beowulf is modest, but upon his return he reports to Hrothgar that he almost lost this fight. He gives the credit to God, who guarded him and allowed him to spot the ancient weapon on the wall. Apart from stating that he slew both "shepherds" of that underwater hall, and that men may now sleep safely, Beowulf has nothing more to add.

He Has Good People Skills. Beowulf listens respectfully to Hrothgar's "sermon" and does not try to compete with it. He may realize that it's not easy for others to deal with his greater strength, and so he allows them to shine when they can. In the same spirit, he returns the borrowed sword, which he managed to bring back through the mere even with his hands full. As previously noted, he is careful to be very polite to Unferth, who probably has not only his own personal feelings to manage, but also a fair amount of political power as the king's counselor or spokesman. In the third section, we will see that Beowulf also paid attention to the court of Hrothgar by sizing up the people and the likely situations, good and bad, that would arise. His invitation to Hrethric (to visit him at Geatland) may even have been prompted by the tensions surrounding the question of succession. He may have picked up on the queen's nervousness, Hrothgar's blunder in proclaiming him "adopted," or Hrothmund's bold assertion of right as the king's nephew. In the third section, Beowulf will spell out the likely outcome of the political marriage that he heard about at Heorot, so it is almost certain that he has not missed the likely outcome when the old king dies.

He Thinks Strategically. Hrothgar is surprised by Beowulf's attention to his own role as official ambassador of Geatland. The Danes are at peace, with the exception of their home-grown monsters, so Beowulf's lavish offer of a thousand spears may be over the top. On the other hand, the Geats are in a precarious position. They are pressed by fierce Swedes to the north, as well as other sea-peoples (perhaps even Danes, who wish to expand into the warm lands of southern Sweden). Hrothgar already told a story of Beowulf's father having to flee a feud among the Swedes, and in the third section, the perilous politics of Geatland will be even more manifest. Could part of Beowulf's decision to go to Denmark have been to secure a powerful ally? Hrothgar alludes to previous strains between Danes and Geats and promises that those days are over. Perhaps this was Beowulf's goal. He thinks large and sees the significance of every action.

Symbolic Settings

In this second section, the action takes place in three different places. The setting of the mere is described in vivid language, and the struggle itself takes place in the underwater hall. Then Beowulf returns to Heorot, where he hears Hrothgar's "sermon." There is a strong symbolic contrast between heaven and hell in these shifts.

As noted above, the description of the mere parallels at least one description of hell. It is not hell as we imagine it, but it suits a "worst place scenario" of people who spend more time outdoors and around dangerous animals than most of us do. It is a hell of fear, discomfort, and uncertainty.

The discovery that Grendel and his mother live not in a cave, but in a hall, introduces a new element to the setting. In the Anglo-Saxon vision of heaven and hell, both God and Satan live in royal halls. God's hall is high, bright, peaceful, gold-adorned, and filled with joyful fellowship and singing. Satan's hall is dark and filled with strife, as his followers come to hate him and fight with each other. The central fact of hall life was community; warriors who slept on benches near each other, who woke and ate together, and who planned, traveled, and fought together developed many bonds of friendship and loyalty. The king's role, of course, was to cement this community with gift-giving. God's hall in heaven is a paradise of perfect community. Satan's hall is a hell of outcasts, who struggle against each other and cannot find love or trust. The only thing worse than being an exile with no hall was to be a member of the war band of Satan in his strife-filled dark hall.

Beowulf, then, poses two halls. One is set on a hill, gold-adorned, and filled with communal feasting and singing. The other is placed under a fearful lake, attended by monsters, and lit with only one fire. The latter is the site of eating flesh and drinking blood. There are no supportive friends there, only Grendel's mother and the dead body of her son. Perhaps it is not as complete as the picture of Satan's dark hall, as it does not have bickering minions and back-stabbing servants, but it is close enough that the image would not have been lost on the audience.

In the Hall of Darkness, Beowulf fights against the kin of Cain. Just as Grendel, the emmisary of evil, had intruded into the Hall of Light, Beowulf intrudes into the Hall of Darkness as an emissary of Light. In lines 1570–1572, as soon as Grendel's mother has been cut down, a light begins to glow. Of course it must be the light of the fire, but it glows "as from heaven clearly shines the firmament's candle." This light is possible after the death of both figures of evil, although the true son, the "firmament's candle," cannot shine into the cave. Symbolically, light has won over darkness.

Back on land in the Hall of Light, Hrothgar sits on his throne and gives out wisdom. Hrothgar is not a symbol of God, but in this image he sits as if on God's throne and is surrounded by peace, light, and loyalty. He holds in his hand the symbol of ancient judgment, when the flood waters covered evil (as now the waters of the mere form the burial place of the monsters). He deals out wisdom that closely parallels the Bible, although it is blended and adapted to pagan Germanic ideals and pragmatic wisdom. In this vision he becomes a figure like the biblical patriarchs, such as King David the harpist and warrior or King Solomon the Wise.

PART THREE: THE DRAGON

The last episode is almost as long as the first, and it follows a very different structure. It alternates between narrated histories and straightforward action, but with two significant additions. The story of how the dragon's hoard was buried appears to be a purely fictional re-creation of the event. The story of the old man whose son has died, whose grief is part of Hrethel's story, is also a piece of apparent fiction. These fictional interludes, with their histories and action, create a sad story that seems to live in a black, white, and gray world.

Elegiac Tone

Tone is created by the narrator's words and the kinds of details that are provided. The prevailing tone of the last episode of *Beowulf* is sad and looks forward with gloom to the disaster ahead. In looking back, the poem suggests that the happy days are gone and that everyone important is dying. A poem or song that mourns a death is called an "elegy," and the tone of this section is elegiac. It constantly mourns for someone who has died and for the coming death of a way of life.

Not all of the deaths are mourned. This episode is full of feuding and includes some grisly details, such as when Beowulf's crushes a Frankish warrior's rib cage. Among the other dead in this section, we number Hygelac, his son Heardred, the Swedish kings Ongentheow, Ohthere, and Onela, and Ohthere's son Eanmund. Beowulf recalls Hygelac with regret and unmistakable sorrow, but his speech is made fifty years after the event, and he has long since made his peace with it. The death that is most openly mourned in the poem is the death that occurred even before the poem's action opened. This is the accidental death of Herebeald, Hygelac's older brother. The sorrow of his father, Hrethel, is painted vividly. Why is this death made to carry the burden of mourning all of the deaths in the section?

In mourning the death of Herebeald, Beowulf recalls the sorrow of his grandfather, Hrethel. Hrethel took his son's death very hard, as it came suddenly and not in battle, when he would have expected and avenged it. Beowulf paints a picture that could be Hrethel himself, but it is usually understood as a fictional portrait of an old man who has also lost a son that he cannot avenge. These lines convey emotion through a series of external images. The house is too large, and the land is too wide; with the beloved son gone, the inner house feels empty. Traveling from Hrethel's loss to the old man's loss, the story depicts a death that results in another death and then the death of a way of life. Most of the deaths in the story are accepted routinely and merely point the way for someone else to take over. These two deaths (Herebeald's and the other son's), however, stop everything. Life cannot go on. How can the old men live in the way they have been accustomed? This death brings about the death of their way of life, and they die of grief.

Another death that ends a way of life is the fictional "Last Survivor" of the nation, who hoarded the dragon's treasure. Here, a plague has ended an entire nation's way of life within a short period of time. The one man who is immune to the plague survives, but his lifestyle cannot survive. His last action is simply to memorialize his people, lest they be forgotten by others who might use their cups, harnesses, and weapons. His dying action is to sit in the barrow he built, look at the treasures, and remember the people who used them. Like the grieving father, he sees a life coming to an end in his own life. Where the father thinks the house is too large now that it is empty, the Last Survivor finds the treasure too numerous now that there is no one to use it. His death ends his nation.

Both of these stories are told in a tone different than that of the usual narrative style. There is a lingering over emotional expression that we do not find in most other passages, as well as a sense of these passages as fiction within "history." This is why they are often considered poems within the poem, as though a singer had stepped up to sing between passages of the saga of *Beowulf*.

The episode builds on this sad tone by telling us how depressed Beowulf became when he heard of the dragon. According to the narrator, it was not like him to be pessimistic. In fact, Beowulf himself tells how many hurdles he has overcome and how many challenges he has faced. He never saw a reason to fear before, not even when a child inherited the kingship of the Geats. He was always confident of doing and being right and of a good outcome. This time he has changed, and he feels a sense of wrongness and dread.

The feuds are told with details that are fearful. Instead of telling us, as before, that Haethcyn was killed in battle, the Geatish messenger reminds Beowulf's thanes just how terrifying it was for them and their fathers to be trapped in Ravenswood as they waited to be gutted and hung on trees. The narrative again slows down to portray the emotional states of these men. Although the ordeal ended at dawn with the arrival of Hygelac blowing his horn, the narrative emphasizes fear and loss.

Finally, the death of Beowulf is told with lingering sorrow. Wiglaf tries to revive him, but he expires. His death is really not sad; he is an old man, and he is allowed to die as he would wish, rather than of an illness. If he had not charged the dragon, then he would soon have led his men out to a last battle. But the narrative tone of sorrow is so strong that we are led to overlook this fact and mourn for his death. The last passage, which shows the sorrow of his people, brings this home even more. When

Scyld Scefing died in the opening lines, his people were sad, but their grief is passed over quickly. Beowulf's death is emphasized as a tragedy.

Foreshadowing

The elegiac tone of the episode is used to foreshadow the death of Beowulf by raising the emotions of fear and sorrow. In each lament, for Herebeald and for the lost nation, there is a sense that this death is bringing about the death of more than just one person. This suggestion is driven home as Beowulf's death comes about.

The elegy for Herebeald introduces the sorrow of an heir's death, followed by the father's death. The lament of the Last Survivor repeats this theme; how in his death, a nation dies. By the time the narrator is reminding the audience (as well as the Geats) why the stakes are high in Beowulf's survival, the tone has already foreshadowed the outcome. In the death of Beowulf, there will be loss to the nation. The details are then provided and explain how through the feuds, at least two neighbors will have an incentive to attack them. Without the emotional tone having set the stage, this would not come across as more than the next challenge. Through the foreshadowing of the previous elegies, the poem shows the emotional burden more than direct words could.

The details of the feud act as foreshadowing of the coming continuation of that feud. When the Geats are terrified in Ravenswood, it is the first time we hear of brave fighting men being truly frightened. They have no king, and they do not have sufficient force to defend themselves. These details foreshadow the predicted Geatish future: another king lost and insufficient force for defense.

Narrative Point of View

The stories of the two Danish monsters and of the feud between the Swedes and the Geats are told through several narrative voices. Each speaker has a different point of view. The tale of Grendel had already been told by the narrator, but the last episode provides the story from Beowulf's point of view. The narrator uses an omniscient voice to tell the bare facts, while Beowulf's character adds more personal details. The feud is told through the narrator, through Beowulf's recollections, and through the unnamed Geatish messenger. Each of these voices can add a perspective to the overall story, and none of them tells it from beginning to end.

This may be a clumsy, patched-together way of telling the story. This was certainly the opinion of early critics, who never considered that an author might be involved in shaping it. They saw the work as nothing more than a much-changed historical document that was pieced together. The more recent opinion from this century—that the poem might have had a final author, if not an author who wrote it from start to finish—allows us to take the narrative point of view more seriously and not just as a clumsy accident.

It is possible that the poet shared with modern authors an interest in how a story may develop through layers. Whether the poet chose to tell his story in parts (and out of order) for this purpose, we do not know. In any case, the story unrolls in a Faulknerian manner. First, a fact is dropped briefly and without precise accuracy. Then another fact is dropped, but we wonder how the two facts are connected. The deaths of Ongentheow and Heardred turned out to be only somewhat connected and in different generations, held together mainly by the role of Hygelac as king. In the second explanation of Beowulf's accession to the throne, another angle comes in: was Beowulf hand-picked by his foe? When Beowulf tells his own story, why does he bring attention to the sorrows of his grandfather, King Hrethel? What analogy might we feel in Beowulf's own sorrows, or in his people's expected sorrows at having no heir after him? There is no line drawn; we can only draw it ourselves. Completely unexpected is the entrance of Wiglaf's sword, as it comes from the other side and is an heirloom of the enemy. How ironic that the sword that helped make Beowulf king, by contributing to the death of his cousin Heardred, is now raised to save him from the dragon! Finally, the greatest detail is provided by the speaker who is most distanced from his tale. The messenger provides the descriptions, the sights, sounds, feelings, and fears, of the Geatish–Swedish wars to help heighten the fears of the present time. The excursion into Geatish politics ends with an anonymous woman, who could represent any individual in any time, and who mourns in advance the sorrows of coming defeat.

FURTHER SUGGESTED READING

Brodeur, Arthur Gilchrist. *The Art of Beowulf*. Berkeley: University of California Press, 1959.

Deskis, Susan. *Beowulf and the Medieval Proverb Tradition*. Tempe, AZ: Medieval and Renaissance Texts and Studies, 1996.

Lee, Alvin A. *Gold-Hall and Earth-Dragon: Beowulf as Metaphor*. Toronto: University of Toronto Press, 1998.

———. *The Guest-Hall of Eden*. New Haven: Yale University Press, 1972.

Shippey, T. A. *Old English Verse*. London: Hutchinson University Library, 1972.

Wehlau, Ruth. *The Riddle of Creation: Metaphor Structures in Old English Poetry*. New York: Peter Lang, 1997.

8

Placing *Beowulf* on a Timeline

WHEN THE *Beowulf* manuscript was rescued from obscurity by Thorkelin in 1815, very little was known about the poem's location in space and time. It was clear that it was a poem of the Anglo-Saxon age, and that it came from somewhere in the heartland of England (as opposed to, say, Ireland or Denmark). Anyone who considered the matter further probably assumed that in a short time scholars would be able to state with certainty the century in which it was produced (if not the exact year) and whether the poem was a product of Mercia or East Anglia. However, the more time passes, the more uncertain the issue appears. We really do not know where or when the poem was produced; the closest we can estimate is within a few hundred miles and about 400 years.

It is startling to a modern reader that many manuscripts were left unsigned and undated in this earlier era. Some old manuscripts are signed. King Alfred, for one, signed some of the translations and compositions he worked on, and we have no doubts about their time and place. Information about Alfred is anchored for us by contemporary records of his reign and by his biographer, Asser. The Venerable Bede, a prolific writer in Latin, is known to have authored many specific works of history and poetry, and he was careful to provide dates for himself (he pioneered the "Anno Domini" dating system). Also anchored in time are Aldhelm and Aelfric, two other well-known writers. On the other hand, four long poems ("Elene," "Christ," "Juliana," and "The Fates of the Apostles") all contain the rune letters for the name "Cynewulf" scattered among the lines; apparently it is a signature. But Cynewulf exists only in these poems; he has no biography or other links to historical time. Scholars can only guess that he lived some time around AD 800 (plus or minus fifty years), and that he probably lived in the kingdom of Mercia.

Many of the famous Anglo-Saxon works have no author. "The Dream of the Rood," an inventive poem about the death of Jesus in the narrative voice of the wooden cross, exists in a cathedral library in Italy. The only clues about its date are in the handwriting style, which tells us little. A few of its lines are carved on a stone cross at Ruthwell (in northern England), but the words used in the poem are not generally marked as northern dialect, and little can be said about where it was composed. Before his death in 1072, the Bishop of Exeter presented to his church a book of collected works that included riddles and many assorted poems. None of these works are signed, and no one can tell where the bishop found them for his collection. Several well-known writers enjoyed composing riddles, and some of the riddles are similar to their known works, but no identification can be made. *The Exeter Book* also includes some of the best-known and most admired short poems ("Deor," "The Wanderer," "The Seafarer") and short love poems ("The Wife's Lament," "The Husband's Message," and "Wulf and Eadwacer"), all of which are unsigned and undated. All we know is that these works were written before the bishop's death.

The problem of where to place Beowulf, in history or geography, is not unique, then. There are differences, however, that make it a more important question. The other poems do not speak of any temporal affairs but seem to exist in an alternate literary universe. Like many modern poems that focus on personal or universal themes, they are timeless. *Beowulf*, on the other hand, purports to be a piece of poetical history, and it is linked with separately attested historical figures: Hrothgar and Hrothulf, Hygelac, the Swedish princes (Ohthere, Onela, and Eadgils), and Eormanric (King of the Goths). Beowulf is not a confirmed historical figure, but it is possible that he really lived. To what degree does this poem relate ancient, forgotten history?

In the same vein, *Beowulf* presents a higher degree of complexity in its themes, partly because it is longer, and partly because it ambitiously addresses a pagan story. To what degree is the poem both pagan and Christian? This question presents one of the most profound points of interpretation, for in assessing the motives of the hero it would be helpful to know whether the poet intended us to admire or criticize Beowulf's pride. It would be helpful to know if vague allusions and unclear phrases are anchored in either biblical or pagan mythology. Further, what is the significance of *Beowulf*'s Scandinavian setting? It is clearly written in Old English, a product of Anglo-Saxon scribes, but how does the poem relate

England and Scandinavia? Did the audience of *Beowulf* consider themselves heirs of the glorious Scylding kings, or were they resentful that Danish Vikings were burning their farms? We could answer these questions if we only knew when it was written.

Beowulf, more than the shorter poems, presents many questions of interpretation that hinge on its date of composition. If it is ancient, then its history may be more accurate than the histories by which we judge it, and perhaps its account of these kings should be used to correct the other poems. If it is not as ancient, then its history may be fictionalized, but its literary voice may be more sophisticated, making critics more justified in finding symbolism and irony. If it is ancient, then it may have been preserved as an artifact of the lost Danish past; if it is not, then it may show us an attitude of nostalgia for a Danish past that was, by then, lost.

TWO CENTURIES OF SCHOLARLY TRENDS

To the first generations of scholars, *Beowulf* was clearly very old. The manuscript's date has never been questioned; the written copy (kept under glass) dates from somewhere around the year 1000. The approximate date of Hygelac's raid is 521, so no composition of *Beowulf* before 600 could be accepted. However, how close to 600 might it have been composed and then preserved in copies until 1000? Victorian Era scholarship favored an oral composition date as early as possible, with folk tales about Beowulf circulating by 600 and a written date between 700 and 750.

There were many reasons to favor this early dating. First, in a time of rapid archeological discovery, there was universal admiration of what was most ancient. In the East, scholars were uncovering Egyptian tombs and translating cuneiform, while boys in Britain were made to study Latin and Greek as the foundation of all knowledge. What if *Beowulf* was the equivalent of Homer's *Odyssey*? What if the two funerals were eyewitness accounts? This was an exciting idea for scholars of the time. Second, during this time there was also an effort to find and preserve folk stories and customs, by the Grimm brothers and many others. Third, during Queen Victoria's reign there was a heightened awareness of being Germanic, because Victoria (who was only three generations removed from native German-speakers) had married Albert, a German prince. Last, in a time of massive cross-referencing studies, the *Beowulf* poet's historical hints about Offa, Ingeld, Hrothgar and many minor tribes (such as the Heathobards, Vendels, and Hugas) would allow for a much fuller picture of the lost centuries before writing was in wide use. Contemporary histories began in the 500s among the Franks, but no one was completely sure about the history and placement of tribes before that time or about non-Franks for a hundred years after that. *Beowulf* seemed to fill in some gaps.

An apparently insurmountable barrier to dating the poem much past 800 was the savagery of the Viking raids that began in 793 and continued until 1016. Why would the Anglo-Saxons have cared about listening to or copying a poem that praised the Danes and the Swedes? This seemed to be the ceiling: after 800 the poem could only have been copied faithfully by a few monks who thought its moral value made it worth preserving. The fact that only one copy exists could be evidence that it was in manuscript form during the Viking Age, when many libraries were burned; before that, it might have been a commonly known work. Its lack of references in contemporary literature (no other writers compare great heroes to Beowulf) could be because its theme grew so unpopular that it was largely forgotten, like a badly out-of-date piece of furniture. One scholar, L. L. Schücking, argued in 1917 that, on the contrary, the work could have been created during the years when a Danish king ruled England. It could have been composed in Old English as a means to teach the new Danish rulers the native language, and it could have been based on the stories preserved among the Danish bards. This idea was not accepted by his generation of scholars, who were persuaded that only an early date was possible.

One of the implications of this earliest dating was that the original poem, in whatever form it first took, had been lost through many changes. The original folk stories had become songs and then had been collected into a rough narrative by various "scops" (singing poets). A cycle of three stories about Beowulf came together and were traditionally sung in sequence with some brief transitional material. After it was written, copyists changed it as they went along. Some misspelled words, while some corrected "wrong" (i.e., original, older) spelling. Some added a few lines of their own to improve the Christian piety of the work. By the time the last editors were at work (around 1000), the poem had about the same resemblance to its original as the current forms of the "King Arthur" myth have to the original brief history of a king who fought the Saxon invasion. The current form of the poem was not the work of any one voice, and it was thoroughly corrupt. This allowed scholarly editors to correct these mistakes with countless guesses about what the text "really" said, or ought to say, or once had said.

Following on the heels of the Victorians, a new generation of scholarship began in the 1920s with the ground-breaking work of Milman Parry. Parry theorized that the living tradition of bards in Serbia could shed light on the lost oral poetic tradition of Greece. He used new portable recording machines to record these Serbian bards as they recited lays of events both long past and relatively recent. He found that they reused certain phrases as building blocks and as filler when they had to think of more lines. Instead of pausing, they included stock phrases that fit the required space. Studying the works of Homer, Parry found that Homer's verse seemed to have the same traits, in which Athena was either "gray-eyed" or "wise," depending on the space the line allowed. Parry determined that there was less originality in Homer than previously thought, but he also determined that the rigidity of these stock phrases (which lasted for centuries of bardic use) could show the prehistory of the Greek language. It was not long before others were applying "Oral-Formulaic" methods to *Beowulf* and looking for ancient clues to the Germanic languages before they were written. If *Beowulf* was the earliest composed Germanic work (Icelandic poems are of later medieval origin), then its phrases could be the only clues left from these language changes. Clearly, these scholars preferred a very ancient dating of *Beowulf*, and their studies of the repeated phrases seem to confirm it. In contrast to the Victorians' tendency to correct the text, scholars working with "Oral-Formulaic" ideas wanted to study how the precise spelling might have preserved ancient clues that even the copyists did not hear or understand.

Around 1980, a new wave of study broke down the old certainties and claimed to provide a more reliable dating method, but one that disagreed with traditional scholarship. In the front of this new trend, Kevin Kiernan's close study (1981) of the original manuscript seemed to open the possibility that the poem was written in much the same way that a modern poem would be written. Kiernan found evidence of many corrections made in both of the individual handwriting styles, and it suggested that the writer of the last section had painstakingly re-edited what the first writer had already edited with corrections. The care put into this text went so far beyond the care used by the same writers for other texts that Kiernan wondered if one of the writers, probably the second, was actually involved in composing the text. If not, then perhaps a living author was working with them and exercising control over his text. To support the theory that the second writer was the author, Kiernan found evidence that this writer had returned to the text years later and not only traced over sections that were fading, but also washed a page to erase it and then wrote changed lines onto the wet parchment. Could this be the hand of an author, rather than a meddling copyist?

The newer generation of scholars viewed authorship questions differently, and were more open to a later composition date. Because modern literary study values the complex "voice" of a work, the scholars of the later twentieth century were open to the possibility that the poem had a voice, rather than many seams and tape marks where multiple copyists had edited it. If the poem had more of a genuine authorship, then its literary values (more emphasized since Tolkien's lecture in 1936) could be taken seriously. A later author, in fact, could be presumed to be more sophisticated, working within a tradition that included the voice of the wooden cross in "The Dream of the Rood" and the varied styles of *The Exeter Book*. A later date could also solve the mystery of why the greatest classic of Anglo-Saxon times is never mentioned in other works: maybe it was composed shortly before the end of the Anglo-Saxon age, or perhaps only fifty years before the Norman Conquest. To this generation of scholars, the heavy emphasis of the Victorians on Germanic roots seemed misplaced. Especially following the world wars, a less primitively Germanic origin seemed more attractive, and a few scholars have even sought roots for *Beowulf* in Celtic myths of Ireland. It is undeniable that the interpretation of literature can be influenced by many ideas circulating in the wider culture. Scholars were more open, therefore, to these possibilities, and less rigid in viewing the poem in only one way. While some scholars reviewed the evidence and were persuaded by Kiernan to accept the date of composition as being later than 900, many others simply chose a position that we cannot know its date. In 1936, Tolkien could state that the dating of *Beowulf* appeared to be one of the most solid offerings of scholarship, but in 2005 it is best to say that we simply cannot know when or how it was composed.

EVIDENCE

There are four essential types of evidence that can be evaluated to determine a working date for the poem. Language and historical evidence, the province of the first century of scholars, are joined by manuscript and psychological evidence. There is ongoing work being done in all of these areas, and language studies are increasingly making use of computer-analysis capabilities. The relative weight a writer puts on these areas of study often determines his or her position on dating.

Language evidence includes study of words, of poetic meter, and of the use of oral formulas. Because we know that languages change over time, we can often date a work by the kinds of words it uses. For example, the King James Bible uses many words that do not exist in any kind of currency now but were common in 1600. In some cases, scholars can determine that a form of a word changed during the Anglo-Saxon period by comparing known early works with known later works. In other cases, by knowing how a word must have been formed in earlier Germanic times, they can label a word as an early or late (more similar to medieval) form. In the same way, there are local charters and decrees that make some generalizations about dialect and spelling possible. Many words can be identified as Mercian, West Saxon, Northumbrian, or Kentish. Either they are spelled in a certain way (Northumbrian tended to use "i" whereas southern forms often used "e"), or else they are local words not used outside that area (most regions today have such words as well). *Beowulf* appears to use West Saxon (Wessex) forms in its general spelling. These West Saxon forms are considered "normal" for Old English texts, because Wessex became politically dominant and its dialect came into widespread use. On the other hand, unusual words do appear throughout the document: are they evidence of Kentish (or Northumbrian or Mercian) slang being used in Wessex, or could they be relics of an older document or the additions of an "outsider" scribe?

As one example of word study, R. W. Chambers (1958) describes the changes in use of the definite article, "the." Over time, speakers of Old English appear to have increased their use of "the" in phrases with a certain (weak) adjective form and a noun. The poems of Cynewulf have far more of these phrases that use the definite article than phrases that are without it. For example, in "Elene," there are as many as sixty-six phrases with the definite article and nine without. "Exodus," another poem (not by Cynewulf) that is considered relatively old and belonging to the first centuries of Christian conversion, has ten phrases with the definite article and fourteen without. *Beowulf* fits in with "Exodus," because it has thirteen of the weak adjective phrases including the definite article, and it has sixty-five without the definite article. By this measure, it could be even older than Exodus, since it uses fewer of the definite article phrases, and this might confirm an early date. However, Chambers points out that on the other side, "The Battle of Maldon" (a poem commemorating a Viking battle in the year 991) is more similar to these "early" poems in its definite article usage, although there is no question that it was composed late in the Anglo-Saxon period. So, is this evidence of a genuine language change, or is it a stylistic form? Could the poets of "The Battle of Maldon" and *Beowulf* have been aware that the missing definite article was an archaic style? Is it possible that they chose this style to give their work an antique feel?

Another form of language evidence comes from the close study of metrical patterns. In its broadest description, Old English poetic meter used four strong (accented) beats per line, with a varying number of unaccented syllables. Each line used alliteration for three of these strong beats; usually the first two, and one out of the third and fourth. But the specific shapes that these lines might take varied a great deal. Some syllables used vowels that were held longer than others, "long" vowels as opposed to "short" ones. The first generation of scholars determined that there were at least five typical types of Old English poetic lines, and some scholars analyzed upwards of twenty types of line arrangements.

Did these metrical habits change over time? If the poems could be arranged with any certainty, then perhaps over several centuries we could see a shift from using certain types of lines, to using others. Then *Beowulf*'s trends could be placed in this timeline. Studies of this type are technical and have not found any consensus, because of the difficulty in creating a timeline for Anglo-Saxon poetry. It is impossible to say with certainty when or where Cynewulf was writing. It is impossible to know if "Exodus" and "Genesis" were composed before "Daniel" and "Judith." Modern scholarship is careful to avoid circularity (making the same assumption that some were earlier and then using that evidence to prove the same thing).

A highly technical example of metrical evidence is Kaluza's Law, which is a description of a particular metrical pattern of long and short syllables. This pattern is assumed to be a continuation of ancient Germanic poetic tradition, just as metrical patterns today were inherited from several centuries of English verse. If the pattern was so traditional that reciting scops did not change it, then it may preserve an ancient pattern of syllables. In that case, discovering how closely *Beowulf* follows the pattern of Kaluza's Law should suggest how ancient and traditional it is. Since the short and long distinctions in these words had in some cases eroded by the time of written Anglo-Saxon history, their use in the poem would support its oral formation in a time before writing; perhaps around 650. In this case, the phrases of *Beowulf* have a high rate of faithfulness to Kaluza's Law, so some scholars point to this metrical evidence as strong support for an early date of composition.

Finally, not all language studies support an early date. Frank (1981) compares Scandinavian verse forms of the tenth and eleventh centuries and finds many parallels. Some words used in key lines in *Beowulf* appear to have a Danish-influenced meaning. The word "lofgeorn" (meaning "praise-eager") occurs only in negative ways in other Old English verse (where it suggests an "attention-hog"), but it is a term of praise in Scandinavian literature, just as it is in *Beowulf*. The very last word of the poem states that Beowulf's highest quality was his eagerness for praise. Further, some of the phrases used in describing the customs of Denmark, such as to "cover the head" of a dead man (*Beowulf*, line 446) or the specific word for Heorot's benches, occur only in Scandinavian sources of this time. Again, Beowulf's statement, "It is time for me to go" (316), is a line of incomplete alliteration, and therefore unusual in

Old English verse. However, it occurs almost word for word several times in Norse poetry. Frank concludes that while the evidence is not watertight, this comparison of words, phrase, and meter would support the idea that *Beowulf* was composed during the time of King Canute or under some other strong Danish influence; perhaps by a poet who had heard Danish legends recited in Canute's hall.

Historical evidence involves comparing manuscripts of different times and places and finding commonalities. *Beowulf* offers a wide field of historical comparison. The royal family of Scyldings, for example, also shows up in the Medieval Latin history of Denmark by Saxo Grammaticus, and in various Icelandic sagas dealing with Helgi (Halga) and Rolf (Hrothulf), and their relatives, Hroar (Hrothgar) and Eric (Hrethric). The Swedes appear as Ali and Athils (Onela and Eadgils) in Icelandic sagas, and Athils is the greatest king, married to a former Scylding queen. The briefly told story of Sigurd (Sigemund) the dragon-slayer and his nephew, Sinfiotli (Fitela), has of course ample parallels in the legends of both Iceland and Germany. Ermanaric (Eormanric) of the Goths, whose necklace Hama stole in the story that describes the Brosing necklace presented to Beowulf, was a historical king. There are at least three descriptions of the giant Hygelac and his unsuccessful raid on the Franks. What can we learn from this sort of evidence?

The earlier scholarship relied on the details in *Beowulf* to correct or fill in historical evidence. Scholars assumed the poem had been close to eyewitnesses. More recent scholarship takes a more skeptical look and examines the possibility that the poet himself leaned on medieval histories to create a sense of antiquity. In one such study, Goffart (1981) examines Hygelac's raid in which he fights against Franks, Frisians, Hetware, and Hugas (the tribe of Daeghrefn, whom Beowulf kills). While early scholarship supposed that the poem preserved the knowledge of little-known ethnic groups (the coastal Hetware and the lost tribe of the Hugas), Goffart examines the evidence for these groups in the histories of the Franks. He concludes that it is very likely that the *Beowulf* poet had read these histories, which were available in England by the mid-900s. In the cases where the earlier histories (Gregory of Tours) and later histories (*Liber Historiae Francorum* and others) disagree about the details of the raid, the *Beowulf* poet sides with the later, not the earlier, histories. It could be that the account in *Beowulf* preserves details that the early histories forgot, but it could also be that the mistakes, omissions, and corruptions of the later histories are mirrored in *Beowulf* because the poet was recreating, not preserving, history. By Goffart's estimate, the poem could not have been written with these historical details before 923, at the earliest.

Another type of historical evidence comes from archeology. Could recent discoveries of Scandinavian and English artifacts shed light on the poem's date? Newton (1993) suggests that the high degree of correspondence between the descriptions of weapons in *Beowulf* and the royal weapons discovered in Sutton Hoo's burial mound could form a real link. Studying the fictionalized East Anglian royal genealogies, he finds a strong overlap with the Scylding royal names. If *Beowulf* was written in East Anglia not long after the last pagan kings ruled, perhaps memories of the splendid hoard and ship funeral could have enhanced the descriptions of weapons and funerals. Newton's argument supports the traditional view of the poem as dating between 700 and 750, since the Sutton Hoo burial dates from around 620.

Manuscript evidence is not widely available because of the condition of the parchment. It is kept under glass and very few can see it. Three manuscript studies, the first done in 1882 by Zupitza and the most recent completed by Kiernan in 1981, have been the only source of manuscript details until recently. There is now a CD-ROM edition of the text that contains high-quality photographs of the manuscript pages. Zupitza "corrected" the text where he felt it was unreadable or corrupt, but modern translators working with the text itself can make their own judgments about what the letters mean. While Kiernan's study of the parchment led him to favor a very late date (in the period of Danish rule), not all of those studying the manuscript have come to that conclusion. The manuscript itself offers far less scope for study than do language, history, or the last category, psychology.

The psychology of the poem is a more recent focus, although writers from all times have made guesses and assumptions. With the literary emphasis on exploring the mind behind a text, studies today ask questions similar to the following: "What is the attitude of the *Beowulf* poet toward pagan religion? Is it more Christian or more pagan?" "How does the attitude toward women compare with other Anglo-Saxon manuscripts?" "Does the tone of *Beowulf* reflect the downfall of the Anglo-Saxon kingdoms, or the triumph of the early Christian period?"

Inevitably, psychological studies blend with other approaches. Kiernan, for example, sees in his theory of the poem a resolution of its attitude to paganism and its tragic tone. The Danish kings were recently converted Christians, and the nations of Iceland and Norway were also recently converted, while Sweden was still pagan. A poem written to please a Danish king would have to be respectful of pagan ancestors, while simultaneously recognizing that they did not have the truth and could not call on the real God. An Anglo-Saxon poet writing in the Danish Age would recall

all too vividly the experience of a nation that suffered invasion while governed by weak kings, including the burning towns, dead bodies, and captured women that defeat entailed. The elegiac tone of the last section could be infused with the tragedy of a defeated people, although the Danish rule was easy and congenial.

In another psychological and historical study, Benson (1967) examines the writings surrounding the great Anglo-Saxon mission to convert the continental Old Saxons to Christianity. Many of the sermons and letters of the time reveal attitudes and concerns that are similar to those shown in documents from more recent missionary efforts. The bishops back at home appeal to the faithful to support the efforts in prayer and giving money, while the mission letters from Boniface and others tell of the kinship they feel with the Saxons and the progress they are making with their message. One letter from Boniface, in particular, seems significant to understanding the *Beowulf* poet's attitude toward paganism. In this letter, he rebukes King Aethelbald of Mercia for sexual immorality, and he tells him that even the pagan Saxons have a higher standard than he does. Although the pagans are ignorant of God's written law, they know in their hearts what God established in the beginning. Boniface seems to mirror the poet's attitude: the pagans are ignorant and cannot be saved without the truth, but when it comes to matters of morality and values, they are to be admired. Benson argues that placing the composition of *Beowulf* during the height of the missionary period, the eighth century, would explain the poet's interest in the continental tribes and his attitude of critical admiration.

There is a growing consensus among current scholars that we may never be able to determine the place and time of the poem, and that the only certainty may be the handwriting date on the manuscript itself, about 1000 to 1025. Without knowing a certain timeline for the other Old English classics, and without finding any historical marker that rules out all other theories, we will go on weighing evidence that points both one way and another. In the meantime, the choices that translators make about the probable date of the poem continue to influence their choices of interpretation of doubtful words.

★

★   ★

IN DEPTH: A DISPUTED WORD

On the often-reproduced first page of the manuscript (see the first page of the *Beowulf* manuscript in Chapter 1), a word in line 6 shows the difficulties of translation. The word is "eorl" (the victim of Scyld Scef-ing's terror). Translators who favor an early composition date generally see this as a form of the proper name "Heruli," a continental tribe that is mostly lost to history. They are supposed to have lived in an area con-venient to Scyld's raids, and they might well have been terrified to see his ships arrive on shore. However, that is the preferred reading only by those who assume that obscure names in the poem preserve an ancient eyewitness account. If the poem has a later date of composition, the word may literally be "earl" (a regional chieftain). In this reading, Scyld took advantage of the local political organization of Scandinavia and terror-ized all of the earls so that he could become dominant in the region. Did the organization into earldoms exist at the time of the composition, or was it composed before this organization occurred? Did the poet hear of the Heruli as the ancient rivals of the Scyldings, or was the poem com-posed long after the Heruli's existence was forgotten? Among recent translations, Heaney (2000) chooses to use the neutral word "foes," as do most others. Liuzza uses "earls," while Slade (2004) uses "Heruli."

FURTHER SUGGESTED READING

Bolton, W. F. *Alcuin and Beowulf: An Eighth Century View*. Brunswick, NJ: Rutgers University Press, 1978.

Chambers, R. W. *Beowulf: An Introduction to the Study of the Poem with a Discussion of the Stories of Offa and Finn*. Cambridge: Cambridge University Press, 1958.

Chase, Colin, ed. *The Dating of Beowulf*. Toronto: University of Toronto, 1981.

Evans, Stephen S. *The Heroic Poetry of Dark-Age Britain: An Introduction to Its Dating, Com-position, and Use as a Historical Source*. Lanham, MD: University Press of America, Inc., 1997.

Foley, John Miles. *Traditional Oral Epic: The Odyssey, Beowulf, and the Serbo-Croatian Return Song*. Berkeley: University of California Press, 1990.

Fulk, Robert D. *A History of Old English Meter*. Philadelphia: University of Pennsylvania Press, 1992. (Explains metrical evidence such as Kaluza's Law.)

Girvan, Ritchie. *Beowulf and the Seventh Century*. London: Methuen, 1971 (first published 1935).

Kiernan, Kevin. *Beowulf and the Beowulf Manuscript*. Brunswick, NJ: Rutgers University Press, 1981.

Niles, John D. *Beowulf: The Poem and Its Tradition*. Cambridge: Harvard University Press, 1983.

Parks, Ward. *Verbal Dueling in Heroic Narrative: The Homeric and Old English Tradition*. Princeton: Princeton University Press, 1990.

Puhvel, Martin. *Beowulf and the Celtic Tradition*. Waterloo, ON: Wilfrid Laurier

Watts, Ann Chalmers. *The Lyre and the Harp: A Comprehensive Reconsideration of Oral Tradition in Homer and Old English Epic Poetry*. New Haven, CT: Yale, 1969.

9

Language and Poetry

THE OLD ENGLISH LANGUAGE

THE LANGUAGE used in England between AD 600 and AD 1100 can be made to appear as either strikingly similar to Modern English or as a completely different language. Old English is the root of Modern English, but in the process of change, much Old English material has been changed and diminished, while many other elements have been added. In order to understand the language of *Beowulf*, a student must understand this blend and be able to "run the movie backward" to see the language as it used to be.

Most students understand that there have been many foreign words borrowed in recent centuries, from "lingerie" and "rodeo," to "curry" and "raccoon." Most students have learned in school about words formed from Latin and Greek roots, but few understand that these words were consciously added to the vocabulary between 1500 and 1800. A growing scientific exploration required a new vocabulary, and since most educated people studied Latin and some Greek, it was easy to form new, precise words from these roots. Thus, a person whose eyes work better for seeing far away is "farsighted," but an apparatus for seeing objects that are far away is a "telescope." The new word has a precise meaning and becomes a word in its own right.

If you could strip away all foreign words and all words created from classical roots, you would still be left with a mix of words. The following is what the preceding paragraph looks like with all foreign-borrowed words (including names) and classical words removed:

"Most students understand that there have been many foreign words borrowed in recent centuries, from . . . and . . . to . . . and . . . Most students have learned in school about words formed from . . . and . . . roots, but few understand that these words were . . . added to the . . . between 1500 and 1800. A growing . . . required a new . . . and since most . . . people studied . . . and some . . . it was easy to form new, precise words from these roots. Thus, a person whose eyes work better for seeing far away is 'farsighted,' but an . . . for displaying an image sent from far away is a . . . The new word has a precise meaning and becomes a word in its own right."

Now, going back to the Middle Ages, a large source of borrowed words came from the settlement of overlords who spoke Medieval French after the Norman Conquest. William I, the Conqueror, was a descendant of Norsemen himself, but he and his men adopted the language of the land they settled in and spoke French, the new form of Latin. This language replaced Old English at the court for several hundred years, but it never replaced it in the small towns and farms. When English began to be written again around 1300, it had taken on a blend of French words and had simplified some of its Old English grammatical system. The core vocabulary, however, was still from Old English. Here is the same passage with the removal of any words derived from Norman French:

"Most . . . understand that there have been many . . . words borrowed in . . . from . . . and . . . to . . . and . . . Most . . . have learned in . . . about words . . . from . . . and . . . roots, but few understand that these words were . . . to the . . . between 1500 and 1800. A growing . . . a new . . . and since most . . . and some . . . it was easy to . . . new . . . words from these roots. Thus, a . . . whose eyes work better for seeing far away is "farsighted," but an . . . for . . . seeing . . . that are far away is a . . . The new word has a . . . meaning and becomes a word in its own right."

As you can see, what is left is the framework of the sentences, including a few nouns and adjectives. The verbs "understand," "borrow," "learn," "be," "has," "work," "see," and "become" are all of Old English origin, as are the prepositions and conjunctions that now litter the page. The numbers, in their full form with "thousand" and "hundred," are also from Old English. Also surviving this weeding-out test are "words," "roots," "eyes," "things," "meaning," and "right." The words from French tended to be more elaborate words, such as "foreign," "recent," "required," and "precise." Some words that entered English more directly from Latin during the early Middle Ages seem less fancy or foreign. For example, "student," "study," and "school" were part of the Latin-learning medieval school environment. To a certain extent, the origin of words corresponds with how difficult we consider them to be for children to learn. In the previous list, only the words "student" and "school" would be thought of as easy words for beginning readers, but most of the words derived from Old English are taught in the first grade.

Old English looks like a foreign language primarily because of the number of words we no longer recognize, differences in how the words are handled within a sentence, and changes in spelling. When first some Danish words, and then many French words, became widespread, some Old English words were no longer used. These words, such as "niman" (to take) and "gar" (spear), must be learned like the vocabulary in any foreign language. Most words in Old English change their form slightly depending on how they are used in a sentence. In Modern English, the change of an internal vowel is still used to indicate tense in some verbs (chose, rang, wrote) and number in some nouns (geese, mice). Similarly, there are still some endings added to indicate position in the logical order of the sentence (who/whom, he/him/his). Old English had all of these features in much greater number and importance. When a word that might otherwise be familiar changes its form, readers might miss the continuity with modern vocabulary. Simple spelling changes can also disguise words that ought to be familiar. The word "ecg" (the first element in Beowulf's father's name, Ecgtheow) means sword. The combination "cg," which is no longer used, is equivalent to our "dge." Therefore, the word is simply the same as edge, the sharp part of a sword or knife. Similarly, once you know that "sc" indicated our sound *sh*, then words like "fisc," "scip," and "Englisc" are easy to understand.

The most obviously different element in Old English writing, besides the difficulty of the script, is the handful of letters that we no longer use. To indicate our sound *th*, the Anglo-Saxons used "ð" (thorn) and "þ" (eth), usually interchangeably. To spell our sound of the short "a" (as in "hat"), they used the letter "æ" (ash). The word "ash" itself, then, would be written "æsc." These letters remain available for most keyboards because they are still used in Modern Icelandic. Unavailable in most fonts, the older form of "w" was a runic letter similar to a "P"; most printed texts have normalized it to look like a modern "w."

Some of the following listed words, taken from the first 100 lines of *Beowulf*, bear a close relation to Modern English words. Some are identical: oft, wide, long, to, word, leaf. The meanings can be somewhat different. For example, "to" could be used to indicate our meanings of "at" and "in." If the special characters were not used, then these three words would also be identical: æfter, ðær, wæs (after, there, was). More common are words that involve one or more letters that are different from the modern word:

cyning	king	*cwen*	queen
god	good	*lif*	life
sang	song	*folc*	folk
hu	how	*worold*	world
heal	hall	*hearpe*	harp
eall	all	*heofon*	heaven
geong	young	*weorc*	work
hlud	loud	*feor-weg*	faraway

There are, among the many verb forms, some that are only a few letters away from our modern forms:

funden	found	*stod*	stood
dydon	did	*dælde*	dealt
gyfen	given	*hyran scolde*	should hear/obey

But, of course, not all Old English words are as transparent as these. Some are completely different:

ellen	brave deeds	*wuldor*	glory
wig	war	*ðeoden*	prince
wine	friend	*fela*	many
yþ	wave	*mod*	mind
here	army	*sinc*	treasure
symbel	feast	*sele*	hall

Like Modern English, Old English had synonyms. In addition to this new word (wine) for "friend," they also used "freond," and two words appear in these lists for "hall."

It is beyond the scope of this work to explain how words were used within sentences and how endings changed as the word's role changed. For ambitious students who wish to explore the original text of *Beowulf* but do not have training in the language, some translations include the Old English on a page facing the Modern English. For help with deciphering the Old English, Michael Alexander's edition of the original text (1995) gives a glossary of words as they appear, rather than a finished translation, to save the step of looking them up in a dictionary.

Royal names were made up of two elements that had positive meanings. Beowulf, for example, is "bee wolf," which is usually thought to suggest a bear. Hrothgar is "glorious spear," Hrothulf is "glorious wolf," and their noble doorkeeper, Wulfgar, is "wolf spear." Wealhtheow's name, "foreign slave," is the puzzling one, as its elements are not positive. In Ecgtheow, "sword slave," the elements are more positive and suggest perhaps an addiction to sword fighting. Unferth is usually taken to mean "not peace" (although it may begin with an "H"). Beowulf's young kinsman, Wiglaf, is "war remnant," which may be a fitting name for a war orphan. Hygelac seems to mean something like "thought gift" or possibly "thought strife," and his queen Hygd is "thought," an old form of our modern word "heed."

By knowing just a few name elements, we can understand the names of several Anglo-Saxon kings. In the line of King Alfred the Great of Wessex, his older brothers and sister all were named "Aethel" as a first element, which means "noble." Alfred, however, was named "Elf counsel." "Raed" meant counsel or advice, and both Alfred's next older brother and his great-grandson were named "Aethelraed," which is more commonly spelled "Ethelred." The famous nickname of his great-grandson Ethelred, the "Unready," does not refer to his slowness in putting on his shoes but to his reception of poor advice ("un-ræd"). Throughout the period of Germanic kings on the continent, in Scandinavia, and in England, certain name elements may have fallen into and out of fashion. In early years, not all royal names followed the pattern of having two elements (Offa, mentioned in *Beowulf*, is an example).

It is uncertain how ordinary people were named, for only a few examples remain. Some documents provide us with short names, such as "Dudda," "Bebba," "Dunne," and "Golde" (a girl's name). Common people may have used such short names, or animal names like "Wulf." These may have been the ancient equivalent of traditional nicknames like Bob and Peg, or Shorty, Red, and Chip.

POETIC LANGUAGE

The main aspects of Old English poetry are stress-based meter, alliteration, and poetic word usage. Old English poetry was radically different from the poetry we know today. Modern English poetry uses a metrical system originally based on Greek verse patterns, such as iambic, trochaic, and anapestic. These patterns are measured in Greek; a set of four metrical patterns is called a tetrameter, a set of five patterns is called a pentameter, and so on. Modern English poetry uses a system of identical or similar sounds in the last syllable of each line; in other words, it uses rhyme. It uses words in poetic ways that are either heavy on analogical ideas or (in contemporary use) intended to startle a reader with incongruity. None of these devices appear in Old English poetry.

English in all of its ages has been a language based on word stress: every word has a syllable that is pronounced with slightly greater emphasis. The arrangement of these stresses into patterns has always been a part of poetry, although the patterns have changed. In Anglo-Saxon times, the pattern was less prescribed and not unlike the nursery rhymes that preserved some of the sounds. In each line there were four main word stresses allowed, and the lines tended to break into halves. The first half was called the "on verse," and the second half was called the "off verse":

Hwaet! we Gar-Dena / in gear-dagum (1)

The number of light, unstressed syllables could vary, and the clever use of these sound variations was one of the skilled poet's tools.

While there is a large number of syllable variations, since the number of unstressed syllables was unrestricted, Old English half-lines tend to fall into five types, usually called by letters A through E. Here, Modern English phrases illustrate them, with the usual scholarly description in parentheses:

A: polished armor   (/x/x, where / is stress and x is not)
B: a hoard of gold   (x/x/)
C: a skilled harpist   (x//x)
D: King Athelstan   (//\x or //x\, where \ is a syllable with slight stress)
E: lost in the hills   (/\x/)

Of course, **A** could also be "polished his armor," since an extra unstressed syllable could always fit, **B** could be "a hoard of some treasures," and so on.

Tying the half-lines together, the significant stresses had to begin with the same sound. Not every stressed word needed to be alliterated, however. In the first half-line, typically two words alliterated, and in the second half-line, the first stressed consonant followed the pattern. There was wide latitude for variation. Consider these lines from the opening of the story of Finn, Hildeburh, and Hengest. Every word that falls into an alliterative pattern is capitalized:

ne Huru Hildeburh Herian ðorfte
Eotena treowe; Unsynnum wearþ
beLoren Leofum æt ðam Linden-plegan
Bearnum ond Broþrum; hie on geByrd hruron
Gare Wunde ðæt Wæs Geomuru ides.
(1071–1075)

Here we can see several distinct patterns. The first, third, and fourth lines in the group follow a typical pattern in which the two stresses consonants are echoed once in the second half-line. The second line illustrates another possibility, in which all vowels are considered to alliterate with each other, so that "Eotena" (Jutes) and "unsynnum" match. However, there is only one alliterative repeat in each half-line, not two. The last line of this passage shows a more complex possibility. The sounds *g* and *w* are repeated in reverse order in the second half-line. As a new complication, "geomuru" was pronounced as though beginning with a "y" instead of a "g." The sound possibilities represented by one letter were treated as though they were the same; as though a modern poet used a sort of sight alliteration between the "s" in "sing" and in "trees."

The sounds of Old English verse, then, were created by this constant interplay of stress patterns and sound similarities. The effects were every bit as sophisticated as the use of metrical variation and internal rhyme in the poetry of T. S. Eliot. The variations have kept scholars busy for 200 years; scholars catalogue the possibilities and try to see if there is any regularity to how these options were used to convey meaning. So much time has passed since the days of the Anglo-Saxon audience that it is difficult to know how they truly perceived these matters. The more sophisticated subtleties of each time are buried with the living men and women who used them, unless they are written down. While Aristotle helpfully catalogued his feelings about Greek poetry, no Anglo-Saxon took up this task, and so it is a matter of highly educated guesswork.

Poetic diction, in Old English poetry, involved an enormous vocabulary. Much of it may have been archaic to the poet, as a modern poet might use "o'er" for the word "over." There appears to have been a large stock of synonyms to draw from to fit the occasion and the place in the line, and if no synonym was convenient, the poet was free to make one up. These made-up phrases, usually called "kennings," are one of the primary features of Old English poetry and make it difficult to translate without artificiality.

In the opening lines of *Beowulf*, three direct uses of the word "sea" are avoided through poetic phrases that imply the sea without using the word. In line 10, Scyld arrives "ofer hron-rade," while in line 200, Beowulf sets out in his new ship "ofer swan-rade." The sea in this case is the road for whales or swans, and the description of both whales and sea birds on the water made it instantly clear what sort of road the poet meant. In line 239, the Danish Coast Guard states that Beowulf has come "ofer lagu-strǽte" (over the water-street). It is likely that these kennings were stock phrases that had been employed in verse well before *Beowulf*, but surely kennings could also be original. To create a recognizable but fresh circumlocution would be a mark of creative flexibility. Because we have only a limited amount of literature from this period, we cannot know if even a phrase used only once in our texts is truly original. Of course, it is also impossible to know if its first use was actually a moment of literary creation, or if it already existed in oral usage. Even in modern times, there are phrases used in everyday conversation that rarely appear in written literature.

Similar to the kennings are the frequent compound expressions. In just the first sixteen lines of Beowulf's fight with Grendel, for example, we find "evening-speech," "fen-lair," "harm-foe," "city-dwellers," "ale-sharing," "wine-hall," "battle-daring," "earth-dwelling" ("fold-bold" in Old English), "iron bonds," and "artful-thought." These are descriptive phrases, rather than circumlocutions: one word modifies the other. They are much closer to our modern words "doghouse" and "mailbox." While the modern compounds have become specific words, the Old English compounds remained mostly fluid so that a poet could create these compounds at will. This was another that allowed for creativity and artistry.

The effect of these poetic techniques is to make Old English poetry a highly civilized, sophisticated art that is difficult to translate. Translators must make many choices in converting it to Modern English, in spite of the closeness of old and modern vocabulary. Can a "kenning" be converted to a reasonable modern equivalent? Should a compound phrase be split, and is there a better modern compound that might recapture the sense of the original? Is there any way to choose words that imitate the original alliteration, or is there any way to create a new one? Is it better to create a more natural-sounding modern sentence and use only the slightest alliteration, or is it better to create an archaic-sounding sentence that rings out the l's or m's the way the old lines did? Can the four strong stresses of the line be preserved in a translation? If either the stresses or the alliteration could be imitated, which is more central to the verse form? (For examples of some of these translation choices, see Chapter 2, "Choosing a Translation.")

The only real way to explore the intricacies of Old English verse is to find a basic textbook and try translating one of the easier texts. Beginners may have the easiest time with *First Steps in Old English* (Pollington, 1997), while more experienced language students may prefer *A Guide to Old English* (Mitchell and Robinson, 1982). The easiest prose occurs in Aelfric's *Colloquy*, a work originally composed in Latin to teach everyday words but "glossed" by some unknown monk with the Old English words (the way a student might pencil English words above a Spanish sentence). The easiest poetry could be "Maxims," the title of two poems that lay out an ideal view of what life should be (the wolf belongs in the forest, the king in his hall, the fish in the sea). Ambitious students may be tempted to jump right into *Beowulf*, a rewarding but very difficult exercise.

FURTHER SUGGESTED READING

Alexander, Michael. *Beowulf*. New York: Penguin Books, 1995.

Bliss, A. J. *The Metre of Beowulf*. Oxford: Blackwell, 1962.

Fulk, Robert D. *A History of Old English Meter*. Philadelphia: University of Pennsylvania Press, 1992. (This includes an explanation of metrical technicalities such as Kaluza's Law.)

Lewis, C. S. "The Alliterative Meter." In *Essential Articles for the Study of Old English Poetry*, eds Jess B. Bessinger, Jr. and Stanley J. Kahrl. Hamden, CT: Archon Books, 1968.

Mitchell, Bruce. *An Invitation to Old English and Anglo-Saxon Literature*. Oxford: Blackwell, 1995.

———. *On Old English*. Oxford: Blackwell, 1988.

Mitchell, Bruce, and Fred C. Robinson. *A Guide to Old English*. Toronto: University of Toronto Press, 1982.

Pollington, Stephen. *First Steps in Old English*. Hockwold-cum-Wilton, UK: Anglo-Saxon Books, 1997.

Pope, John C. *The Rhythm of Beowulf*. New Haven: Yale University Press, 1942. (This explains the meter with musical notation.)

Robinson, Orrin C. *Old English and Its Closest Relatives*. Stanford: Stanford University Press, 1992.

Shippey, T. A. *Old English Verse*. London: Hutchinson, 1972.

10

Religion in *Beowulf*

To the extent that *Beowulf* presents any religion at all, it is a blend of Christian and pagan ideas and feelings. Just what the blend consists of is a matter of some debate. Is the poem originally pagan but altered to a Christian form? Or is it originally Christian, depicting ancient pagan life as historical fiction? Or does it show us the patchwork of Christian and pagan beliefs still alive in its audience?

While Anglo-Saxon Christianity is well documented, the earlier pagan practices are not. It is impossible to determine exactly what parts of the poem show pagan influence, when no one knows what that influence would look like. We lack sources on pagan beliefs and practices simply because the pagan Germanic tribes did not use writing; and when writing came with the Celtic and Roman missionaries, it was not used to write about paganism. There are hints of what the Anglo-Saxons believed before Christian conversion, which we usually supplement with the fuller, but much later, records of Norse paganism. We know the history of the Christian conversion and how Christian beliefs developed. By putting together the facts and conjectures, we can form a sense of the religious belief of *Beowulf*.

PAGAN BELIEFS

Because there are so few records left, any description of pagan practices must be one-half guesswork. We can read a Christian description of the pagan calendar of months, some anecdotes in historical chronicles, and the hints that show up in books of medical remedies and charms. Of course we can draw on the Norse belief system, but we do not know how closely this system resembled English practice. Norse beliefs, as given in the medieval Icelandic poems and prose, could be very similar to English pagan beliefs, or they could represent some changes in emphasis. They were written down several centuries later and in a different place.

We know that the basic outline of the Norse pagan gods was used in early England. Four days of the week are named for Tiw, Woden, Thor, and Freya (spelling varies). In the Norse system, Woden, more commonly spelled Odin in Icelandic sources, was the king of gods and also the lord of poetry and death. Thor, the god of lightning and thunder, seems to carry his hammer in England as well as in Iceland. Frey and Freya were brother and sister, and the god and goddess of love. Tiw, or Tyr, was a god of war. These names also show up as the names of places in England: Woden's many place names include Wednesbury and Wansdyke; Thundersley and Thundridge are named for Thor; Tuesley and Tysoe are named for Tiw; and Fryup and Frobury are named for Freya.

According to legend, Odin, presumably the same as Woden, once hung himself on the "World Ash Tree" for nine days until he became the master of secret runes. An Anglo-Saxon collection of herbal medicines and spoken charms preserves a reference to this feat in the Nine Herbs Charm. This charm is unique in naming Woden directly. An infection is personified in the form of a snake, and the charm states that Woden struck the snake with nine "glory-twigs" and it flew into nine pieces, which represents the healing of the infection. The charm instructs the healer to cut runes of the herbs he is using into nine sticks. The repeated use of the number nine is supposed to recall the nine days that Woden hung. Woden/Odin was also the master of runic mysteries, from the knowledge he gained on the World Ash Tree, and these runes were supposed to have their power when they were cut into wood. Norse Odin is associated with ravens and is the god of battle and victory.

Thor and Tiw ("Tyr" in Norse) were gods of fighting. Tiw's spear-shaped rune and Thor's hammer are found as emblems on weapons all through the English pagan period. Tiw was honored by sword dances, and we find pictures of men dancing with swords as decorations on some helmets from this period. Norse stories tell of Thor making raids on the frost giants with his mighty hammer and driving a chariot pulled by mighty goats. These same stories could have been part of early Anglo-Saxon fireside tales.

Less is known about some gods who may have been more important to the Germans of the Eastern coastal plain, who migrated to England.

The "Runic Poem," which explains the names of each rune, includes a god named Ing, who "was first among the East-Danes seen, till he later departed over the sea." The name of Ing appears in *Beowulf* as one of the nicknames of the Danes: the "Ingwines," or friends of Ing. Who was Ing? Ing may have been another name of Frey, the god of war and love. Swedish mythology considers them the same person. "Frea" means simply "Lord" in Old English and isn't really a proper name.

One intriguing fact about Frey is that his totem animal was the boar. The boar figures prominently in *Beowulf* as a fighting symbol on armor. The description of Beowulf's gear in the early poem mentions boar images on the war band's helms. We know that some of the helmets found by archeologists have boar figures on them. The fine helmet at Sutton Hoo has figures of boars over the eyepieces, and the helmet found at Benty Grange has a small sculpture of a boar as a crest. One of the two Geatish warriors who struck down Ongentheow in the feuds is named Eofor (the Boar). Guided by Norse mythology, we think more of Thor and his mighty hammer or Odin the King, but it is clear that warriors who were ordering helms put more value on the Boar.

Tacitus states that the eastern Germanic tribes worshipped a goddess, Isis, with an image inside a ship. The goddess that they worshipped was not the Egyptian Isis, but rather an Earth Mother figure that other sources call Nerthus. This Earth goddess was probably mixed with Norse beliefs about Ing/Frey's sister, Freya, goddess of love. The little we can tell about this worship suggests that its center was probably in the land of the Ingwines (the Danes). As Tacitus reports, there was a secret image of the goddess in a wagon (not a ship) drawn by two cows. The priest tended this wagon and allowed the cows to pull it where they wished. Where the wagon stopped, the goddess was said to be present, until the priest was ready to head the cows back to the secret lake where the image lived. After slaves washed down the wagon, they were drowned in the sacred lake. Human sacrifice was almost certainly a feature of earth worship. The bodies recovered from Danish bogs, having been ritually killed by strangling, could have been offered to the Earth Mother in a place where they knew the earth would draw the body down and out of sight, as it sank in the bog and "Nerthus" took her offering.

Even during Christian Anglo-Saxon times, there were rituals to heal a "sick field" that called on the "earth's mother." All through the Middle Ages, there were country customs of Harvest Queens and May Queens. As late as the 1800s, some country people of England still celebrated harvest time with a robed shock of wheat in a wagon. These customs are almost certainly festivals based on the old pagan festivals of earth worship, even if the country folk no longer believed in the pagan gods as such. It is likely, too, that in the minds of the everyday Anglo-Saxons, the customs honoring the Harvest Queen, or Nerthus/Freya, were more important than those honoring Woden or Thor.

Herbert (1994) suggests that one part of *Beowulf* that may directly be an expression of an old pagan myth. The poem opens with the death of Scyld, the son of Scef and the father of another Beowulf. There are a few independent accounts of this person who arrived in a boat. In these others, the baby who arrived in a boat was not Scyld, but Scef; and the son of Scyld was not Beowulf, but Beow. These different accounts must be based on some original story that is lost to us. It may be the story of Sheaf (of grain) who arrived as a gift from the gods, and, through his son Shield, gave the people Beow (Barley). Perhaps this version reflects an old, even forgotten, myth. If the round Shield could represent the round sun, then the sun is needed to warm the sheaf of seeds to produce a crop of barley. Another reason to believe that the story shows us a pagan myth is that the later people of Denmark had no such story of their founding kings. The story is only found in English sources; the English may have known it as a myth associated with the country that they came from, the country of the Ingwines. There is no question, however, that a farming myth like this was far from the mind of the *Beowulf* poet. The confusion surrounding Scyld and his father, and the "error" in the name of Scyld's son (Beowulf rather than Beow), reveal that the poet knew nothing more than the basic story of the family.

Supernatural creatures abounded in the pagan world view. It is clear that the pagan Anglo-Saxons believed in many fantastical creatures such as elves, giants, trolls, and all kinds of monsters (see Chapter 3, "Grendel"). Their view of world history may have included the Norse scenario in which the old gods died after fighting a doomed battle. It certainly included the three Fates who governed history. We know only the North Germanic names for these "Three Sisters," but it is clear that the Angles and Saxons must have used similar names. They were called, essentially, "Was," "Being," and "Shall Be"; or in Norse, "Wyrd," "Verdandi," and "Skuld." There is no record of what the early English called two of the Fates, but "Wyrd" remains in the Old English language as the word for "Fate."

The "Three Sisters" is a concept that is found all over the European world. By any names, they are the immortal sisters who control history. One is very old and represents the past that controls the conditions of the present. One is grown but not old and represents the present and the necessities of our everyday life. One is young but mysterious, perhaps with a covered face, and represents the unknown future that the others control. The Three Sisters are most often shown in the process of weaving cloth, an image of time. They occur in Greek and Roman literature, as well as in *Macbeth* and in the fairy tale "Sleeping Beauty." These Fates were always ageless and above the gods. Their decrees could not be escaped. Whatever stories the Anglo-Saxons knew about the Fates, we know that they used the name "Wyrd" to mean the inescapable decree of the day of one's death.

The pagan Germanic tribes' values, however, were based on heroic action. The other side of Wyrd is that since fate cannot be changed, it can usually be ignored. If a warrior is fated to die, then he will die, but if he is not fated to die, then courage will help him become famous and honored. They valued bold action, not passive acceptance. Bold action was often needed in defense of the greatest good, the king and his hall. Bold action, not passive acceptance, complemented the loyalty that they required at every level.

Loyalty, the highest Germanic value, also meant loyalty in a marriage. When princesses married kings they had never met, they remained faithful for life. Tacitus described how the entire society banded together to persecute adultery, deeming it disloyalty of the worst kind. Tacitus admired this ethic, just as later English missionaries admired the same ethic in pagan Saxons (in modern Germany). Loyalty also meant the duty to vengeance if one's kin or lord were slain. This duty was absolute and resulted in complex feuds in which each generation committed new murders to be revenged. Pagan Anglo-Saxon culture was not a safe place for mistakes.

Christian Conversion

The Christian conversion of the pagan Anglo-Saxons was mostly peaceful. On the island of Britain, they were surrounded by Christian kingdoms. To the west, Ireland had been Christian since St. Patrick, a Briton, had served there as a slave and then come back as a free missionary. To the east, the Franks had become Christians with the rest of the Roman Empire. As the period of migration to Britain ended, two missions began to bring the Christian religion to the fierce Germanic pagans.

In AD 597, a small group of Roman monks arrived in the coastal land of Kent, which had been settled by Hengest's descendents (according to legend). The monks were sent by Pope Gregory, who had seen blond slave boys arriving in Rome and was determined to send missionaries to this people who were previously unknown. His pun is famous: hearing that they were "Angles," he called them "Angels"; hearing they were from a kingdom called Deira, he stated they must be saved "de ira," or from the wrath of God. The small band of missionary monks was afraid that the people of Kent were far from angelic and considered turning back to avoid certain death. To their surprise, they found that King Aethelbert of Kent was married to a Frankish princess who had her own Christian priest and church. The King decided that he would not stop them from freely preaching since they had taken the trouble to come so far for what they felt was the truth, so he allowed them to set up a base at his queen's church. Since that time, Canterbury has been the center of the English church.

Far to the north, the child Oswald (son of the King of Northumbria) fled into exile on the Irish island of Iona. There he became a Christian. When he returned in 636 to take back his kingship, he brought a band of monks led by Aidan. They founded a monastery on the rainy, cold island of Lindisfarne, off the Atlantic coast of northern Britain. The spirituality and holiness of Aidan's monks became legendary, and gradually the people of Northumbria were converted. The Christian faith spread, through Roman or Irish priests, until it was the dominant faith by 650. By 700, all of the Anglo-Saxon kingdoms professed Christianity.

Early on, Pope Gregory advised his missionaries on how to deal with the newly-converted English. He suggested that the monks should not make the people give up their usual customs. If a place had been sacred to their gods, the monks should build a church there because they were already used to going there. If there was a holiday or festival, they should find a Christian saint or event that they could substitute, and thus keep the same festival. The Pope felt that it would be asking too much for these people to give up all of their customs with little to substitute. The resulting synthesis of customs and beliefs not only gave us many familiar holidays, but it also at once preserved and masked the pagan customs. We may still practice some aspects of Yule (such as eating pork on New Year's Day), but the reason why we do this has long since been obscured. Christmas and Easter were both created on this model: Easter is the name of an Anglo-Saxon pagan goddess. While we all know her name, we know little about her. Her spring festival was transformed into the feast of Christ's resurrection, giving us an odd, modern blend of religious and springtime imagery.

Christian and Pagan Values Blend

Many of the pagan values fit well into the new Christian teachings. We can understand how the early English viewed the new religion by reading the poetic versions of Bible stories that they eventually created. God is the king and lives in the hall of heaven. The angels are his war band, and Satan is the warrior who betrayed his lord and tries to stir up a civil war in the hall. Adam's lack of loyalty to his lord causes him to be exiled; Noah's loyalty to God is rewarded. Jesus is the young warrior who comes to earth to fight with Satan, and he succeeds by leaping onto the cross so eagerly that it almost falls over (as in "The Dream of the Rood"). Each Bible story was seen through the prism of Germanic values of loyalty and bold action. Just as with the Easter festival, there seemed little need for real change. Similarly, the Christian teaching of marriage fit into their scheme well, since both systems emphasized making and keeping vows. For those entering monasteries, making and keeping vows was not a foreign concept, and the head of the religious order became the new Lord to whom loyalty was due. Probably the high amount of overlap in ethical values was one of the reasons that the conversion was so apparently easy.

The pagan value that did not fit into this scheme was revenge. The kin's duty to vengeance was contrary to Jesus' teaching to love an enemy and forgive a sin. The law codes of the English kingdoms began to encourage payment rather than murderous revenge. Some monks were reluctant to tell Bible stories that described vengeance. At least one scribe deliberately mistranslated a Psalm that discusses revenge; the wording was changed into something more positive and peaceful. In spite of this care, feuds continued all through the Christian centuries. It is likely that this point was never resolved except in the most devout followers, but it remained a point where the cultural values and religion clashed.

The new converts had to decide if the Christian religion interfered with their habits of war. In most cases, they did not see a problem with fighting even other Christian believers or making alliances with pagans to wage war. Even some of the monks had been warriors, and they still continued to fight if attacked. They felt no contradiction in praying for victory before a battle. One notable exception to this ethic was King Edmund of Northumbria during the time of Viking attacks, who found himself unable to mount a defense and chose to die a martyr's death by meeting the Vikings alone and unarmed. Most of the Christian kings continued to fight against not only invaders, but each other.

Pagan beliefs, just like pagan holidays, sometimes found a new home. Perhaps some country folk whispered to each other that Woden had hung on a tree just like Christ, or that Jesus and his mother Mary were like Ing and his mother Nerthus. Just as the gods had once blessed the harvest, the new Creator God sent the sunshine to bring the same harvest. The harvest ritual could go on in the name of the Father, complete with a robed shock of wheat or barley. A boar could be roasted for Yule, and God's blessing could be asked for a prosperous new year. Even monsters could be fitted into the Christian world (through Cain), and elves that persecuted innocent men with sickness or poor harvest were just spirits of Satan. "Wyrd," the controlling arm of Fate, became God's will and decree. The idea continued but with a different face. The word continued, too; it was no longer the name of a goddess but of an idea. Every Anglo-Saxon knew that some men were doomed to die and became "fey," and then nothing could save them. "Wyrd" was accepted as one of the facts of life.

This is not to say that the Anglo-Saxons, the early English, were not devout Christians. In any culture, level of belief varies among individuals, both with personal devotion and with education. But overall, even if some country folk still cut runes into their weapons, the people of Mercia, Northumbria, Wessex, and the other kingdoms were orthodox, cheerful believers in the new faith. The century after conversion, they began sending out missionaries to their relatives, the Saxons. These missionaries met with success but also with some failures, and some died. They were embraced as saints, and enthusiasm for converting the heathen continued. Pope Gregory had recommended not confrontation with paganism, but synthesizing its customs with Christian teaching. If his aim was the overall conversion not just of people but of society as a whole, then it worked.

CAEDMON

A significant change in English literature came about when an illiterate cowherd had a vision. While today we may be skeptical about such stories, it is told in detail in Bede's *Ecclesiastical History*, and it is told with full confidence in the truth of what happened. Among the peasants who staffed the monastery farm at Whitby in Northumberland, there was a shy, illiterate man named Caedmon who always left the room when people called out for song. He did not know any songs and was afraid of being put on the spot. One night, an angel appeared to him and commanded him to sing. He found that he could sing, and his first song was a hymn of praise for creation. The abbess of the monastery heard of his song, examined him, and decided to relieve him of all cowherd duties so that he could compose more songs. Caedmon's original hymn was preserved in several dialects in different manuscripts, and it could be described as one of the biggest hit songs of the Anglo-Saxon period.

What was remarkable about Caedmon's hymn was that no one had yet thought of using their traditional poetry to sing about God. The Roman and Irish monks had brought the news of God through Latin, and Latin was clearly God's language. An educated monk like Bede could learn to write Latin poetry or read the Latin Bible, but no one thought of using their everyday language to create religious songs or poems. It is because Caedmon received this gift from an angel that the abbess and her council proclaimed his poetry to be acceptable and worthy of imitation.

Caedmon's hymn kept the old Germanic poetic form of meter and alliteration (see Chapter 9, "Language and Poetry"). It used phrases that were originally used in war poetry but were adapted for church use. For example, God is the "heaven-kingdom's guardian," just as a secular king might be the "glorious kingdom's guardian" or the "Geatish kingdom's guardian." The poem uses seven different substitutions for God's name, and the last one uses the term "frea," which means "Lord," but may have been the common name for the god Ing as well (see previous discussion). Caedmon freely used pagan habits and words to create Christian verse. The strongly accented words, colorful phrases, and repeated initial sounds are purely Germanic and have nothing to do with Latin verse.

Caedmon went on to sing other songs based on Bible stories that the monks read to him. As his amazing creations were written down and passed to other monasteries, he reformed literature. Even with the loss of many old manuscripts through time, we have two versions of Genesis and many other Bible passages that have not only been translated, but also recast into Old English verse. It is possible that Caedmon himself wrote some of these poems, but no one can know for sure, since manuscripts were rarely signed. By bringing together the oral tradition of Germanic verse and the writing abilities of the monks, the monastery at Whitby began a new tradition of genuine "English" Christian literature. This literature was a synthesis of native and foreign beliefs and customs. We can trace this same kind of synthesis throughout *Beowulf*.

BELIEF IN *BEOWULF*

During the nineteenth century, scholars viewed *Beowulf* as a relic of the lost pagan days. Any references to a Christian God were considered to be later insertions by monks who recopied the manuscript and touched it up to make it more acceptable. Most *Beowulf* scholars studied and speculated about which words and lines were "interpolations" and which lines were original. After Tolkien's 1936 lecture and paper, scholarship began to take the poem seriously as literature, and scholars began to study what was actually in the text, rather than what might have been in the text at a previous time. While *Beowulf* was still seen as very old (Tolkien himself dated it to 750), it began to be seen as more uniformly Christian. The pendulum swung so far to the other side that some papers presented Beowulf as a symbol of Jesus. With the more recent acceptance of later dates of composition, the poem's original Christian composition is more often accepted. It is probably a product of the Anglo-Saxon Christian values and reflects the inconsistencies and blends of the culture, not the changes made by a monk.

In *Beowulf* there are only two direct references to Bible stories. One is the connection of Grendel to the curse of Cain. The other is a fleeting reference to the Flood of Noah as Hrothgar is gazing on the giant sword hilt. Both stories are in Genesis; there are no references to Jesus, or even to Moses or King David. Some scholars speculate that the author of the poem was not well educated and did not know very many Bible stories. Others suggest the opposite and claim that because the stories he selected were not the best known, he must have been very well educated; perhaps in a monastery like Whitby. Another possibility is that these stories had a more pagan feel to the poet, since they spoke of revenge, kin slaying, and grand-scale disaster. The author may have chosen them because they best fit his story.

Christian references are more numerous in the first half of the poem. The poem is sprinkled with casual references to God, and it uses many phrases to name God. He is the "Almighty," the "Shepherd of Souls," "Holy God," the "Creator," the "Father," and many more. In the tradition of Caedmon, these names are not very different from the names for Hrothgar: the "Helm of the Scyldings," the "mighty one," and the "giver of treasure." They are notably Christian, however, not merely recast names of Hrothgar. Whether they were once used for the pagan gods is an open question. We can never know, since any oral poetry in Old English was lost.

The characters in the first part of the poem piously thank God for sending a hero to fight the monster or for victory in the fight. These comments give the poem much of its Christian coloring and also set up some of the tension in interpreting their meaning. We know that a historical Hrothgar could not have thanked the Bible's God of creation, so either the poet created an anachronism or the original poem said something different. The attitude of the Anglo-Saxons to their pagan Saxon relatives suggests that the poet may have written the anachronism as a tribute to the nobility of some pagans. It could be a suggestion that Hrothgar and Beowulf would have thanked the correct deity, if they had only known how.

There is no question that the text calls the Danes pagans, even while putting Christian-sounding words in their mouths. In the opening pages, lines 90–98 describe the Danes singing a song of Creation (perhaps Caedmon's song) in their new hall, while less than 100 lines later, they are sacrificing to pagan idols. Lines 175–188 may contain the most overt statement of religious belief. Using the narrator's voice, instead of the Danes' words, the poem tells us that in their desperation they turned to pagan gods and even prayed to the devil. In spite of their later words about the Almighty God, the narrator says that they did not know the true God, the Creator. Lest we think that his admiration for the noble pagans has made him sanction their religion, the narrator tells us that such things will only lead to fiery torment. To make it more explicit, he addresses the reader and exclaims how blessed is the one who can turn to the true God in time of need. There is no question that the narrator, in creating the anachronism of Hrothgar's thanks to the Creator, knew that he was being unhistorical.

The narrator himself demonstrates blended pagan and Christian beliefs in other ways. The pagan word "wyrd" and God's decree are used interchangeably. For example, when Hrothgar and Beowulf make speeches about his plans and prospects (440–572), the outcome of the fight with Grendel is said to be either in the hands of the Lord, or wyrd. Beowulf uses both words in one speech (440, 455). Does he mean "Wyrd," the goddess, one of the "Three Sisters," or "wyrd," an impersonal sense of fate which could simply be God's will? He firmly attributes his survival among the sea monsters to "wyrd," which had not doomed him. Later, in telling about the fight, Beowulf comments that the "Creator" allowed Grendel to escape. The narrator's voice tells us first that the sleeping men did not know the grim "wyrd" that awaited at Grendel's mother's approach, and second that when Beowulf escaped from the clutches of Grendel's mother, it was the "Lord" who decided the outcome. In the fight against the dragon, it is "wyrd" that controls the outcome (2526, 2574). Perhaps the word "wyrd" had come to mean a sense of inevitability, but the decree of God put a face on it. While the pagan warriors had known that "Wyrd" was either for or against them, the Christian warrior could comfort himself that a personal God looked down on him and controlled "wyrd" itself.

The narrator of the poem clearly shows a great interest in both fighting and treasure. In a time when fighting between the kingdoms, as well as fighting to defend against outside invaders, was so common, it is not surprising that both pagans and Christians would show an interest in hearing the details of a fight. While monks voluntarily lived in poverty, treasure was still highly valued in Christian society. In the coffin of St. Cuthbert of Northumbria, archeologists found a golden cross of fine workmanship and great value. Even the saintliest kings, such as King Alfred of Wessex, commissioned new jewels and treasures as their prosperity increased. And yet, as unsurprising as these interests are, they are clearly native Anglo-Saxon interests, not specifically Christian interests. They reflect the blended society's values rather than values based on the teachings of Jesus, who advised his followers to store spiritual treasure in heaven.

A poem based on the teachings of Jesus (as the monks must have expressed them) might have emphasized forgiveness, meekness, or kindness. Jesus spoke against vengeance very specifically. *Beowulf* comes down on both sides on the question of revenge. While Beowulf declares that revenge is better than mourning, the narrator shows less enthusiasm. Grendel's mother, after killing a Dane, took back her son's arm in clear token of her motive of vengeance for his death; the narrator comments that it is not a good exchange when both sides must trade the lives of their friends. Is this a Christian sentiment in opposition to the pagan values of the feud, or did the participants in most feuds view the tit-for-tat deaths as a bad exchange? While the narrator sighs over the deaths, he does not make any negative commentary on Beowulf's actions and seems to admit the correctness of revenge in this case, however sad it may be. He does not turn to the audience and comment that the hero's anger was understandable, but revenge will not win the favor of the Creator. The narrator either approves of the feud or is silent on the matter.

Loyalty and bold action, the two highest values of the war band, are the poem's highest values. Beowulf's bold action is praised at every turn, as he trusts "wyrd" for the outcome and forges ahead in his fight, his swim, or his battle. Loyalty takes center stage in the last episode, when Wiglaf stands up with Beowulf to fight the dragon. Wiglaf's harsh words against the other retainers spell out the code of the war band very clearly: when the king gives you treasures, you owe him your life, regardless of the circumstances. Is this a Christian sentiment? It is not part of the teachings of Jesus in their original form. But to the Anglo-Saxons, who saw Jesus as the leader of a new kind of war band and his followers as sworn retainers and thanes, it was part of his teachings. When Jesus said, "Take up your cross and follow me," and, "I will give you a heavenly mansion," the Anglo-Saxons heard new wording and applications for the law of the war band.

It is almost impossible to pick apart the values of the poem and label one part pagan or traditional and another Christian. The poem appears to present the same blended, patchwork philosophy as the Anglo-Saxon church and society. Until the poem can be definitively dated, we are left with the ambiguities of the text itself.

FURTHER SUGGESTED READING

Cavill, Paul. *Anglo-Saxon Christianity*. London: Fount Publications, 1999.

Cherniss, Michael D. *Ingeld and Christ: Heroic Concepts and Values in Old English Christian Poetry*. The Hague: Mouton, 1972.

Cox, Betty S. *Cruces of Beowulf*. The Hague: Mouton, 1971.

Crossley-Holland, Kevin. *The Norse Myths*. New York: Pantheon, 1981.

Damon, John Edward. *Soldiers, Saints, and Holy Warriors*. Burlington, VT: Ashgate, 2003.

Guerber, H. A. *Myths of the Norsemen: From the Eddas and Sagas*. New York: Dover Publications, Inc., 1992.

Herbert, Kathleen. *Looking for the Lost Gods of England*. Hockwold-cum-Wilton, UK: Anglo-Saxon Books, 1994.

Klaeber, Friedrich. *The Christian Elements in Beowulf*. Trans. Paul Battles. Kalamazoo, MI: Western Michigan Unversity, 1996.

Linsell, Tony and Brian Partridge. *Anglo-Saxon Mythology, Migration and Magic*. Hockwold-cum-Wilton, UK: Anglo-Saxon Books, 1994.

Mayr-Harting, Henry. *The Coming of Christianity to Anglo-Saxon England*. State College: Pennsylvania State University Press, 1991.

North, Richard. *Heathen Gods in Old English Literature*. Cambridge: Cambridge University Press, 1997.

Parker, Mary A. *Beowulf and Christianity*. New York: Lang, 1987.

Wilson, David M. *Anglo-Saxon Paganism*. Oxford: Routledge, 1993.

I I

Anglo-Saxon Culture

KINDS OF CULTURAL EVIDENCE

W E KNOW ONLY A LITTLE ABOUT Germanic culture before the conversion to Christianity and the introduction of writing. What we know comes from outsiders, for example the Roman historian, Tacitus. Tacitus described the Germanic tribes that the Romans encountered in the region of modern France and Germany around the year AD 70. As the Franks were converted, they began to write their histories; likewise, with conversion the English also began to write about their history and culture. Written sources from inside the Norse and Icelandic countries were even later, and most date from the tenth or eleventh centuries at the earliest.

With any examination of an ancient culture, there are two sources of evidence: written and archeological. This evidence may have been left deliberately, in the form of a carefully arranged burial or an organized history. It may also have been left more or less accidentally, like the rubble of a house or a trash pit, or a personal letter that survived the centuries. Ideally, the evidence of written history and archeology will agree with one another. For example, the type of tool mentioned in a letter will be uncovered in a dig, or the fort whose defense is described in an poem can be excavated. However, these ideal conditions seldom occur, and if written and archeological evidence conflict, an interpretative decision must be made. Which is accurate: the written information or the archeological findings? Did the writer bend the truth, or has the artifact not yet been found? Are we misinterpreting the objects or the writer?

Some cultural items are more numerous than others, based on what they were made from. Pottery keeps well when it is buried in the ground, so what is usually easiest to determine is what sort of cremation urns or pottery dishes were used. Metal may rust, but in some conditions it survives in a tarnished, crusted state. Wood, leather, and cloth rarely survive. Since the early Germanic people, of Beowulf's time, used these materials for much of their daily life, relatively little of their material culture can be found in a museum. They built houses with wood or mud rather than stone. They ate with wooden utensils rather than pottery. Some of their metal weapon or tool parts have survived in graves, and we can reconstruct the wooden parts from those findings. Some rare coffin burials (notably those of St. Cuthbert of Northumbria and Queen Arnegunde of the Franks) preserved cloth. The best-preserved artifacts are those that the people themselves valued most: gold and jewels. We have strings of amber beads and golden brooches that have lost nothing in their centuries below ground.

The bogs of Denmark and the low-lying Atlantic shores are a gruesome but effective preservation medium. Whole bodies have been recovered from the bogs, fully clothed and wearing their own tanned skin and hair. No one knows for sure who these mummies were, but the evidence suggests that they were prisoners of war and were strangled as a sacrifice. They may not have been Germanic; they could have belonged to any of the other neighboring tribes, such as the Celts or Picts.

DAILY WORK

There is ample record of the daily lives of early English people. There are wills and other legal documents, riddles that describe objects of daily life, and Aelfric's *Colloquy*. The *Colloquy* is a Latin document that discusses common occupations to teach the Latin words for tools and daily vocabulary. An anonymous monk inked in Old English words above the Latin, as a student might pencil English words in the margin of a Spanish book. Because of these markings, we can assemble a simple Old English text that describes what many common workers did. Another remarkable document that survived is a description of a generalized estate around 1000. It explains what each type of worker was due as compensation. The operation of a typical Anglo-Saxon estate is revealed, and some of the details even show us the customs of the country people.

The social system involved a complex system of hierarchy and obligations. At the top of the social ladder was the nobleman, or the thane. Like Beowulf, he owned many "hides." To be considered a thane, an

Anglo-Saxon noble had to own at least five hides (about a square mile). Some noblemen, of course, owned much more, as they were the forerunners of the modern dukes and earls of entire counties. The thane had his principal tenants, and they shared in his duties to the king. The thane typically had to pay for the equipping of a ship to do coast-guard duty (important in a time of piracy). He had to keep up fortifications of various kinds and make sure bridges were repaired. His principal tenants would share in these duties (more in the hands-on side than through funding). While the thane was to help maintain the king's deer fences, his tenants had to make sure the fence posts got cut. The thane, of course, had the duty of military service and personal attendance to the king for part of the year. Both the thane and his tenants shared in duties to the church. Apart from financial support of the official church, they had duties of charitable support for the poor.

The thane's wife or daughter had the same network of duties. Although one poem states that a woman's place was at her embroidery, a noblewoman could inherit land, and some women owned large estates. Among the wills and documents, there is one that records a land-owning mother who refused to grant a certain tract of land to her son and instead gave it to a female relative of her choosing. The most famous women of the time included King Alfred's daughter, Aethelflaed, and the Abbess Hild (or Hilda). Aetheflaed, widow of the Aldorman of Mercia, ruled Mercia and led a defense against the Vikings. She is known in history as the Lady of the Mercians, and she was as powerful as any king. Abbess Hild, who was born to a noble family, ruled a monastic community of both women and men at Whitby. Her community included the poet Caedmon, and his fame was partly due to her patronage and encouragement. While they also created large amounts of skilled embroidery, there is no doubt that Anglo-Saxon women had some degree of independence and power and were at the same social level as the men in their lives.

Some workers had duties on the thane's acreage, and their duties were quite different. Beekeepers, swineherds, cowherds, and all sorts of lower-level farmhands lived on the estate (often with their own garden plot). The ones whose duties did not seem time-consuming (beekeepers and swineherds) were expected to drop everything and help out with odd jobs, and they were to have a horse on hand for this purpose. Perhaps they worked on the bridges, fences, and fortifications. They may have been the people called on to repair wagons or other tools. In return, they were allowed to keep a set portion of the honey or pigs that they tended. If tenant farmers made use of the swineherd's services, they had to tip him loaves of bread.

Lower still on the social ladder were serfs with specific jobs; they were not much more than slaves. They worked hard and got little for it. The plowman in Aelfric's *Colloquy* complains of his lot and says he must work terribly hard because he is not free. The estate document bears him out; the payment a thane owed to his sower were nothing more than some extra seed, and the payments to an oxherd did not extend beyond allowing him to pasture his own oxen in the herd while moonlighting to earn his own shoes. The cowherd could pasture his own cows with the thane's herd, and the cheesemaker (probably the cowherd's wife) was allowed a certain number of her cheeses but had to make the thane's butter, as well. Granary-keepers were allowed the spilled grain, foresters were allowed to cut and sell firewood from trees blown down in storms, and hay-wardens could have a certain plot of hay right in the thick of the thane's hay fields (to give them an incentive to do a good job). As it is likely that some of these roles overlapped (perhaps a tenant farmer could be a forester in his spare time), the daily lives of these laborers were filled with long hours of hard work.

On the thane's side, he owed these hard-working, poor folk many small gifts that perhaps made their lives bearable. The thane might be expected to give them winter supplies, as well as Easter supplies. The workers expected certain feasts at harvest and after plowing. After mowing, they expected a tip and a meal at the haystack. Other tips were also expected, such as a free log from the wagon at woodcutting time. It was the little details that made the tenants and servants view a thane as good or bad; their opinion was not based on his moral character. In a medieval society, everyone had duties to perform for everyone else, and a large part of morality was based on the punctuality in carrying out these tasks. If the cheesemaker had to supply the thane with good butter, then she certainly expected a fine lunch to be supplied when she helped at hay time.

Slaves could be born into a slave's family or they could be prisoners of war. Commonly, they were children sold into slavery to pay their parents' debts, or adults sold into slavery as punishment for crimes. As the Christian era continued, some Anglo-Saxons felt sorry for owning slaves. Some left provisions in their wills to free their slaves.

The only women's work that the estate document describes is the cheesemaker. Aelfric's *Colloquy* overlooks women altogether. We can assume that the wives and daughters of the farmers and other workers were involved in the hard work of daily life. We can learn a little bit about their lives from the riddles, which mention daily details in giving (misleading) clues. In one riddle, there is a butter churn; in another, a girl goes out to the garden to pull an onion that makes her eyes water when she cuts it. Of course, raising children must have occupied a great deal of the women's time.

Towns allowed for many other workers who were not dependent on the thane's estate. The *Colloquy*, which is written as a series of interviews, finds a hunter, a fisherman, a fowler, a merchant, a shoemaker, a saltmaker, a baker, and a cook. The hunter works directly for the king by supplying his table with wild game. But the others appear to be townspeople who sell their services. The merchant explains carefully that his plan is to buy low and sell high, while the fisherman describes the many types of sea life he can catch and how he sells them in the city. The names of his fish often ring true to modern ears, including eels, herring, lobsters, and crabs; many of these words are almost unchanged. Each craftsman argues that his craft is very important to the community. Perhaps the farm workers used their spare acres to eke out some extra food and exchange their goods for salt, shoes, and fish.

Names of animals and tools have changed little, mainly in spelling. The fisherman uses a boat, net, and angle; the hunter uses traps. The fowler lures hawks with birdlime and whistling; the cowherd makes butter and cheese. Tools like hammers, axes, and saws had similar forms and names, as did many farm animals (such as ox, cow, swine, and sheep). Many old words associated with farm work, handicrafts, ships, and boats have been preserved simply because so little changed in the related habits and technology before the twentieth century.

Below this network of "free" and "unfree" professions there was a class of criminals. The story of the martyrdom of King Edmund of East Anglia at the hands of Vikings includes a story of how thieves tried to break into the church built over his grave. They were stopped, of course, by the dead saint, who froze them into poses with their tools. One had a hammer, one was working with a file, one carried a spade, and one stood on a ladder. The image of thieves breaking into a building at night has not changed much over many centuries.

Every criminal class implies some kind of structure aimed at keeping order. The primary agent for keeping order in a town was called a Reeve, and since many market towns were located on the water, the Reeve was also in charge of the port. The duties of a Reeve might include the actions of the guard who met Beowulf on the Danish coast, who was responsible for finding out who was coming into the port and why. The Reeve was also responsible for following up complaints in the market and keeping order. The Reeve of a "shire" (comparable to an American "township") was a Shire-Reeve, which was shortened over many years to "sheriff."

Parallel to this secular structure, Christian England had many priests and monastic communities. At the top were the saints, who battled monsters and demons and performed many good works and miracles, and just below them were the bishops, the thanes of the church. Monasteries were somewhat independent and self-supporting, and were ruled by abbots. Local priests, as well as religious communities, were supported by the landowners' church fees and tithes. The monastic communities were also the centers for preserving and copying manuscripts, and we certainly owe the survival of *Beowulf* to some monastery's diligence in maintaining its library.

It may surprise some readers that women in Anglo-Saxon times could own property, lead monasteries, and so on. We often have an image that women in past times were always oppressed, but this is not true. By Tacitus' account, the Germanic tribes considered their women to be very powerful in their own right. Tacitus states that some women were thought to have mystical power as seers, a claim borne out by other accounts. When the men went into battle, the women stood nearby and cheered them on, urging them to fight harder. Tacitus explains that because the men only wanted to fight and were slothful about farming, they allowed their women to run the estates with the help of the old men. Whether this is a fair characterization of the Germanic men, it is true that from earliest times the Anglo-Saxons and other Germanic peoples allowed women to own land and manage households. The ring of keys hanging on a woman's belt was a sign of her real authority, and some accounts make it clear that she had the keys to the man's chests of treasures, not just to the kitchen.

The poetic term for a king's daughter or sister who is given in marriage to form an alliance is a "peace-weaver." The king who received the bride was required to give her a large amount of treasure to seal the bargain, and often this treasure included estates. The bride was expected to carry her nation's honor on her shoulders and make a good impression everywhere she went. Some of these foreign brides achieved great influence and wealth, and some ruled on their own. Some of them were seen as sources of power, so much so that an invading king would go to great lengths to marry them. Canute, the Danish king who conquered England in 1016, married the English king's widow, who had been a Norman "peace-weaver" princess.

In a Byzantine Greek history by Procopius, there is a very early story (although sketchy and unreliable in its details) of an Anglo-Saxon princess. The story is dated around Beowulf's time; perhaps twenty years after the death of Hygelac. A young king among the coastal lands, at the mouth of the Rhine River, became entangled in two marriage alliances at the same time. He married a Frankish princess (the sister of Hygelac's slayer), while officially "married" to a princess of the "Angles." He had sent the betrothal gold to Angle-land (England), but he married the Frankish princess before the Anglo-Saxon bride could arrive. The Anglo-Saxon princess responded by personally leading a military invasion, and when her men had tracked down the bridegroom she demanded an explanation and required him to send the Frankish bride home. The "peace-weavers" were not doormats.

In Anglo-Saxon times, women worked and traveled and led lives as full as the men's lives. In a time when no one had much control over what happened, the women had as much control as most men. They functioned as near-equals to the men in their lives all across the social order.

EDUCATION AND THE CHURCH

Before the arrival of Christianity, education meant oral learning. A boy like Beowulf would have learned many stories and histories in his grandfather's court, and he would have learned the traditions of law. Education meant learning a trade, whether it was skill with weapons, or goldsmithing, or farming.

The centers of learning were the towns that rose around trade routes and around royal residences. There is evidence that these towns in the sixth century were far from being a cluster of poor huts and instead were large and prosperous. They were centers of manufacturing as well as of trade, including glassmaking, blacksmithing (of weapons as well as tools), goldsmithing, polishing amber and garnet (local Scandinavian resources), and manufacturing small items like combs. They also built ships, a key craft in times when water was the main highway. Priests usually kept the traditions of teaching not only religion, but also law. In medieval Iceland, "priest" was the term for lawyer. Royal centers, religious centers, and law schools would therefore come together at places like Heorot or Uppsala (the capital of the Swedes).

Writing existed only as runic scripts. Runes were made in imitation of Latin letters, but they had been created through slight contact during the early years; perhaps in Tacitus' time. Runes bear only a vague resemblance to Roman letters and include many added symbols. They were mostly used to mark someone's property or to make a memorial in a public place. Of course, they also had a magical property connected with Odin/Woden and were probably most used in the temple centers by priests. To cut runes into something could mean to cast a spell. Runic writing

RUNES

F U TH O R C G W

H N I (J) (IH) (X) P S

T B E M L NG D OE

AE A EA Y ST Q

Chart of the Anglo-Saxon runic system, commonly called "futhorc" (also spelled "futhark") after the first six letters. (Stephen Pollington, *Rudiments of Runelore*. Hockwold-cum-Wilton: Anglo-Saxon Books, 1995.)

was never used to keep histories or write down legends. It was not even much used for communication, personal letters, or public documents.

After the arrival of Christianity, writing in Latin became the primary feat of education. Monasteries were the new centers of learning, and traditions of law expanded to tap into Roman law as brought in Latin documents. The Anglo-Saxon kings quickly made use of writing to create written law codes. We have around ten different law codes of varying place and time, beginning with King Aethelbert of Kent. He quickly realized the usefulness of the monks' writing skills and wrote out a list of fines for many different crimes. Perhaps to make use of writing for people without any hope of learning Latin, Latin letters were adapted to express Old English sounds, with the addition of a few runic symbols. Unlike the runic tradition, Latin-influenced use of writing was pervasive and preserved letters, jokes, poetry, law codes, and Bible commentaries.

King Alfred is famous for his love of learning. As a small child he had traveled to Rome to meet the Pope, and he had seen the wonders of the

Roman world. When he was older, his mother showed him and his brothers a book. It had pictures and a jeweled cover. She promised it to the child who could first learn to read (or recite) its contents, and Alfred won. As an adult, he admitted that he had not learned to read very well, but when he was not fighting a war, he spent many hours learning to read, and more. He doggedly studied Latin and attempted his own translations of Latin works into Old English. He sponsored a school for his and his thanes' children and brought many scholars together to preserve old texts. The *Anglo-Saxon Chronicle*, our best historical record of the times, was probably begun in Alfred's time.

FOOD

Food in the time of Beowulf and Hrothgar must have been similar to food in later Anglo-Saxon times. The Germanic tribes depended on hunting and raising grain and dairy. Although Tacitus reported that the Germans of the year 100 were not fond of farming and avoided it, the tribal lands of the continent must have had many small farms to supply the bread, cheese, and ale that feasting required.

Wheat, rye, and barley were the staple grains of the time. Wheat was preferred in England for its better taste and lighter texture. Bread, called "hlaf" in Old English (our word "loaf" comes from this), was more like the artisan bread than like commercial bread sold in plastic bags. In a time when metal was precious, bread would not be baked in a pan of any kind but rather as a lump on a board. An oven was a luxury that most individuals could not afford. While early bread must have been baked on a flat stone over a fire (similar to tortillas or chapattis), by Anglo-Saxon times villages had bakers and ovens. The large medieval oven could surround multiple loaves of bread with even heat for real baking. Accounts of how much a worker should be paid or how much was owed to the church or the king will always mention a large number of loaves. Two loaves of bread per day was considered normal rations for a working adult.

Bread was eaten with meat or cheese. People all over the known world raised cattle, and the ancient word for money stemmed from the word for cattle ("fee" is derived from this ancient word). Cattle would not have been eaten for meat until their other uses were expended: their main contribution was milk and its preserved forms, cheese and butter. These two foods have changed so little that a time traveler to Anglo-Saxon England could ask for them with our modern words and be perfectly understood. We can picture a peasant's lunch consisting of large slices of a round loaf of coarse bread with large slices of a round cheese.

Meat for a feast like Hrothgar's was probably wild meat from hunting, especially deer, but as wild animals grew less common through the later centuries and farming became more established, meat at feasts more likely came from farms. Beef rated the highest, but pork and chicken were also considered good. Mutton was a poor man's meat. Anglo-Saxon farmers kept sheep, pigs, chickens, goats, and various fowl like ducks and geese. Pigs were expected to forage in the forest and live on acorns, so they were easy to keep. Farmers made sausages from scrap meat, since the covering on a sausage preserved it longer.

Farmers also grew all sorts of fruits and vegetables. There is no record of what Hrothgar might have served at his feast, or if anyone made sure to include a green vegetable. It is likely that some sort of fancy dish made from fruit would have been included. Anglo-Saxons cultivated apples, cherries, plums, and other fruits and berries. Just as their animals were probably smaller and leaner than modern animals, the fruits were not the large hybrids we see today. We know that onions were a common vegetable, due to a riddle preserved in Old English to which the answer is "an onion" (one clue is that it makes the eyes water). Cabbages were grown in England, but they were leafier than the hard, round heads we know today. They may have had some form of lettuce, radishes, beets, turnips, asparagus, and possibly cucumbers (Charlemagne grew them in France). Beans and peas were dried and included in soup and stew during the winter and spring. There were a limited number of herbs for seasoning and especially for medicines. The cheapness and popularity of onions made them the most likely side dish for the peasant's lunch on a summer day.

Fish were probably more plentiful in the first millennium than they are now. Hrothgar's court, on an island surrounded by sea, could easily have served fish or eels at the feast. The Anglo-Saxons could count on finding eels and lampreys in the lakes and streams, and they fished using hooks, nets, and traps for all kinds of sea life. Some hardy fishermen went out in groups of boats to catch whales in the sea. The other major contribution of the sea was salt, which was useful for taste but also for preserving.

What defines early Germanic and Anglo-Saxon food best for a modern audience is not what they had, but what they did not have. They had salt, but pepper was an expensive and rare import from Asia. They did not drink coffee, tea, or chocolate, which were discovered later in Asia and America. They probably did not grow carrots, and they certainly did not grow corn, broccoli, tomatoes, or potatoes. Most shocking is that they did not have sugar, since sugarcane was unknown. The only sweeteners were natural fruit sugar and honey. Honey was not easy to find, and it would not have been consumed very often. Among the charms and spells, we can read a charm for making a swarm of bees stay on a specific piece of property, so that only the property owner might benefit from their industry. Honey was needed to make mead, the highly prized, sweet alcoholic drink that Hrothgar served Beowulf.

An Anglo-Saxon feast was probably similar to Hrothgar's feast. It would have entailed large pieces of beef and venison roasted over the fire, with a stew of eels or a large, baked fish, a great deal of bread, the best butter and cheese, and many dishes created from the garden. There might have been applesauce to accompany the slightly dried-out meat, baked fruit and honey desserts, and spicy chopped onion and leek side dishes. Most importantly, there would have been ale and mead, as much of it as the women and slaves could prepare and store. It probably took several days to prepare a feast, unless the cooking crew was already prepared to make large meals and only needed warning to serve the best.

BUILDINGS

What did Hrothgar's hall look like? We do not know, because the early Germanic tribes built entirely with wood and there is now no trace of most of these buildings. They made no pictures and few descriptions, and so most discussion of their architecture is educated guesswork. This guesswork is based on the few clues that we find in works like *Beowulf*, the foundations of old buildings that archeologists can uncover, and some rare remaining buildings.

The most common remaining buildings are churches that are built with stone. One small, wooden Anglo-Saxon church remains, but there are many stone churches from these early centuries. They are identified by characteristic stonework techniques, particularly by how the corners were joined. Some of the churches have patches of old plaster inside with a few murals preserved. These murals are faded and sometimes overlooked, especially if they have been covered in some way. Many of the old churches have additions built in later times; the original Anglo-Saxon work may be a small chapel seemingly tacked onto a larger, Gothic church. Stonework seems to be something that the Anglo-Saxons learned from the Roman and British times, however, and there is no evidence that a sixth century hall on a Danish island would have used stonework.

Building foundations have been uncovered all over England and the European continent. Although dirt covered the foundations, careful excavation can reveal where the post holes and other foundation digging had been located. In many cases, there are other objects inside the outlines of the house. The most common kind is a small house's outline with stone or ceramic "doughnuts" inside it, along with bones and perhaps other small tools or stray beads. These small buildings had very deep foundations and are generally called Sunken Feature Buildings (SFBs). There is evidence that their walls did not rise more than a few feet and that their roofs were built low to the ground. In some rural marshlands of England, cottages with this construction were used into the 1800s; the roofs seemed to reach to the ground, because much of the house was underground. On the other hand, some archeologists believe that many or most SFBs had a wood floor built across the "cellar" and were just ordinary cottages. Evidence for either view entails examination of the doorways and of wood fragments that may or may not be remains of these floorboards. The variety of objects found in the sunken pits may reflect what the occupants kept in the pit or the things they tossed under the floorboards to be rid of them.

In any case, the mystery of the "doughnuts" was easily solved. Weaving looms all over Europe were large frames that rested against the wall, and the weft hung down to the floor. In order to keep these vertical strings tight, heavy stone weights were tied to each group of threads. These stone "doughnuts" are the weights, and they are often found still in a line, perhaps where they were dropped to the floor after the cloth was cut off. Were the loom weights simply abandoned when the family moved? Did the settlement get attacked and the weights get left behind because they were not worth looting? Did the house collapse, and the weights were not worth going back in for?

The existence of the loom weights, as well as other random small tools and stray beads (evidence that women were working in the huts), makes most archeologists believe that the SFBs were usually workshops, not living space. This is probably more certain when they occur scattered around the foundation of a larger building. The typical central building foundation in continental digs appears to include living space for humans and animals together. Certainly in remote, cold places like Iceland and Greenland, living spaces were this way because the heat from the cows kept the house warmer. English building foundations do not seem to allow space for animals, and the buildings are smaller. It is likely that the Anglo-Saxons broke with tradition and began to keep animals in separate barns, encouraged perhaps by a climate-warming trend during these centuries.

We know the least about large royal halls. They were constructed of wood, with huge trees turned into roof-supporting beams. The deep

Anglo-Saxon cottage, modeled after the reconstructed buildings at
West Stow village, a living history museum in East Anglia, England.
(Illustration by Ellen J. McHenry.)

holes dug for these massive posts have sometimes survived, since the dirt
was hard-packed by the posts and more loosely filled with dirt later. In
one dig in southern Sweden (in Slöinge), a large chunk of the post itself
remained and is now petrified. Its rings could still be counted, and this
information allowed the house to be dated to the year 710. The house
was thirty meters long, and the post holes were up to a meter across in
double rows. In the same region, another excavation turned up houses
even larger, up to thirty-five meters long. The houses were all long and
narrow and had doors at either short end. The walls curved slightly,
making the middle of the long house wider than its ends. There are
remains of central hearths, probably used more for light and heat than
for cooking. These central fires would have filled the houses with smoke,
since there were no real chimneys and only holes in the roof to let the
smoke out. The hall where the petrified post was preserved was probably a royal hall. There are many small gold figures with an apparent religious purpose; their presence suggests that some religious rites went on
here. In Old Norse times, these findings would indicate a king's residence.
Unfortunately, there is no written record to help us link this settlement
with kingdoms mentioned in *Beowulf*.

In England, only one large, early royal hall has been excavated. It is
in Northumbria at Yeavering. The site was discovered through aerial
photos that showed the crops slightly different in color in patches. The
dirt that had covered the ancient foundation retained water differently
according to what was underneath, and the wheat or hay above it showed
this difference in lighter or darker color. The excavation uncovered a very
large building on a plan quite unlike the long halls in southern Sweden.

It is much wider and had doors on all four walls. It probably had a higher roof, and the weight of the building could not be supported entirely by the posts and walls. All around the perimeter, there are small holes for supporting beams, as though someone went around the building and propped the walls up with two-by-fours. Behind the hall, and perhaps connected to it by a fence, there was a smaller hall that was either a barn or a smaller house for sleeping. Behind both of these buildings, there was a collection of buildings now considered to be a temple. Most surprisingly, there was a section of a wooden amphitheater. It was not round like a modern stadium but a wedge of sloped seating. The whole group of buildings was surrounded by a palisade and had defensive earthworks.

Because we can identify that this excavated site was in fact Yeavering, the royal residence of King Edwin of Northumbria, we know some of its history. King Edwin married a Christian princess of Kent and allowed the Roman missionary, Paulinus, to come. Paulinus sought to persuade Edwin to be baptized, and Bede's *Ecclesiastical History* tells us a story that might have taken place in either the hall or in its wedge-shaped amphitheater. (Some archeologists suggest that the amphitheater was specially built for Paulinus's preaching.) Edwin brought his thanes together to hear Paulinus and decide if he should accept the new religion. One of them, according to Bede, stated that since the new religion brought information about the afterlife, they should accept it. If they were sitting in the hall, he may have gestured with his arm as he reminded them all of what it was like when a bird flew through the open door at one end and out the other. Inside the hall was firelight and safety, but outside the hall there could be stormy weather. Just as the bird was only briefly in a place of light and warmth, so, too, was human life only briefly on this earth; and where the bird or soul comes from, or to where it goes, no one could know. Therefore, said the thane, any religion that can tell us this is to be valued.

King Edwin was baptized, but in 633, he was attacked by King Penda of Mercia and King Cadwallon of Wales. King Edwin died in battle and the two victors invaded the town, killed the inhabitants, and burned the buildings to the ground. Archeologists can even identify the place where the fire was deliberately set to bring down the wooden amphitheater. Ironically, this fire may have saved the site for future discovery. The place was abandoned and allowed to be overgrown and eventually planted as a farm field. If the site had not been destroyed and abandoned, it might have grown up into a medieval town, and all records of Yeavering as a royal hall would have been lost.

For all that we know about Yeavering, the one thing we do not know is what it looked like. We can locate where the supporting posts stood, but what did the walls look like? How was the roof shaped, and was it thatched or shingled? Was it only constructed of wood, or was it also made of plaster? Were the beams decoratively carved? The royal site in Slöinge, Sweden, has scraps of gold foil decoration, which suggest that the wooden beams may have been partly covered with gold. There are no such clues at Yeavering, perhaps because the buildings were looted before they were set on fire. While many different models have been suggested, the most popular model shows a large wooden building with a central roof section over the narrow central area and lower roof sections over the broader wings. The main door faces out on the defensive earthworks and pagan burial ground.

In the late 1980's, an archeological team in Denmark discovered the foundation of a large hall that may have been the model for Heorot, near Lejre on the large island of Sjaelland (Zealand). It is shaped like the long, slender Swedish halls, but on a larger scale. While the Swedish halls were typically 100 feet (about thirty meters) long, this hall was closer to 145 feet (48 meters) long. This remarkably large size matches with the description given in *Beowulf*.

The trees for its construction would have been cut in an old forest, and if there were no trees tall or thick enough on the island, the king would use his wealth to import them. With a long row of double posts, the hall would have needed more large beams to tie them together and support the roof. Like the royal hall in Slöinge, Heorot was supposed to have gold covering the wooden beams. The roof would have a steep pitch to shed heavy snowfalls and overhanging eaves to shed rain and snow away from the walls. At either end there would be two windows to let in light and allow smoke to escape.

Much of what we know about the interior of a hall comes from *Beowulf*, and we know more details from medieval Icelandic stories. The hall was not used for cooking, which was done in the outbuildings. It was used for feasting and as a dormitory for the resident warriors. Tables and benches seem to have been movable and perhaps were easily stored somewhere else. In a long, narrow hall with fire pits down the center, there may not have been much walking space with the tables set up. There was probably a permanently raised platform where the king's seat was set up; most accounts picture the king sitting higher than the other feasters. Along the sides of the halls, there may have been a permanent raised platform for sleeping. In the poem, the Geats go to sleep in beds, and there are pillows and blankets present as well. Perhaps the walls were lined with storage chests in which the blankets and some dishes were kept. The chests may have served as beds.

Heorot's floor is finished with wood, not packed dirt (1317). It may be colored in some way (1725); maybe painted or laid out in patterns of contrasting wood colors, like tiles. Perhaps communal and royal halls usually used a flooring material, because the constant traffic would have worn down a dirt floor too quickly or the frequent feasting would have kept it muddy and uneven. Ordinary cottages may have used flooring or may have used packed dirt.

Even the best of halls must have been dark, with the only light coming from the high windows, the two doors, and the fires. One reason for the high-pitched roof may have been so that the smoke would rise above the height of the people. We should not picture the hall interiors as bare or primitive, however. The dishes found at many sites are highly decorated and include glass cups. There may have been decorations hanging on the walls and roof, either trophy weapons (such as those in Grendel's cave) or woven hangings. Swedish cottages used to hang white, embroidered cloth across the roof beams on festive occasions, and it is possible that Scandinavian halls such as Heorot did the same. The poem tells us that gold-woven tapestries hung down; gold could be beaten to fine threads that were worked into the cloth to catch the light.

CLOTHING

Most clothing must have been homemade; woven on the upright looms with hanging weights. Women spun wool and flax. Silk was a later import, known in Anglo-Saxon times but very expensive. Extremely little cloth has survived from this time. There are sometimes cloth fibers in graves, most notably in the coffin of a Frankish princess and in the coffin of St. Cuthbert of Northumbria. St. Cuthbert's silk may have been put in long after his death, and the scrap preserved in the Frankish coffin is so small that not much more than its content and color can be known. Sometimes scraps of cloth survive at the end of a belt or strap, as they are sheltered by a clasp.

Most of what we know about early clothing is deduced from the metal objects that survived in graves. Iron tended to rust away, but gold was preserved well, as was bronze; therefore, we know more about the clothing habits of the wealthy. Of course, into early Christian times some burials were cremations (as described in *Beowulf*). A cremation destroyed not only the body and its cloth, but also the golden objects. In well-preserved inhumation (burial of the body) graves, metal clasps and pins show us how clothing had been fastened and decorated and suggest how it was worn. Styles of clothing may vary a great deal between different places and times, as well as between individuals. Since people may have traveled, a burial in one place may reflect a style of clothing worn in another place. When we find a grave in Sweden or in Kent, we can usually place the grave within a hundred years but not much closer than that. To make matters more confusing, people may have been buried with objects that were much older than they were or with things that were not theirs. Even worse, they may have been buried in ways that they did not normally dress; perhaps with more or less jewelry than usual.

We do have drawings of people from later Anglo-Saxon times. We can be fairly sure how people looked by the ninth and tenth centuries. Men wore narrow trousers under a tunic or shirt and a cloak. Even humble workers were expected to own and wear shoes and gloves, but hats did not seem to be popular. Men were buried with very little jewelry, perhaps only a ring on a finger. Pictures show many of them with moustaches and carefully combed long hair and some with beards. Women in these pictures appear to be swathed in cloth, with an outer long tunic over an inner dress. Like men they wore cloaks, but on their heads they usually had a hood or draped scarf. They had belts that substituted for modern pockets, with hanging bags or chains to carry important keys or tools. Women wore more jewelry than men. They wore strings of beads or gold rings, and they usually had large, showy brooches (decorative pins) to secure cloaks. Some of these gold or bronze brooches survived as grave goods.

Clothes were made of linen or wool. Wool took dye better and was therefore not only warmer but more decorative. Natural dyes allowed them to wear red, blue, several shades of brown, and colors that could be made with blends of these dyes. Straps and the edges of sleeves were often made of decorative, tablet weaving.

There are no drawings for the earlier period, when Angles, Saxons, and Jutes were migrating to England, and Beowulf was presumably traveling to Heorot. We must reconstruct clothing based on grave goods, mainly by the clasps and brooches left behind. There are few clues for men's dress in this early period, so we can only guess that their attire was reasonably similar to the pictured Anglo-Saxons. Women's clothing seems to have changed more.

During this early period, a typical woman's grave included two round "saucer" brooches and a large, cross-shaped brooch. The saucer brooches, which were inscribed with many decorative patterns and might have included jewels, rested near the shoulders, while the cross-shaped brooch was on the chest, usually off-center. The saucer brooches appear to have either fastened or decorated the tunic that went over the underdress.

Two women's brooches. Silver saucer brooch is based on one found at
Beeston Tor, Staffordshire, England. Square-headed brooch is based on
one found at Berinsfield, Oxfordshire, England. (Illustration by L. D. Staver.)

Perhaps the saucer brooches were only decorative; often, strings of amber
beads hung between them. Since necklaces were for gold display, saucer
brooches could have been used for displaying amber. Some of them dis-
played not only amber, but also coin shapes made of silver, like charms
on a bracelet. While a wealthy woman's tunic must have been decorated
and bright, the underdress was probably simple. Its sleeves may have
been cut to let the hands through and then pinned with sleeve clips that
are found in some graves.

The larger cross-shaped pins are usually called "square-headed brooches."
They are used to estimate the date of a grave, because they went through
so many changes over time. Beginning with a simple design that may

have copied Roman military cloak pins, they had a large square top where the pin was fixed in back, an arched area for the pierced cloth to bunch up in, and then the foot where the pin fastened (like a big safety pin). Over two centuries, the brooches became more and more decorative, larger, and fancier in every way. The goldsmith work can be breathtaking, as it is filled with scrolls and animal figures. Because of the placement of these brooches in the grave, they seem to have fastened a cloak in front but slightly off to one shoulder. Perhaps the heaviness of the pin helped balance the weight of the heavy wool cloak as it dragged behind.

The women of the Danish and Swedish lands may have covered their heads like later Anglo-Saxon women, or they may not have. Royal women may have worn headbands to display yet more gold, garnet, amber, and silver; one Frankish royal grave appears to have a headband like a small crown or hat. Wealhtheow is described as laden with gold, and she may have hung gold and amber in strings around her hair or on an elaborate hat, as well as on her neck, chest, waist, arms, and fingers. Amber bead strings could have been used to hold her hair up in a dazzling display of wealth and power. Dressing their women as richly as possible seems to have been one of the ways that Germanic men showed their status and wealth (see illustration of Germanic noble lady in Chapter 3).

WEAPONS

Weapons were the most precious possessions of Germanic men in the pagan period and continued to be valued into the Anglo-Saxon Christian period, too. The ancient words for "man" and "woman" were both based on a generic "mann," meaning human being. A woman was a "wifmann," or weaving man, a person who spun and wove cloth. A man was a "waepnedmann," or weapon man, a person who bore weapons. While women were often buried with symbols of their cloth making, men were usually buried with some kind of weapon. These burials varied from the rich display of the Sutton Hoo burial to a lowly spear tucked in next to a dead, poor man.

Through written records and grave goods, we know that the spear was considered the basic weapon of this period. Spears could be used in hunting, too; especially against the fierce boar that had to be struck before his tusks got close enough to hurt anyone. The next most basic weapon was a long knife, which was worn tucked into the belt and also served hunting and crafts purposes. A shield had no function in hunting, because it was only for defense. Higher-status warriors had helms and swords; perhaps this is why *Beowulf* goes into such detail concerning treasure swords

Weapons. (*A*) Arrows; (*B*) Long bow; (*C*) Spear; (*D*) Sword; (*E*) Sheath;
(*F, G*) Two styles of sax (or "seax"); (*H*) Leather-covered, painted wooden shield;
(*I*) Fighting ax. (Illustration by L. D. Staver.)

and patterned helmets but passes over shields and spears in silence. Ideally, a fighting man needed something he could throw (such as a bow
and arrows or a spear), something he could hold (like a knife, sword, or
axe), and something for defense (like a shield, helmet, or chain mail).
(For an example of a Germanic warrior with weapons, see illustration in
Chapter 3.)

   The spear was the symbol of a free man. It was given to a boy as he
reached adolescence and was forbidden for slaves to carry. Including a
spear in a grave may not have implied a belief in its use in the next life
as much as it represented a habit of burying a man with his main status

symbol (like dressing him in a suit and tie). Slaves were buried without spears, and free men were buried with them. The spear was made of wood; *Beowulf* states that their spears were made of gray ash wood. There were regular hand-held thrusting spears and smaller throwing-spears (like darts or javelins). Spears varied in size, from six to eleven feet. They had long points made of iron that were locally produced and varied in shape and style. Partway down the wooden shaft, the owner probably wound a strip of leather around it tightly as a grip and left a loop free. This loop could help the warrior carry it when his hands were full. The end of the wooden shaft was often covered in iron, so that it would not split if it thumped on the ground. The spear was an all-purpose, inexpensive weapon. It could be used in a wall of shields, sticking out so that the enemies would meet the spear's point before they reached the shield.

The sword did not change greatly from Beowulf's time to the later Anglo-Saxon period, except in its workmanship and decoration. A Germanic sword, like a Roman sword, was a straight, thin blade that was sharp on both edges. At the grasping end it tapered into a tongue, or "tang," which had to be fastened to a hilt. In Beowulf's time, hilts were beginning to include metal, rather than just bone or wood. A hilt had to be strong so that it would not break in battle and render the sword useless. There was usually a guard between the hilt and the blade to keep the hand from moving down too far and getting cut, and at the end of the thin handle there was a pyramid-shaped pommel to cover the end of the tang. This pommel was the main place for showing status through rich decoration. The pommel might have extensive gold designs, or, like the sword in the Sutton Hoo burial, it could have a gold design inlaid with colored garnets. Pommels of Beowulf's period are individual works of art; some are simple, and some are inconceivably ornate. Some of these pommels were pressed down over a leather handle-strap. Swords were stored in leather-covered wooden scabbards that were often lined with wool to prevent rust. They were worn on the chest with a shoulder strap and only moved to hang at the belt in later Anglo-Saxon times.

The short sword (or long knife) was called a "sax" (also spelled "seax" in Old English) and is thought to be the root of the tribe of "Saxons." It may have been the original sword used by these tribes, who depended on the spear for their main fighting power. The sax would be there for hand-to-hand fighting and also for a hunting knife. It remained in widespread use all through the Anglo-Saxon period. It was a single-edged blade, often decorated and carried in a leather sheath.

Shields were made of wood. Wood had the advantage of stopping arrows well and was cheap and easy to replace. However, a wooden shield also could be easily broken in a prolonged fight with swords and even more so with axes. The wooden shield had a central, metal part that held it together and formed a handle in the back, where it was gripped in the warrior's fist. This part is called a boss, and in Anglo-Saxon times it was large and pointed like a spike. Perhaps this feature was for defensive use, and it may have turned aside spears from the central handle, thereby protecting the user's hand. In graves, the boss is the only remaining part after the wood has rotted away; it was riveted to a central hole in the board. The wooden board itself was made of a light, tough wood that was resistant to splintering (such as poplar, willow, or maple). Individual boards were held together tightly not only by a riveted strip of metal, but also by the application of wet leather that shrank around them and pressed them together more tightly. It is likely that they were painted with some sort of design. Shields were used not just for individual protection, but also in a "shield wall," where warriors pressed close together with their spears pointing out so that they could block all darts and other blows until, at last, the shield wall broke. The success of some battles depended on keeping the shield wall together as long as possible.

Beowulf wears a helmet and a coat of chain mail, and it is clear from archeological finds (and lack of them) that these were the most expensive items in the weapons catalog. Most warriors went to battle with some combination of hand-held tools but not with any serious protective gear on their bodies. They may have used leather for some protection, as it would protect them from slight wounds. The construction of a metal helmet and a coat of interlocked metal rings must have been the work of a team of smiths for weeks and must have cost a small fortune. It is no wonder that these pieces of gear were handed down from father to son and carefully looted from fallen enemies.

A helmet was made of many different plates riveted together. Some of them had a metal frame and plates of bone riveted between. The central top ridge that went from the face to the nape of the neck was the main frame, while a side ridge often went from ear to ear. Plates could be riveted to these ridges, and then wedge-shaped plates could be riveted between these to create a round head shape. All of the existing helmets include a long extension down over the nose and hinged flaps covering the ears and part of the cheeks. The Sutton Hoo helmet has a full faceplate with eyeholes, a formed nose, and a mouth hole. This helmet must have been not only more expensive, but harder to fight in, as it restricted vision.

There are only four confirmed helmets found in Anglo-Saxon burials.

There are only two instances of chain mail: one a fringe of chain work at the back of a helmet, and the other the chain shirt of the Sutton Hoo burial. To make chain mail, a smith had to hammer iron into thin wire and form small rings by wrapping the wire around a rod. Each ring, cut apart from the rest, had to be linked with others in an Olympic-rings type of interlock and then riveted or welded to fasten it. Both of the examples of Anglo-Saxon chain-mail alternate riveting and welding, ring by ring. The chain-mail "byrnie" of Sutton Hoo has 20,000 rings in it. It would have required regular oiling to keep the rings from rusting together, and it weighed about twenty-five pounds. Audiences must have winced when Beowulf leaped into the mere wearing his armor. Not only would it have weighed down the swimmer, but when he emerged, someone was going to have to clean pond slime from its thousands of rings and dry and oil it so that it would not rust.

Two other forms of weapons were used at least some of the time. Fighting axes may have been used in Beowulf's time, but they did not become a main weapon until the later Viking Age. Viking attackers wielded two-headed fighting axes against the spears and swords of the Anglo-Saxon defenders. More importantly, the bow and arrow was in use for hunting and war, although we have less record of it compared to spears and swords. Some archeological finds turn up arrowheads, while others turn up bows, but very few graves seem to have included obvious small arrowheads. However, in *Beowulf* and in other poems, as well as in pictures, bows seem to have been used as a part of military strategy to divide the shield wall. Anglo-Saxon bows were long but may not have been drawn back with as much force as later English bows were. It is likely that bows were used in battle mainly by way of using what many men already owned: a hunting bow. The bow was never a prestige weapon until the English used it with deadly force against French knights in 1346.

FURTHER SUGGESTED READING

Banham, Debby. *Food and Drink in Anglo-Saxon England.* Stroud, UK: Tempus Publishing, 2004.

Bazelmans, Jos. *By Weapons Made Worthy: Lords, Retainers, and Their Relationship to Beowulf.* Amsterdam: Amsterdam University Press, 1999.

Blair, Peter Hunter. *An Introduction to Anglo-Saxon England.* Cambridge: Cambridge University Press, 1956.

Brown, David. *Anglo-Saxon England.* Totowa, NJ: Rowman and Littlefield, 1978.

Bruce-Mitford, Rupert. *Aspects of Anglo-Saxon Archaeology: Sutton Hoo and Other Discoveries.* New York: Harper's Magazine Press, 1974.

———. *The Sutton Hoo Ship-Burial: A Handbook.* London: The Trustees of the British Museum, 1968.

Campbell, James, ed. *The Anglo-Saxons*. Ithaca: Cornell University Press, 1982.

Carver, Martin. *Sutton Hoo: Burial Ground of Kings?* Philadelphia: University of Pennsylvania Press, 1998.

Clemoes, Peter and Kathleen Hughes, eds. *England before the Conquest: Studies in Primary Sources Presented to Dorothy Whitelock*. Cambridge: The University Press, 1971.

Crossley-Holland, Kevin. *The Anglo-Saxon World: An Anthology*. Oxford: Oxford University Press, 1999. (Includes Aelfric's *Colloquy*, the estate document, wills, and riddles.)

————. *Notes on The Anglo-Saxon World*. Totowa, NJ: Barnes and Noble Books, 1983.

Fell, Christine. *Women in Anglo-Saxon England*. Bloomington: Indiana University Press, 1984.

Fisher, D. J. V. *The Anglo-Saxon Age c. 400–1042*. London: Longman Group Ltd., 1973.

Green, Charles. *Sutton Hoo: The Excavation of a Royal Ship Burial*. Totowa, NJ: Barnes and Noble Books, 1963.

Harrison, Mark. *Anglo-Saxon Thegn: AD 449–1066*. Botley, UK: Osprey Publishing, 2001.

Haywood, John. *Dark Age Naval Power: A Reassessment of Frankish and Anglo-Saxon Seafaring Activity*. Hockwold-cum-Wilton, UK: Anglo-Saxon Books, 1999.

Herbert, Kathleen. *Peace-Weavers and Shield-Maidens: Women in Early English Society*. Hockwold-cum-Wilton, UK: Anglo-Saxon Books, 1997.

Hill, David. *An Atlas of Anglo-Saxon England*. Toronto: University of Toronto Press, 1981.

Hodges, Robert. *The Anglo-Saxon Achievement*. Ithaca: Cornell University Press, 1989.

Hooke, Della. *The Landscape of Anglo-Saxon England*. London: Leicester University Press, 1998.

Lacey, Robert and Danny Danziger. *The Year 1000*. Boston: Little, Brown, 1999. (Very readable, good general information on Anglo-Saxon life.)

Laing, Lloyd and Jennifer. *Anglo-Saxon England*. London: Routledge, 1979.

Leahy, Kevin. *Anglo-Saxon Crafts*. Stroud, UK: Tempus Publishing, 2003.

Owen-Crocker, Gale R. *Dress in Anglo-Saxon England*. Oxford: Boydell Press, 2004.

Page, R. I. *Life in Anglo-Saxon England*. New York: G. P. Putnam's Sons, 1970.

Pollington, Stephen. *Rudiments of Runelore*. Hockwold-cum-Wilton, UK: Anglo-Saxon Books, 1995.

————. *The English Warrior: From Earliest Times Till 1066*. Hockwold-cum-Wilton, UK: Anglo-Saxon Books, 1996.

————. *The Mead Hall: Feasting in Anglo-Saxon Tradition*. Hockwold-cum-Wilton, UK: Anglo-Saxon Books, 2003.

Quennell, Marjorie and C. H. B. Quennell. *Everyday Life in Roman and Anglo-Saxon Times*. New York: Dorset Press, 1959.

Savelli, Mary. *Tastes of Anglo-Saxon England*. Hockwold-cum-Wilton, UK: Anglo-Saxon Books, 2002.

Stephenson, I. P. *The Anglo-Saxon Shield*. London: Trafalgar Square, 2004.

Underwood, Richard. *Anglo-Saxon Weapons and Warfare*. London: Trafalgar Square, 1999.

Whitelock, Dorothy. *The Beginnings of English Society*. Baltimore: Penguin Books, 1952.

————, ed. *English Historical Documents, ca. 500–1042*. Vol. I. New York: Oxford University Press, 1955.

Wilson, David M. *The Anglo-Saxons*. New York: Praeger, 1960.

12

Modern Adaptations of *Beowulf*

Dᴜʀɪɴɢ ᴛʜᴇ ᴛᴡᴇɴᴛɪᴇᴛʜ ᴄᴇɴᴛᴜʀʏ, some adaptations of the poem and its world began to be published. These adaptations include books, graphic art, and film. They include faithful adaptations of the story that attempt to bring its style up to date to make it easier to read, and they also include interpretations of the story from other angles. The least obvious and most famous adaptation is the work of J. R. R. Tolkien. The following reviews are arranged to cover first books, then graphic art, and last film. A full review of the world of Tolkien can be found in Chapter 13.

BOOKS

Beowulf Is My Name, by Frederick R. Rebsamen, 1971.
Rebsamen's straight translation of the epic poem was published in 1991, but this earlier version is part translation, part adaptation. Many of the questions that the original poem leaves unanswered are addressed here. Who was Beowulf before he came to Denmark, and why did he come? What were his thoughts? How did he feel about the raid on Frankia? How would the story have been told if the narrator had been Beowulf himself? Rebsamen's version sticks close to the original but tries to answer these questions. It is written in prose, not poetry, and it reads smoothly.

Beowulf: A Likeness, by Randolph Swearer, Raymond Oliver, and
      Marijane Osborn, 1990.
The central feature of this adaptation is Raymond Oliver's poetic interpretation of the story. As Swearer explains in a preface, the purpose of the work is to "explore the poem's silences." Oliver's stanzas, often rhymed, describe the sights, smells, and other sensations of Heorot (here simplified to "Hart"). Among other "silences" this poem fills in,

Hrothgar's understanding of the Christian God is expanded with references to Old English Christian works, and Beowulf's ascension to ruling the Geats is marked by his marriage to the widow, Hygd. The facing pages of this oversize volume are filled with stunning images created mostly from artifacts. Pages of Beowulf's manuscript, reconstructed weapons, ships, and halls, ancient wood carvings, photographs of Scandinavia, and old woodcut illustrations are artistically arranged. Osborn's essay on the setting of the poem in the real world of Scandinavia completes a graceful adaptation.

Grendel, by John Gardner, 1971.

As the title suggests, this short novel is about Grendel, not Beowulf. It is told in the first person, partly as a narrative and explanation of the past years leading up to the conflict, and partly in the present tense up to the moment of his death. Gardner's Grendel is a highly self-aware monster, and if self awareness is one of the defining traits of humanity, then this Grendel is a human monster.

Self awareness is Grendel's burden. He can speak but usually chooses not to communicate; he lives with a more beast-like nonverbal mother. He is drowned by a flood of mental speech as he tries to understand his condition and his place in the world. Living among beasts when he was young, he fit in with them as a more intelligent beast himself. When the Danes first came to settle, he found them and their reaction to him startling and fascinating. He watches them for many years, creeping close enough to see and hear. Grendel cannot understand why they go to war, but he watches them grow wealthy and build their great hall. He is especially fascinated when a poet, "the Shaper," comes to the court and uses his song to redefine people's actions. The ragged, inglorious fighting that Grendel had watched turns into the glorious founding of a kingdom by a mythical Scyld, through his skillful use of words. Grendel has no place in this re-imagined kingdom, and the glorification of man leaves him no place except with the beasts, or with the "dark side" (Cain's race). From this point on, Grendel's fascination becomes tormented as he tries to understand his role in life.

Two characters from the original poem become major characters: the dragon and Unferth. The grieving and confused Grendel goes first to the dragon, who is ages old and very wise. The dragon confuses him more with existentialist advice and a flood of even more sophisticated words. His advice is that no action matters in the long years of the world, and that Grendel can accept playing his role of antihero or turn to the dragon's own pursuit of collecting gold. Grendel, who believed in the values that the Shaper sang, finds himself more confused and angry than ever when he is told that the solution to his question is nothingness. Whether from this advice or from some magic, Grendel now finds himself charmed against iron and able to walk among men without fear. He finds this state more isolating than ever.

Grendel's solution is to become the antihero: "the Wrecker of Kings." After guards attack him when he comes to eavesdrop, he decides to begin raiding the hall. Unferth is the only hero who tries to stand up to him after a few murderous raids. In Gardner's depiction, Grendel's strength against Unferth is not in his arms and teeth, but in his power of speech. Wavering between beast and human, Grendel decides to speak to Unferth and mocks his heroism in a tone reminiscent of the dragon's. When Unferth comes to the underwater cave to pursue the fight, Grendel again denies him a hero's role. After mocking the idea of heroic values, he waits for Unferth to fall asleep and takes him back to the surface. In this exchange, sparing Unferth becomes his weapon against something more powerful than Unferth's sword: the idea that something great and noble might exist.

Gardner includes many names from *Beowulf* as minor characters. Wealhtheow arrives as a peacemaking princess of unbelievable beauty and shakes up Grendel's world again. Grendel, having accepted his role as demon, does not want to admit anything noble or lovely and wishes vainly to cast down the young queen from the pedestal that even he places her on. Hrothulf arrives as an orphaned teenager (like Grendel unsure of his role), and like Grendel, he is tempted by a peasant who speaks with the tone of the dragon, urging him to revolution. Hrothgar, of course, is the aged king, once strong in pillaging surrounding tribes but now weak, tired, and unsure of what to do.

One challenge of writing a book based on a known story is that the ending is already known: in the end, Grendel must die. The interest here is not in how the great hall will finally be rid of the monster, but in how Grendel's mental story will play out. Rejecting heroic values that cast him as the villain, he becomes a cynical antihero, and in the end he grows bored. He cannot believe in the glorious past or in enduring love, but he cannot completely debunk them, either. After the Shaper's death, he finds life a burden of self-aware tedium. The inevitable arrival of the foreign hero casts Grendel at last in his proper role and allows him to fulfill himself by going to meet Beowulf, hoping at last to kill the embodiment of heroic values. What kills Grendel in the end is as much Beowulf's words as his wrestling. As they fight, Beowulf makes it clear that he is fighting for the reality of a moral system, for the eventual triumph of human ideals. Grendel's mind is divided: he wants to believe in these things, but in order for them to triumph, he must expire.

This novel treats the original poem with great respect. The characters, people, and story line are all preserved and even given visible freshening. Hrothulf, a mere name in the poem, becomes a believably melancholy fourteen-year-old playing with his baby cousins. Unferth's bitterness, and his apparent blend of bravery and cowardice, are explained through his moral defeat. The psychological story, however, is entirely modern. The dragon speaks in the voice of an existentialist philosopher, and the peasant who tempts Hrothulf uses the language of modern revolution. Grendel's hyper-verbal stream of consciousness belongs to a modern novel, not to an ancient epic. At times he constructs poems or dramatic scripts, and at all times his tone is sophisticated, ironic, and poetic. His conflict of self-definition expresses a modern question: Who am I? Am I who others say I am?

Eaters of the Dead, by Michael Crichton, 1976.

Eaters of the Dead, newly released as *The Thirteenth Warrior*, attempts to retell Beowulf's story through the foreign voice of the Arab Ibn Fadlan. The new story, while recognizable, is changed to a point of confusion, at least for unwary readers. The confusion begins with the novel's format. It is apparently a manuscript translated from Arabic and Latin and written around AD 922 by an Arab emissary from Baghdad, who was sent to meet with the King of the Bulgars and was caught up on a side adventure. The novel opens with an introduction that appears to be a scholarly history of the manuscript, and it sounds like real histories of manuscript fragments. There are places, names, and dates, but they are all fictional. All through the novel this pretense is maintained, with fictional scholarly footnotes on the translation and a fictional appendix. Only in a brief acknowledgement to the translators of the real Ibn Fadlan manuscript does Crichton state that only the first three chapters are drawn from this material.

The real manuscript describes some people called the "Rus," who were probably Scandinavians. During the Viking Age (AD 800–1000), Scandinavians settled along the

Volga River and founded the first kingdom of Kiev. Ibn Fadlan met a group of these Rus and described them as very tall and blond, tattooed, and always armed. His Muslim customs of washing made him see the Rus as unusually dirty and disgusting, and he describes in detail both their slave markets and the funeral customs he observed. No one knows if the customs he saw were those actually followed by the Norse in Scandinavia, or if they were a local variant; some scholars believe that the people he describes were an ethnic blend of Scandinavian and Volga Khazar.

Crichton's novel continues the tone of Ibn Fadlan's narrative and tells how the Rus entangled him in an adventure. An emissary from the North comes to them, asking for help against some mysterious foe. With the help of an old woman's fortune-telling, an expedition forms around the warrior Buliwyf, but for luck they require a thirteenth member who is not Rus. They choose Ibn Fadlan, who was only passing through. Traveling by ship and horse, they journey back to their homelands and to the hall of Rothgar. Here they find that a cannibalistic nighttime foe is killing not only warriors but farmers, children, and animals. The band of warriors must withstand several attacks, and finally, acting on the advice of a dwarf, they attack the foe in an underwater cave.

Although the story is recognizable, there are more differences than similarities. The monster is not a single entity but a community of primitive semi-human creatures. They attack in a realistic, human way, in large numbers and with weapons. Defenses such as wooden palisades are useful. Buliwyf does not fight alone, but the whole band tries to defend the hall and loses several warriors. The "dragon" is a massive attack at night, carrying torches to set the hall on fire. The only supernatural beings are the dwarves (who live in a cave), and there is no motive given to the foe apart from cannibalism.

Names from *Beowulf* show up in altered spellings, but the new relationships might confuse a reader who tries to use them to understand the original poem. For example, "Higlac" is Buliwyf's father, and Wulfgar (the doorkeeper in the original story) is a son of Rothgar. Rothgar has five sons instead of two; Unferth is not named but is presumably the herald said to be helping the son, "Wiglif," to conspire against his father. The warrior band includes familiar names like Edgtho (the original Beowulf's father) and Rethel (the original Hygelac's father).

Cultural details are the most misleading on two levels. *Beowulf* is set in the Dark Ages (no later than AD 600), but Ibn Fadlan's account is set in the later Viking Age (AD 922). This difference alone could change cultural customs, since most cultures change over the course of 300 years. However, most of the narrator's cultural comments are fictional. Since they continue in the voice of the real Ibn Fadlan, they sound like authoritative descriptions. The narrator tells us that the Northmen believed, said, or did various things. A careful reader may realize that the superstition about mist is only for the sake of the story, but the same reader may not realize that other beliefs about death or gods are also fictional. The narrator appears to describe as an eyewitness how the Northmen treated their slaves and how they handled sexual matters, but these descriptions are also fictional. Crichton's narrator contradicts other eyewitnesses, such as Tacitus and Boniface, in stating that adultery was openly tolerated, and we do not have any record of how Scandinavians treated slaves. There are many more small details like this, such as how the "Rus" traveled, dressed, and ate.

Some details show Crichton's research and are accurate according to what we know from other sources. The general building (wood) and terrain are accurate, and Ibn Fadlan sees realistic "northern lights" display in the night sky. Tacitus wrote that Germanic warriors did not farm, and Crichton's "Trelburg" is a wooden fort with no agriculture.

We know from Tacitus that some women were considered seers, a detail which Crichton uses in the person of the "Angel of Death" (whose auguries set up the thirteen warriors for the expedition). We know from many Germanic sources that their writing (runes) were cut or carved into wood or stone and were considered magical. Crichton's Northmen regard writing with suspicion and consider it a kind of magic.

Many readers will enjoy Crichton's story, but it should be read with the understanding that it is not well-researched historical fiction, but rather fiction masquerading as history.

GRAPHIC ART

Beowulf, drawn by Michael Uslan and Ricardo Villamonte for DC Comics, 1975.

This comic uses Gardner's *Grendel,* along with the original poem, as a source of ideas. Unferth is a treacherous villain, Grendel is a tormented monster with a vaguely human form, and Beowulf is a traditional comic-book hero who wears a horned skull helmet. The comic added a female warrior to make up for the heavily male-oriented original poem. After describing Grendel's defeat, the comic created further adventures of "Beowulf the Dragon-Slayer."

Beowulf, drawn by Jerry Bingham for First Comics Inc., 1984.

Bingham's version is a graphic novel, not a serial comic that required further adventures. His Beowulf wears a horned helmet and fur loincloth, but the art is a more serious attempt at translating the story into a picture form. Grendel is similarly a monster in vaguely human form with large muscles and long claws. The huge, Chinese-looking dragon towers over Beowulf with fangs as long as the hero's head.

The Collected Beowulf, drawn by Gareth Hinds for The Comic.com, 2000.

Originally in three separate comics, this graphic novel is also available in a single paperback edition. Hinds' Beowulf wears armor modeled after recent archeological finds and is faithful to the period and setting. His Grendel is darker and less human than the earlier graphic representations, with yellow eyes and fangs in a skull-like face. The story and characters are all from the original, and rather than inventing dialogue, Hinds uses the 1910 translation by Francis Gummere to tell the story where narrative is needed.

Each part uses a different art technique, and most effectively, the elegiac third episode is expressed mainly in gray and black. Combining realism and the sense that this story is from a book, he uses star charts to fill in the night skies over Heorot and includes labeled constellations. Blue-green water backgrounds give the "mere" scenes a watery feeling, even when the pictured action is taking place on land. (The sea monster that Beowulf's men shoot looks like the Loch Ness Monster.) The dragon is snake-like with a bird-like head.

The most provocative scene illustrates Hrothgar's "Sermon." As Hrothgar speaks of the certainty of downfall and death even to the courageous, he and Beowulf look at an image of New York City's skyline with clouds of smoke billowing behind. Drawn before the terrorist attack on the World Trade Center, the artist's vision suggests that any center of success and pride becomes a vulnerable target. Whether the attack is through pollution, war, or natural disaster, Hrothgar's warning to remember your mortality is always timely. There is no time that does not require courage and wisdom; even a time that no longer believes in demons and dragons.

Beowulf wrestles with Grendel, pinning him by the arm.
(© Gareth Hinds/Thecomic.com)

Hinds represents the message of Hrothgar's "sermon" with
modern symbols of pride and success that may be vulnerable to destruction.
This drawing was completed before the 2001 attack on the World Trade Center.
(© Gareth Hinds/Thecomic.com)

FILM

Grendel, Grendel, Grendel, directed by Alexander Stitt, 1980.

This animated film of Gardner's novel was made in Australia and features the voice of
Peter Ustinov. It is a musical and follows Gardner's novel, *Grendel* (though not the original *Beowulf*), faithfully.

The Thirteenth Warrior, directed by John McTiernan, 1999.

Michael Crichton produced and helped direct this film version of his novel, *Eaters of the
Dead*. It stars Antonio Banderas as Ibn Fadlan, Vladimir Kulich as Buliwyf, and Dennis

Beowulf battles the dragon in the surf outside the barrow's entrance.
(© Gareth Hinds/Thecomic.com)

Storhoi as Ibn Fadlan's interpreter and friend, Herger. The film is a faithful representation
of the novel.

As with the novel, the film includes some aspects of historical accuracy and some
flights of fancy. For example, the chain mail that Ibn Fadlan wears is more historical
than the armor that the Norsemen wear, which often uses elements of later medieval
periods. On the other hand, the duel ("holmgang" in Norse) in which several wooden
shields are split, is reasonably accurate. The time period portrayed is Viking Age, about
the year 900, not the earlier Dark Ages time of 550–600. Its connection to the story of
Beowulf is thin enough that many viewers do not realize that the link is intended.

Beowulf, directed by Graham Baker, 1999.

This film stars Christopher Lambert and uses the setting of *Beowulf,* a castle under attack
by an evil demon, but then alters it from that point. The source of the evil is thought
to be inside the hall itself, so the castle is quarantined by a besieging army. Beowulf
arrives alone, unlike in the poem, and he is supernatural and "damned," not heroic. He
has difficulty fighting the demon, because it is able to move through walls and acts unpre-
dictably. The source of evil turns out to be Rothgar himself, and Grendel's mother is
played not as a monster, but as a temptress. This film does not relate well to the poem
Beowulf and is not recommended for classrooms.

Beowulf and Grendel, directed by Sturla Gunnarsson, 2005.

This film, starring Gerard Butler as Beowulf and Stellan Skarsgård as Hrothgar, is intended to be a faithful reproduction of the poem. The characters are mostly intact from the poem, but the film supplies motivation for Grendel (who is a kind of Bigfoot). Hrothgar's men have killed his father and terrified the young monster, thus creating an avenger who will later terrorize their hall. Filmed in Iceland, the movie strives to be faithful in its historical details and setting.

FURTHER SUGGESTED READING

Montgomery, James E. "Ibn Fadlan and the Rusiyyah." *Journal of Arabic and Islamic Studies* 3, 2000.

Smyser, H. M. "Ibn Fadlan's Account of the Rus with Some Commentary and Some Allusions to Beowulf." In *Franciplegius: Medieval and Linguistic Studies in Honor of Francis Peabody Magoun, Jr.*, eds. Jess B. Bessinger Jr. and Robert P. Creed, 1965. (Includes the Ibn Fadlan manuscript; informal versions of the manuscript are also available online.)

13

The Beowulfian World of J. R. R. Tolkien

J. R. R. TOLKIEN was Professor of Anglo-Saxon at Oxford University from 1926 until his retirement in 1956, and he was the first-ranked *Beowulf* scholar of his generation. His view of the poem's meaning changed the direction of scholarship after 1936. It is surprising to realize that he never created a complete translation of the poem but allowed his ideas on its meaning to live only in the many lectures he gave. However, he left behind two works of fiction that he is remembered for more than for his scholarship: *The Hobbit* and *The Lord of the Rings*. These stories never mention *Beowulf* and never use comprehensive parallels to its story, but they form the most complete development of the cultural, literary, and moral world of *Beowulf*.

While some modern adapters have tried to bring the epic story into the modern setting of ideas or writing style, Tolkien chose to keep many of these ideas and styles, and adapted them into a new story. His fiction shares some of the same strengths and weaknesses as *Beowulf*, and many readers find that if they like one, they will like the other. Tolkien used many sources in Anglo-Saxon, Icelandic, and even Finnish literature. He admired the Finnish folk epic *Kalevala* and wished to recreate its magic in a new epic story for England. He drew some names and events from Icelandic prose and poetry. But it is still Anglo-Saxon poems and ideas that most shaped his stories, and *Beowulf* itself that lends more details and motifs than any other work.

NAMES

Beyond direct influence from *Beowulf*, the Old English language shaped many of the words Tolkien used to create the fictional world. He wanted to make his writing sound like it was from an earlier era by using words that would sound "old" to modern readers. "Middle Earth" itself is borrowed from Anglo-Saxon and other Norse mythology. It is the Middangeard (or "Midgard" in Norse); the middle realm suspended between the highest home of the gods, and the underworld of the unhappy dead. In Old English, "middangeard" simply means the earth.

To make the hobbits seem like a medieval form of English country folk, he used some names with old, half-forgotten Anglo-Saxon meanings. "Hobbit" itself, although it is a name that Tolkien thought of spontaneously, comes with an Old English explanation: "hole builder" (holbytla). Sam Gamgee's full name, Samwise, means "stupid" in Old English, while the Gaffer's full name, Hamfast, means "homebound." Some of the other hobbit names, such as Meriadoc, have a Welsh sound, which indicates that these hobbits came from borderlands with different traditions. Most place names in the Shire are English country names based in Old English geographical words.

Tolkien's concept for the people of Rohan was that they had come from the Far North. Their language was, to the hobbits, foreign and yet familiar, an earlier form of their own speech. To suggest this relationship, Tolkien used Old English words and names for the language of Rohan. While the name "Rohan" is Elvish (invented by Tolkien) and thus the name used by outsiders, the people of Rohan call themselves "Éotheod" (formed from Old English "eoh," horse, and "theod," people). The king's name, Théoden, means "prince," and the other noble names of Rohan could come from any Old English poem. Théodred is "people-counsel"; Éomer is "horse-famous"; Éowyn is "horse-joy." Erkenbrand, the lord of Westfold, has a Frankish-sounding name that means "jeweled-torch." These names follow the traditional pattern of Anglo-Saxon, Gothic, and Frankish aristocratic compound names. Meduseld, the royal hall, is modeled after Heorot in many ways, and its name comes from one of the words used in *Beowulf* for a "mead hall" (3065). Its town, Edoras, indicates in Old English that it is enclosed, for "eodor" means wall or boundary. The land of Rohan is called the Mark, which means a region with a boundary, and the same word is the root of the ancient Midlands kingdom of Mercia. The warriors of the Mark always fight on horseback in a troop called an Éored, which means "troop" in Old English and suggests horses (eoh) at its root. The horses, too, have Old English names.

The royal horses are Mearas, which is another Old English word for horses (giving us our modern word "mare"). Their leader is Shadowfax, which is spelled in Modern English but has the Old English meaning of "shadow-hair." Éomer lends horses to Aragorn and Legolas, and these horses are named Hasufel ("gray-coat") and Arod ("honored").

Places and creatures around Rohan also have Old English names. It is not surprising that the places around Westfold are Mount Thrihyrne (Three-Horn) and its fortress is the Hornburg (Horn-fortification). The tree shepherds (called "Onodrim" in Elvish) are generally called ents, which means "giants" in Old English. Their most hated neighbors, who cut trees out of spite, are the orcs, whose name is also drawn from Old English. Although its origin is in Latin, where "orcus" is a word for "demon," the Anglo-Saxons had adopted this word and it occurs in *Beowulf* (112) in the list of creatures that arose in the descent of Cain.

More surprisingly, the wizard Saruman has an Old English name. "Searu" had a range of meanings that included skill, cleverness, trick, and treachery. This range emphasizes both his technical advances and his treachery. A Modern English translation of his name could be "Techno-Man" or "Tricky-Man." *Beowulf* uses compounds of "searu" in many places. These words can indicate good, well-made things (such as the inlaid floor at Heorot or the good chain-mail coats), and they can indicate things that are well-made but have an evil quality (like Grendel's dragon-skin bag). However, "Searu" is mostly used in negative contexts. In line 3102, Wiglaf describes the cursed dragon's hoard as "cunning gems," and in line 2738, Beowulf denies ever seeking out "searu-nithas" (meaning intrigues or plots against someone else). The names of Saruman's places are Old English as well. He lives at Isengard, the "Iron-Yard" on the banks of the river Isen ("Iron"). Perhaps the iron in the nearby mountains provides a source of materials for his industrial advances. His tower, which was built by the Elves, is called "Orthanc," which also means "skill" or "cunning." Beowulf's chain-mail byrnie is not only made with "searu" (skill), it is also made with "orthanc."

Another set of names was taken not from *Beowulf* nor directly from Old English, but from the related mythology of Iceland and Norway. The medieval Norse poem "Voluspa" lists legendary dwarves, and there you will find most of the group that Bilbo travels with to the Lonely Mountain, as well as Gandalf, the wizard. These names must have seemed ready-made for adaptation, and their Norse origin gives them an authentic feel.

MONSTERS

Tolkien shared with the *Beowulf* poet a similar attitude toward monsters: humans are capable of choosing right and wrong, and most animals are not (although magical animals in some of Tolkien's works may be exceptions). Monsters, however, are only capable of immoral action. They cannot choose right or wrong but appear only capable of choosing wrong. Monsters live to attack and must be killed at all opportunities. While killing a human might be wrong (especially if he is your kin or if he has done nothing against you), and killing an animal might be wasteful (if not needed for food), killing a monster is always right. Monsters are defined as wrong in their being, a part of the fantasy world where black and white are clearer than they are in the real world. The only good monster is a dead one.

It is hard to trace a direct analogue to Grendel in Tolkien's works. Rather, he includes various characters that have Grendel-like attributes. Foremost are the trolls, whose bodies are said to be as hard as stone, and who will turn back to stone in the light of the sun. Trolls are large and they eat people (and hobbits), but the comic presentation of them in *The Hobbit* does not seem very Grendel-like. More reminiscent of *Beowulf* is the unnamed troll who helps in the attack at Moria and whose strength is able to tear away a door.

In *The Hobbit*, the dragon, Smaug, is developed in a more direct and important way than the trolls were. Unlike *Beowulf*'s dragon, this dragon has the power of speech, but otherwise its habits are very much the same. Both dragons came from the north to settle into a large hoard of gold, although *Beowulf*'s dragon found his hoard unguarded and hidden in a barrow, while Smaug had to attack and drive off the resident dwarves. Both dragons sleep in a room with their hoard, and although the epic does not specify that the dragon curled up on the gold itself, it is reasonably implied. Both dragons have a detailed knowledge of the contents of the hoard; both overreact to the loss of a small part of it. In fact, both dragons lose the same item: a golden, jeweled cup. Faced with this loss and unable to find the thief, both dragons respond with random, large-scale destruction. They soar into the night sky and come down with fire to burn whole towns. Their ends, of course, are not the same. *Beowulf*'s dragon returns to its barrow safely only to be attacked at home by the aging hero, while the dragon of *The Hobbit* is killed in flight by an arrow. The epic does not make use of Tolkien's tradition that jewels stuck to the underbody of a dragon, although this detail could have been a common belief at the time.

In line 112 of *Beowulf*, the kin of Cain includes giants (not ents in this case), elves, and orcs. Tolkien did not follow *Beowulf* in portraying elves as monsters but included other elements of the Anglo-Saxon tradition about elves. "Elfsheen" was an adjective for a woman's beauty, while elves were also known to cause diseases such as "water-elf disease" or "elf-sogoth" (lunacy). Elves were said to be the source of stone arrow-heads found around England from more primitive times, and these arrows were called "elf-shot" or "elf bolts." Tolkien's conclusion from all sources of elf stories, both ancient and medieval, was clearly that elves were nei-ther good nor bad. Like humans, they made moral choices. They were tall, extremely fair skinned, and inherently dangerous. They lived in an Elfland that could never quite be reached but was sometimes glimpsed.

The most classic English elf scenes occur in *The Hobbit*, when Bilbo and the dwarves can hear the hunting horns of the Mirkwood elves and sometimes see them feasting, but they can never meet or speak with them. The elves have ways of disappearing; they remain in their own realm unless they wish for contact with humans. Similarly, Galadriel's land of Lothlorien is not a place that someone can enter just by going there. Few are permitted to enter, and many will pass by without ever being aware of Elfland. Elrond's Rivendell is more accessible, but it is still across a raging river and set into the hills, and the elves have the power of traveling undetected when they wish not to mix with humans. They are not magical in the sense that they cannot do tricks of fire like Gandalf or vanish like Bilbo, but they do exist in another kind of reality.

Orcs offered Tolkien a wide range of imagination. His orcs are cor-rupted forms of elves, perhaps bringing together attributes of *Beowulf*'s "ylfas and orcneas" (elves and demons). They are not as large or as pow-erful as Grendel, although they, too, shun the light. They may eat human flesh, but this is not their defining trait in the way that it is the trolls'. Orcs, like demons, can only make evil choices, although in their intel-ligence they are higher than the animals. Orcs are never good even to their own kind but choose cruelty, mockery, and treachery. Haunting the forested mountains as the elves haunt the forests, orcs are a dark coun-terpart to Tolkien's good elves. As mini-Grendels, they are always fair game for attack and extermination.

The author of the *Liber Monstrorum* (an Anglo-Saxon work on strange beasts, written in Latin) might have included Beorn, the shape-changer, as a monster. These legendary figures of Germanic stories may have continued a prehistoric tradition of totem animals for certain tribes, gen-erally fierce ones such as wolves or bears. The hero, Sigurd, and his nephew, Sinfiotli, for example, wore wolf skins and turned into wolves on some of their adventures. The "Saga of Hrolf Kraki" includes a hero often compared to Beowulf himself, Bothvar Bjarki. Bothvar is the son of a shape-changing man/bear named Bjorn (pronounced "byorn") and a woman named Bera. In his adventures, he kills a dragon and is able to overcome many strong men like Beowulf (whose name, "bee-wolf," is usually taken to indicate a bear). In a last battle, Bothvar himself takes a bear-shape for a time, and in that shape he is able to overcome more enemies than when he is in man's shape. Tolkien's man/bear is named for Bothvar's father, Bjorn, which means "noble man" and is similar in sound to "bera" (bear). Like Beowulf and the Norse shape-changers, Beorn is a fierce fighter and larger and stronger than other men even when he is in man-shape.

TRADITIONS AND CUSTOMS

The first Germanic writing was the script we call runic, which imitated Latin letters, but with many changes and additions. The ability to cut runes was part of magic and spell-casting, and long after Latin script was used to write Old English, runes retained the ancient, magical connotation. Runes occur in the world of Tolkien as ancient scripts and magical writing. Just as there were different regional traditions of runes in northern Europe, Tolkien's elves use a runic script that differs from dwarf runes, and both are different from the ancient runes of the Northern Kingdom of men.

A knife from Mordor with runes cut into it provides one of the closest parallels to *Beowulf*. This knife melts after a piece of it pierces Frodo's shoulder, and the hilt is all that remains to show Elrond. Like Hrothgar, Elrond and Aragorn try to read the runes to understand the history of the weapon and how its magic works. Both swords have ancient runes and are from a more ancient time; however, the Beowulfian runic sword is from pre-flood times and made by giants, while the Mordor knife is small and comes from a land that is more like hell.

Other weapons provide links of tradition with *Beowulf*. Like the swords in the epic, many of the swords in *The Lord of the Rings* are named. Anduril, the "Sword that was Broken," is carried into battle with the Old–English-named Guthwinë ("good friend") and Herugrim ("ravager-grim"), the royal swords of Rohan. Boromir and Gandalf carry named weapons, and even Bilbo names his long knife "Sting." Sting is found in an ancient hoard; like the giant sword, it is hung on the walls of the trolls' cave. The younger hobbits (in *The Fellowship of the Ring*) get weapons from a barrow. Like the treasure in the barrow of *Beowulf*, this ancient treasure is cursed, and the curse must be broken if they are to use the weapons freely. Perhaps the Geats would have been less reluctant to keep the treasure hoard if Tom Bombadil had spoken a spell over it to end its curse. The attitude toward weapons in Tolkien's works is the same as in the epic. Weapons are almost magical and have individual histories and powers. Older weapons are probably finer, which of course is not literally true, since human history shows us a pattern of improvement and invention across time. Both epic stories are based on the idea of a more ancient civilization that had more wonderful treasures, and that power consists partly in tapping into this more ancient time and gaining continuity across the ages.

In addition to the treasure-barrows, other burials are also reminiscent of Beowulfian scenes. There are three major burials in the epic: Scyld's funeral ship launch, the funeral pyres for Hildeburh's brother and son, and Beowulf's funeral with pyre and mounded barrow. Tolkien shows us not only the ancient barrows on the Barrow-Downs, but also the royal burials of Boromir, Théoden, and Denethor. Each of these funeral scenes borrows elements from *Beowulf*. From Scyld's ship comes the smaller-scale, adapted boat burial of Boromir. There are no lavish treasures beyond what he carries, so these treasures are arrayed in symbolic fashion. Like Scyld's ship, Boromir's elvish canoe is pushed out into the current to go where it will. Like the ship, no man knows where it ended up, as it floated successfully over the waterfall and down the river to the sea. Denethor's suicidal pyre is most like the fires of Hildeburh's story: full of despair. While Hildeburh's brother and son were certainly dressed in treasures, the emphasis in the story is on the flames that engulfed their bodies, and this emphasis is carried into the death of Denethor in an oil-soaked fire.

The most Beowulfian funeral is the state burial of King Théoden. The creation of mounds is not only reminiscent of Beowulf's barrow, but also of the mounds excavated at Sutton Hoo. There, royal graves were laid side by side in rows, although we do not know if they were as orderly as the royal mounds of Rohan. Rohan's mounds show the two main dynasties of the royal house, and all of the names are in Old English. Théoden is, of course, buried with treasure and weapons. His barrow is built of stone and covered with a mound of grass, like Beowulf's. There is no indication that his body was burned, but Anglo-Saxon customs allowed for both kinds of burials: cremation and inhumation. (Archeologists of the future Middle Earth would certainly be thankful for inhumation.)

Burials are not the only traditional Anglo-Saxon customs carried on in parts of Middle Earth. The places most similar to Anglo-Saxon England are Beorn's homestead in *The Hobbit*, the Mark of Rohan, and of course the Shire (although it is more like medieval England). Beorn's household is similar to a wealthy thane's farmstead, with three major exceptions. First, Beorn, being half-animal himself, does not eat meat, which the Anglo-Saxons ate with great appetite. Second, Beorn's homestead of course also lacks the familiar servants and slaves of a thane's farm, since he is served by enchanted animals. His house is a Germanic hall, which is thatched, supported with interior pillars, and lit only by fires in central pits. The animals set up tables for the guests, much as Hrothgar's servants set up tables for the celebratory feast after Grendel's defeat, and Beorn's story-telling over mead is like a scop's songs after a feast. The third main difference is Beorn's lack of interest in finery. Every thane aspired to own as much gold and decorated things as he could afford, and most could afford a fair amount. Beorn is a combination of peasant farmer and aristocratic lord. He does not live by plunder but practices subsistence farming. His household is in some ways an idealized picture of the best of Anglo-Saxon country life.

If Beorn shows us idealized farm life, then the royal hall of Meduseld, in *The Two Towers*, shows us the most idealized image of the Anglo-Saxon aristocracy. Like Heorot, Meduseld is decorated with gold and shines from afar. Visitors follow a paved road to its doors, where a door warden challenges them and requires them to leave weapons in the outer chamber with the rest of the guards. The interior of Meduseld is like Heorot, too: its floor is paved with colored stones, its pillars are decorated, and woven tapestries adorn the walls. There is a long hearth in the middle and a raised platform where the king's chair sits.

The customs of Meduseld, and even some of its dialogue, are directly parallel to Heorot's. In "The King of the Golden Hall," the door warden Hama, like Wulfgar, must first ask the king's permission for the visitors to enter, even after the king knows their names. Like the coast guard who first encountered Beowulf and had to decide whether to allow him to proceed, Háma brings out a proverb to support his own judgment: "Yet in doubt a man of worth will trust to his own wisdom." This statement is similar, though not identical, to *Beowulf*'s "a sharp shield-warrior must be a judge of both things, words and deeds, if he would think well" (286–289). Twice, in the greetings of Rohan's royal court, we read sentences of Old English. "Westu hal" means "Be thou well." When Théoden departs, Eowyn tells him, "Ferthu Théoden hal," which means "Travel, Théoden, well."

Like Unferth (the "thyle" who sits at Hrothgar's feet), Wormtongue is first seen sitting at Théoden's feet. Like Unferth, he greets the visitors with a slanderous version of their actions, in particular twisting Gandalf's role as Sauron's antagonist into a "storm-crow" (which is perhaps similar to the modern nickname "ambulance-chaser"). Like Unferth, he presses his attack and seeks to discredit the visitors and charge them with malice and weakness. Although Unferth goes on to improve his character, Wormtongue must be cast down, sent away, and turned into an exile. His name, Grima, means "helmet" or "mask." Just as a masked helmet struck fear into an opponent by covering the wearer's thoughts and intentions, Grima's deceitful, unrevealing face is able to create fear in the king through his secret treason.

Éowyn acts as hostess in the place of a queen, but because the story is about the disruption of war, there are few scenes that show her in this role. She is standing in the hall when they arrive and is described as very pale and blonde (as Tacitus and others described the Germanic tribes). As Aragorn sets out on the Paths of the Dead, she brings him a cup of parting and hands it to him ritually. Finally, at Théoden's funeral feast, she serves a ceremonial cup to the new king, her brother Éomer. Éowyn, of course, has more of a warlike role in this story than the women of *Beowulf*. Tolkien makes use of the Norse tradition of the "shieldmaiden," who is able to handle weapons and may fight. In the end, Éowyn also plays the traditional role of princess bride, as she cements the alliance of Rohan and Gondor by marrying the new Prince of Ithilien.

The customs of Rohan mostly revolve around horses and fighting, and in this respect they are less like the Anglo-Saxons than the eastern Goths. While the Anglo-Saxons used horses for travel, they did not use them for war. However, a poem (now called "Maxims I") mentions horses in a long list of phrases that state the way life ought to be. Just as a king ought to be on the gift chair, says the poem, an earl ought to be on horseback. In fact, the poem uses the word that Tolkien picked up for the Rohan fighting formation: the "eored." The "eored" ought to stay in formation, says the poet, and a good man ought to be sure to have a good horse at all times. The Danes of *Beowulf* certainly care about horses. They bring to mind the Riders of Rohan, as they spontaneously race their horses to celebrate the death of Grendel. Among Hrothgar's gifts were eight horses; one was fitted with harness for a king.

Common to the men of Rohan and Gondor is a love of horns. Boromir's custom is to blow a horn on setting out and when he needs help. Théoden makes a point of blowing horns at dawn when he is about to ride out of the Hornburg to battle orcs; Erkenbrand's horn answers him. As the men of Rohan ride into Gondor, arriving in the nick of time, they blow their horns again. The calling, echoing horns create a sound to accompany the ideal of heroic battle, especially at dawn with a new hope rising. This image is found in *Beowulf* when the Geats, like many of Tolkien's characters, are trapped in a forest at night and know they will die in the morning. All night they hear the jeers and threats of the Swedes, but at dawn they hear the horns of Hygelac's unexpected rescue, perhaps on horseback: "Solace came along with the sunrise, after they heard Hygelac's horn and trumpet sounding the charge" (2942–2944). The motif of hope coming with the dawn is repeated many times by Tolkien, often with horns blowing.

LITERARY MODELS

One of the striking features of *Beowulf* is its suggestion, through its partial and embedded stories, of a world older and deeper than itself. Some of them are long enough to hold together as a story, such as the lay of Hildeburh and the fight at Finnsburg. Others are so short as to be barely understandable, such as the reference to Hama's theft of the necklace. These embedded stories and references connect the story of Beowulf to a time even further in the past. If we read the poem in full, with its many digressions, we can never forget that it was part of an actual world, not just a story.

Tolkien wanted to imitate this sense for his works, so he followed the same strategy. Like the *Beowulf* poet, he included many partial songs and stories; legends about long-ago people who were ancient even to the characters in his own story. These legends connect the story to a wider, deeper history and give it a sense of reality. Just as some of the embedded legends in *Beowulf* echo themes of the story, some of Tolkien's legends were created to echo and strengthen his themes (like the lay of Beren and Luthien, whose story tells us about another fight against an overwhelming evil).

Some of these songs and stories are even drawn from Old English sources, if not from *Beowulf* itself. "Eärendil the Mariner" is a legend sung in *The Fellowship of the Ring*. It is the story of an elf who sailed to a supernatural island in the Far East and was turned into a star. Tolkien found this name in the poem now called "Christ A." The lines sing to "Earendel," a star that is "brightest of angels, over Middle Earth sent to men" (104–105). Tolkien simply invented a myth for the star and then took the unusual step of linking the myth to his elves (Eärendil was Elrond's father).

The style and general content of other embedded songs come from Old English sources, such as two songs in *The Two Towers*. In the chapter "Treebeard" the ent Treebeard recites to Pippin and Merry a list of the living peoples, in which hobbits have been forgotten. Among the later entries he recalls, "Bear bee-hunter, boar the fighter, / Hound is hungry, hare is fearful / . . . Eagle in eyrie, ox in pasture, / Hart horn-crowned, hawk is swiftest." This list is very similar to the poems that describe the idealized life of what ought to be, now called "Maxims I" and "Maxims II." "Maxims II" tells us, "Dragon must be in a mound / Old, proud in his ornaments. Fish must be in water / to spawn its young. . . . Bear must be in wilderness / old and terrible. . . . Bird must be aloft / to soar in the air. Salmon must be rapids / to squirm with trout . . ." (lines 26–40). The ent's song is a Middle Earth variant of the Old English list.

Aragorn recalls the history of Rohan in "The King of the Golden Hall," and sings a song from their legends: "Where now the horse and rider? Where is the horn that was blowing?" The style and content of his song are similar to the lament of "The Wanderer." This speaker describes a ruined, empty hall and asks, "Where now is the horse? Where the warrior? Where is the gift-giver? Where the delights of the feast?" There are echoes, too, of *Beowulf*'s "Lay of the Last Survivor," who looks on his treasure before burying the last remains of his vanished tribe. He laments the loss of the horse that wore the harness, the warrior that polished the helmet, and even the hawk that wore the hood.

IDEAS

The main theme of *The Lord of the Rings* is the nobility of continuing to fight against an overwhelming foe, even when all hope seems lost. The plot is constructed to teach the reader that the most hopeless way might be the only way that will succeed. It is never right to give up, because the next dawn may bring help unlooked-for. It is never right to give up, because others depend on your actions, and even in defeat you may bring about some good that will benefit them. These same ideas are dominant in *Beowulf*. Beowulf goes into each battle not knowing if he will survive, and in fact he plans ahead for the event of his death. He knows in each case, however, that he can only bring good to his society by going forward and that weaker people depend on him. Especially in his last fight, when he feels his death approaching, he goes forward with the idea of ridding the land of an evil, destructive force. Beowulf cannot escape the ironic outcome that by defeating the dragon, he is about to bring an even greater evil down upon his people. However, with time will come new heroes; his part is done, and now young men like Wiglaf must carry on the fight, even if it is a losing one. This cycle is present in Tolkien's imagined world. When each old hero (such as Gil-galad, Beren, or Isildur) dies, his people are exposed to many evils. A new hero must arise and press forward, even when there does not seem to be hope of prevailing, because his people depend on him. Each generation must cleanse the world of the evil that is before them, but new evil and danger will always arise for new heroes to manage. The message of both stories is that we must never give up, lose hope, or think only of ourselves.

In *Beowulf*, there are many hints of a guiding hand, perhaps divine, behind the nominally random, chance events. The characters and narrator speak of "Wyrd" (translated as "fate" or "luck"). (See Chapter 10, "Religion in *Beowulf*," for a more complete discussion of "Wyrd.") At the same time, they sometimes attribute the hand behind the scenes to God. With either the pagan or the Christian belief, clearly the characters and narrator do not believe in chance, random events. When the sword comes to Beowulf's hand to kill Grendel's mother, this event comes from God. When young Beowulf survived his struggle with sea monsters, it was due to "Wyrd" sparing him. The actors in any visible scene can count on an invisible hand, only they do not know in advance if it is for them or against them.

This theme is also carried out fully in Tolkien's work. The characters do not mention any God by name, but they believe in some invisible hand, as is made clear in *The Fellowship of the Ring*, "Bilbo was *meant* to find the Ring, and not by its maker," says Gandalf, in "The Shadow of the Past." When Frodo volunteers to take the Ring on its hazardous quest, in "The Council of Elrond," Elrond says, "I think that this task is appointed for you, Frodo." The hint of a power outside Middle-Earth also occurs in *The Two Towers*. When Gandalf reappears in "The White Rider," after he had seemed to be dead, he explains, "I was sent back." None of these characters suggest, as openly as Beowulf does, who might have meant, appointed, or sent. All of them hint at a higher power of some kind, but none of them name it. Again and again we see the intervention of luck, or fate, or "Wyrd": Frodo slips away from his fellowship at the exact moment a band of orcs comes to kidnap him, his friends are carried rapidly to a place where they may meet an Ent who can help save Rohan, and Frodo and Sam manage to enter a pass into Mordor exactly at a time when it is less guarded and its troops are distracted. As Beowulf himself would point out, "luck" only helps them because their courage was not daunted, and they continued to press boldly on. "Wyrd often spares an undoomed man, when his courage endures!" (572–573).

Finally, the same uncertain religious outlook prevails in both works. While *Beowulf*'s speakers may often mention the true Creator, the Lord, and so on, there is no religious ritual in the story. No soothsayer gives an oracle about the hero's chances of success, and no pagan god is thanked with any ritual sacrifices, even though the narrator mentions that the Danes did that (175). The poem presents an almost religion-free life, apart from the verbal references. Tolkien's world, too, is almost religion-free. There are no rituals marking seasons or holy days, and no prayers to any god. From the Shire to Rohan to Gondor, there are no signs of traditional religion. Perhaps the only literature in Old English that portrays such a world is *Beowulf*, in its attempt to present a pagan world that is yet acceptable to Christian readers.

Tolkien's imaginary world owes much to *Beowulf*. He borrowed some of its creatures, words, setting, concepts, and literary traditions and transformed them into a powerfully real story. He did not update or rewrite the story, but he cut from its cloth a new suit.

IN DEPTH: THE ANGLO-SAXON HOBBIT CALENDAR

In Appendix D of the third volume, *The Return of the King*, Tolkien provides a sample of the Shire calendar. This calendar is directly modeled after the ancient Anglo-Saxon calendar. Tolkien spelled the words in the way he guessed they might have been spelled if they had remained in use. Syllables were dropped and some name elements were changed as successive generations guessed at what the names may once have meant.

Shire Name	Anglo-Saxon Name	Meaning
Afteryule	Æfter Geola	Month after winter festival of Geol/Yule
Solmath	Solmonaþ	Sun month (or "Month of Cakes")
Rethe	Hreþmonaþ	Month of Hrethe (perhaps earth goddess)
Astron	Eastermonaþ	Month of Eostre (goddess, not much known)
Thrimidge	Þrimilcemonaþ	Month of three milkings of cows per day
Forelithe	Ærra Liþa	Month before summer solstice (Liþa)
Afterlithe	Æfterra Liþa	Month after the summer solstice
Wedmath	Weodmonaþ	Weed month
Halimath	Haligmonaþ	Holy month (probably harvest festival)
Winterfilth	Winterfylleþ	First full moon of winter
Blotmath	Blotmonaþ	Month for butchering extra livestock
Foreyule	Ærra Geola	Month before winter festival of Geol/Yule

FURTHER SUGGESTED READING

Chance, Jane, ed. *Tolkien and the Invention of Myth: A Reader*. Lexington, KY: University Press of Kentucky, 2004.

Clark, George and Daniel Timmons, eds. *J. R. R. Tolkien and His Literary Resonances: Views of Middle Earth*. Westport, CT: Greenwood Press, 2000.

Shippey, T. A. *The Road to Middle-Earth*. New York: Houghton Mifflin, 2003.

Tolkien, J. R. R. *Beowulf and the Critics*, ed. Michael D. C. Drout. Tempe, AZ: Arizona Center for Medieval and Renaissance Studies, 2002. (Provides alternate drafts of Tolkien's 1936 lecture.)

Zimbardo, Rose A. and Neil D. Isaacs, eds. *Understanding the Lord of the Rings: The Best of Tolkien Criticism*. Boston: Houghton Mifflin, 2004.

Glossary of Names

Pronunciation guide: Sounds that are different from modern usage are described below. In brackets are the letters that are used to indicate the sound. (Syllables with word stress are written in all capitals.)

E: This sound is the Continental "e," which is closest to the (American) sounds in "lay" and "leg." When it comes at the end of a word, it remains as a short "e," not silent. [ay, e]

A: This sound is the Continental "a," which is closest to the sound in "father." [ah]

I: This sound is the Continental "i," which is closest to the sound in "see." It can also be the short "i" in "dip." [ee, i]

O: This sound is like the "o" sounds in "rope" and "hop." [o]

U: This sound is like the "u" sounds in "pool" and "pull." [u]

AE: This sound is like the (American) short "a" in "hat." [a]

EO: The best way to imitate the Old English diphthong "eo" is to begin with the sound of the (American) short "e" or long "a." Hold this sound and then round your lips to an "o," allowing the sound to glide. The emphasis should be on the initial "e" sound. [eo]

EA: The best way to imitate the Old English diphthong "ea" is to begin with the sound of the (American) short "e" or long "a." Hold this sound and then lower your tongue to form the sound "ah," allowing the sound to glide. The emphasis should be on the initial "e" sound. A less difficult "ay" sound may be substituted. [ea, ay]

TH: Same as modern "th." [TH for sound in "thin," th for sound in "that"]

G: Most of the time, "g" is the modern "g" sound, but at times when a "i" or "e" follows, it becomes a "y" sound. [g, y]

Characters with speaking lines:

Beowulf [BEO-wulf]: Hero of the poem, a nobleman of the Geats; nephew to King Hygelac and grandson of King Hrethel; he is first a young hero and then an aged king.

Coast Watchman of the Danes (unnamed): Coast guard; the "reeve" of the Danish shore, he gives Beowulf an escort to the royal hall.

Hrothgar [HROth-gahr]: Aged King of the Danes, a Scylding; married to Wealhtheow, father of Hrethric, Hrothmund, and Freawaru; Lord of Heorot; his troubles with Grendel open the story.

Hygelac [HEE-ye-lahk]: King of the Geats; uncle to Beowulf; husband of Hygd and father of Heardred and a daughter; he welcomes Beowulf home before dying during a raid against the Franks.

Last Survivor: The last member of a tribe that died out; he buried the treasures of his people in a barrow later occupied by the dragon.

Messenger (unnamed): He brings word of Beowulf's death to the Geats, predicts disaster at the hands of the Swedes.

Unferth [UN-ferTH]: Also spelled Hunferth; a nobleman at the Danish court of Heorot; "thyle" of Hrothgar, possibly a spokesman; he challenges Beowulf with a public insult and later lends Beowulf a sword.

Wealhtheow [WEAL-THeo]: Queen of Hrothgar, lady of Heorot; mother of Freawaru, Hrethric and Hrothmund; she offers a ceremonial cup to Beowulf, receives his oath, and rewards his effort.

Wiglaf [WEE-lahf]: Young warrior of the Geats; a relative of Beowulf on his father's side; he helps Beowulf against the dragon.

Wulfgar [WULF-gahr]: Nobleman of the Wendels; official door keeper of Heorot; he brings Beowulf into the hall with an introduction.

Characters with no speaking lines:

Aelfhere [ALF-he-re]: Kinsman of Weohstan and Wiglaf.

Aeschere [ASH-he-re]: Thane of Hrothgar, brother to Yrmenlaf.

Beanstan [BEAN-stahn, or BAYN-stahn]: Breca's father.

Beowulf (Beow) Scylding [BEO-wulf, or BEO, SHEEL-ding]: Legendary King of the Danes, son of Scyld Scefing; father of Healfdene; his name may be Beow, although it is written as Beowulf.

Breca [BRE-cah]: Prince of the Brondings; Beowulf's childhood friend; he competed in a distance race on the ocean against Beowulf.

Cain [CAYN]: Bible character, son of Adam and Eve; Cain killed his brother Abel out of jealousy and was cursed and banished; the Anglo-Saxons and other medieval people believed that monsters were descended from Cain.

Daeghrefn [DAY-revn]: Frankish warrior, killed by Beowulf in battle after the fall of Hygelac.

Eadgils [EAD-yils]: Son of Ohthere, brother of Eanmund; his quest for revenge on his uncle Onela led to a continued feud between Swedes and Geats.

Eanmund [EAN-mund]: Son of Ohthere, brother of Eadgils; his quest for revenge on his uncle, Onela, led to a continued feud between Swedes and Geats; he was killed by Weohstan.

Ecglaf [EDG-lahf]: Father of Unferth.

Ecgtheow [EDG-theo]: Father of Beowulf; son-in-law of Hrethel (King of Geats).

Ecgwala [EDG-wah-lah]: Legendary Danish king.

Eofor [EO-vor]: Brother to Wulf; slayer of Ongentheow, married to Hygelac's daughter.

Eomer [EO-mer]: Son of Offa, King of Anglia.

Eormanric [EOR-mahn-rich]: King of the Ostrogoths; he is mentioned in the story of the legendary Brosing necklace.

Finn [FIN]: Son of Folcwalda; legendary King of the Frisians; married to Hildeburh, a Scylding princess; his home at Finnsburg was the site of a two-stage feud and massacre between Jutes, Danes, and Frisians, subject of a poet's song at Heorot.

Fitela [FEE-te-lah]: Nephew (and son in some versions) to Sigemund; his Norse name is Sinfiotli.

Folcwalda [FOLK-wahl-dah]: Deceased/Legendary King of Frisia, father of Finn.

Freawaru [FREA-wah-ru, or FRAY-wah-ru]: Princess of the Danes, daughter of Hrothgar.

Froda [FRO-dah]: Father to Ingeld, Prince of the Heathobards.

Garmund [GAHR-mund]: Father to Offa, King of Anglia.

Grendel [GREN-del]: Water troll, "kin of Cain," who attacks Heorot at night.

Grendel's mother: Water-troll, mother of Grendel; she lives in an underwater cave.

Guthlaf [GUth-lahf]: Thane of Hengest.

Haethcyn [HATH-keen]: King of the Geats, son of Hrethel, brother of Hygelac; he killed his brother Herebeald by an accidental arrow shot and was killed in battle by Ongentheow.

Halga [HAHL-gah]: Brother of Hrothgar, prince of the Scyldings; he is dead at the time of the story's action; father of Hrothulf.

Hama [HAH-mah]: Ostrogoth who stole the Brosinga necklace from King Eormanric.

Healfdene [HEALF-de-ne]: Legendary King of the Danes, son of Beowulf (or Beow) Scylding; father of Hrothgar, Heorogar, Halga, and a daughter.

Heardred [HEAR-dred, or HAYR-dred]: Prince and then King of Geats, son of Hygelac; he was killed by Onela and Beowulf became king.

Heatholaf [HEAth-o-lahf, or HAYth-o-lahf]: Swedish or Geatish warrior killed by Ecgtheow before Beowulf's birth; Hrothgar helped pay to end the feud.

Hemming [HEM-ming]: Kinsman of Offa, King of Anglia.

Hengest [HEN-gest]: Legendary Jutish warrior, considered one of the settlers of the Isle of Britain; companion of Hnaef on his disastrous journey to Finnsburg; he set in motion the second stage of the feud between Jutes, Danes, and Frisians, subject of a poet's song at Heorot.

Heorogar [HEO-ro-gahr]: Deceased brother of Hrothgar; father of Heoroward.

Heorot [HEO-rot]: Royal hall of Hrothgar.

Heoroweard [HEO-ro-wahrd]: Son of Hrothgar's brother, Heorogard.

Herebeald [HE-re-beahld]: Son of Hrethel (King of the Geats), brother of Hygelac; he was killed by his brother, Haethcyn, by an accidental arrow shot.

Heremod [HE-re-mod]: Legendary King of the Danes; he lost his rule due to selfishness and treason and was driven away.

Hereric [HE-re-rich]: Brother of Hygd, uncle of Heardred.

Hildeburh [HIL-de-bur(h)]: Deceased/Legendary Queen of the Frisians, wife of Finn; sister to Hnaef and daughter of Hoc; her home at Finnsburg was the site of the two-stage feud and massacre between Jutes, Danes, and Frisians, subject of a poet's song at Heorot.

Hnaef [HNAF]: Legendary King of the Danes, a Scylding; brother to Hildeburh; his journey to visit Hildeburh at Finnsburg in Frisia was the occasion of a two-stage feud and massacre between Jutes, Danes, and Frisians, subject of a poet's song at Heorot.

Hoc [HOK]: Deceased/Legendary King of the Danes, a Scylding; father of Hnaef and Hildeburh, subject of the poet's song at Heorot.

Hondscio [HOND-shoo]: Geatish warrior, companion of Beowulf; he was the only Geat killed by Grendel before Beowulf began the fight.

Hrethel [HRE-thel]: Deceased King of the Geats; father of Herebeald, Haethcyn, Hygelac, and a daughter; grandfather of Beowulf.

Hrethric [HREth-rich]: Prince of the Danes, older son of Hrothgar.

Hrothmund [HROth-mund]: Prince of the Danes, younger son of Hrothgar.

Hrothulf [HROth-ulf]: Son of Halga, nephew of Hrothgar; he lives at Heorot and is a leading warrior; legends hint that he later seized the throne.

Hrunting [HRUN-ting]: Sword lent to Beowulf from Unferth in the fight against Grendel's mother.

Hunferth [UN-ferth]: Alternate spelling of Unferth; the manuscript uses a silent H.

Hunlafing [HUN-lahf-ing]: Thane of Hengest, or Hengest's sword.

Hygd [HEED]: Geatish queen, wife of Hygelac; sister of Hereric; mother of Heardred and a daughter.

Ingeld [ING-geld]: Prince of the Heathobards, a neighboring nation to the Danes; future husband of Freawaru; their wedding will be the scene of a feuding massacre.

Modthryth [MOD-threeth]: See Thryth.

Naegling [NAY-gling]: Sword of Beowulf that failed against the dragon.

Offa [O-fah]: King of Anglia, a legendary heroic warrior; husband to Thryth.

Ohthere [O-THe-re]: Son of Ongentheow, brother of Onela; he was killed by Onela and his sons, Eadgils and Eanmund, tried to avenge him.

Onela [O-nel-ah]: "Battle-Scylfing" King of the Swedes; son of Ongentheow; brother-in-law to Hrothgar of the Danes.

Ongentheow [ON-yen-theo]: Aged King of the Swedes; father of Onela and Ohthere; he killed Haethcyn (King of the Geats and brother of Hygelac) and was killed by Wulf and Eofor.

Oslaf [OZ-lahf]: Thane of Hengest.

Scyld Scefing [SHEELD SHAY-fing]: Legendary King of the Danes; father to Beowulf (or Beow), founder of the Scylding Kings; ancestor to Hrothgar; he arrived as a baby in a boat and later requested a burial in a ship that was launched to return him to the sea.

Sigemund [SEE-ye-mund]: Legendary Germanic hero, son of Waels; among many exploits, he killed a dragon.

Thryth [THREETH]: Legendary princess, wife of King Offa of Anglia; her haughty and unruly behavior labeled her as a negative example. Her name may be Modthryth; the text is unclear.

Weland [WAY-lahnd]: Legendary Germanic smith who made Beowulf's chain mail.

Weohstan [WEO-stahn]: Father of Wiglaf.

Withergyld [WIth-er-yild]: Deceased Heathobard warrior, fallen in previous feud with the Danes; remembering him helped restart the feud.

Wonred [WON-red]: Father to Wulf and Eofor.

Wulf [WULF]: Brother to Eofor; he helped his brother kill Ongentheow.

Yrmenlaf [EER-men-lahf]: Brother to Aeschere, thane of Hrothgar.

Nations and families:

Brondings: People of Breca (Beowulf's childhood friend).

Danes: Ring-Danes, West-Danes, East-Danes, Bright-Danes, South-Danes, North-Danes, Spear-Danes; people centered on the islands and part of the peninsula of modern Denmark; also called the Scyldings (after the ruling family) and the Ingwines.

Eotens [EO-tens]: Jutes, or giants.

Finns: People centered in modern Finland.

Franks: People of central France and Germany; a Germanic kingdom first converted to Christianity.

Frisians [FREE-zhans]: People centered along the coast of modern Netherlands.

Geats [YEATS, or YAY-ahts]: War-Geats, Weder-Geats, Sea-Geats; people centered in southern and coastal Sweden.

Gifthas [YIF-thahs]: People of East Germany.

Heathobards [HEAth-o-bahrds, or HAYth-o-bahrds]: People of Ingeld, possibly located in the north of modern Germany, along the coast near Denmark.

Heathoreams [HEAth-o-reams, HAYth-o-rayms]: Place where Breca landed after the sea contest against Beowulf; modern location is unknown.

Helmings: People of Wealhtheow (Queen of Hrothgar).

Hetware [HET-wah-re]: People located near the mouth of the Rhine River.

Hrethlings [HREth-lings]: The ruling family of Geats.

Hugas [HU-gahs]: Allies of the Frisians, possibly the Franks.

Ingwines [ING-wi-nes]: The Danes.

Jutes [YUTS]: People centered around the islands and peninsula of modern Denmark.

Scyldings [SHEELD-ings]: Honor-Scyldings, Victory-Scyldings; the ruling family of the Danes.

Scylfings [SHEEL-fings]: Battle-Scylfings; the ruling family of the Swedes.

Waegmundings [WAY-mund-ings]: Family of Beowulf's father, and of Wiglaf, possibly located near the Swedes.

Weders [WE-ders]: The Geats.

Wendels: People of Wulfgar, the doorkeeper of Heorot.

Wylfings [WIL-fings]: The people of Heatholaf, who was killed by Ecgtheow years before the poem's action.

Works Cited

Alexander, Michael. *Beowulf.* New York: Penguin Books, 1995.

Benson, Larry D. "The Pagan Coloring of Beowulf." *Old English Poetry: Fifteen Essays,* ed. Robert P. Creed. Providence: Brown University Press, 1967. (Also published in *The Beowulf Reader*, ed. Peter S. Baker. New York: Garland Publishing, 2000.)

Chadwick, H. M. *The Cult of Othin.* Cambridge: Cambridge University Press, 1899. (This classic is also available online.)

Chambers, R. W. *Beowulf: An Introduction to the Study of the Poem with a Discussion of the Stories of Offa and Finn.* Cambridge: Cambridge University Press, 1958.

Chase, Colin, ed. *The Dating of Beowulf.* Toronto: University of Toronto, 1981.

Damico, Helen. *Beowulf's Wealhtheow and the Valkyrie Tradition.* Madison: The University of Wisconsin Press, 1984.

Frank, Roberta. "Skaldic Verse and the Date of *Beowulf.*" In *The Dating of Beowulf*, ed. Colin Chase. Toronto: University of Toronto, 1981.

Goffart, Walter. "Hetware and Hugas: Datable Anachronisms in *Beowulf.*" In *The Dating of Beowulf*, ed. Colin Chase. Toronto: University of Toronto, 1981.

Kiernan, Kevin. *Beowulf and the Beowulf Manuscript.* Brunswick: Rutgers University Press, 1981.

Newton, Sam. *The Origins of Beowulf and the Pre-Viking Kingdom of East Anglia.* Cambridge: D. S. Brewer, 1993.

Orchard, Andy. *Pride and Prodigies: Studies in the monsters of the Beowulf manuscript.* Toronto: University of Toronto Press, 1995.

Parry, Milman. *The Making of Homeric Verse: The Collected Papers of Milman Parry.* Oxford: Clarendon Press, 1971.

Pollington, Stephen. *Rudiments of Runelore.* Hockwold-cum-Wilton, UK: Anglo-Saxon Books, 1995.

Robinson, Fred C. "Elements of the Marvelous in the Characterization of Beowulf: A Reconsideration of the Textual Evidence." In *Old English Studies in Honour of John C. Pope*, eds. Robert B. Burlin and Edward B. Irving Jr. Toronto: University of Toronto Press, 1974. (Reprinted in *The Beowulf Reader,* ed. Peter S. Baker. New York: Garland, 2000.)

Tolkien, J. R. R. "*Beowulf:* The Monsters and the Critics." *Proceedings of the British Academy* 22, 1936. (This essay is reprinted in several collections).

————. *The Fellowship of the Ring.* New York: Ballantine, 1965.

————. *Finn and Hengest: the Fragment and the Episode.* ed. Alan Bliss. Boston: Houghton Mifflin, 1983.

————. *The Hobbit.* New York: Ballantine, 1965.

————. *The Return of the King.* New York: Ballantine, 1965.

————. *The Two Towers.* New York: Ballantine, 1965.

Schücking, Levin L. "Wann entstand der Beowulf? Glossen, Zweifel, und Fragen." *Beiträge zur Geschichte der deutschen Sprache und Literatur* 42 (1917), 347–410.

TRANSLATIONS

Alexander, Michael. *Beowulf: A Verse Translation.* London: Penguin Books, 1973.

Bradley, S. A. J. *Anglo-Saxon Poetry.* London: Dent, 1982.

Earle, John. *The Deeds of Beowulf: An English Epic of the Eighth Century Done into Modern Prose.* Oxford: Clarendon Press, 1892.

Gummere, Francis B. "Beowulf," *The Five-Foot Shelf of Books: Epic and Saga.* New York: Collier & Sons, 1910.

Heaney, Seamus. *Beowulf.* New York: W. W. Norton and Co., 2000.

Kemble, J. M. *A Translation of the Anglo-Saxon Poem of Beowulf.* London: William Pickering, 1835.

Liuzza, R. M. *Beowulf: A New Verse Translation.* Peterborough: Broadview Press, 2000.

Morris, William and A. J. Wyatt. *The Tale of Beowulf.* London: Longmans, Green and Co., 1895.

Raffel, Burton. *Beowulf.* New York: The New American Library, 1963.

Rebsamen, Frederick. *Beowulf.* New York: HarperCollins, 1991.

Slade, Benjamin. *Beowulf on Steorarume (Beowulf in Cyberspace).* www.heorot.dk, 2002.

Sullivan, Alan and Timothy Murphy. *Beowulf.* New York: Pearson Education, Inc., 2004.

Wright, David. *Beowulf.* New York: Penguin Books, 1957.

MODERN ADAPTATIONS

Beowulf. Dir. Graham Baker. Dimension/Miramax, 1999.

Beowulf and Grendel. Dir. Sturla Gunnarson. To be released 2005.

Bingham, Jerry. *Beowulf.* First Comics Inc., 1984.

Crichton, Michael. *Eaters of the Dead.* New York: Alfred A. Knopf, Inc., 1976.

Gardner, John. *Grendel.* New York: Ballantine Books, 1971.

Grendel, Grendel, Grendel. Dir. Alexander Stitt. 1980.

Hinds, Gareth. *The Collected Beowulf.* Cambridge: The Comic.com, 1999–2000.

Rebsamen, Frederick R. *Beowulf Is My Name.* New York: Holt, Rinehart, Winston, 1971.

Swearer, Randolph, Raymond Oliver, and Marijane Osborn. *Beowulf: A Likeness.* New Haven: Yale University Press, 1990.

The Thirteenth Warrior. Dir. John McTiernan. Walt Disney Productions, 1999.

Uslan, Michael and Ricardo Villamonte. *Beowulf.* DC Comics, 1975.

Index

About the Author

RUTH JOHNSTON STAVER is an independent scholar who specializes in Old English language and literature. She has extensive experience teaching Advanced Placement English Literature and has published on such topics as historical linguistics.